ID0948472

Boomtown Blues

BOOMTOWN BLUES

Colorado Oil Shale, 1885–1985

Andrew Gulliford

Foreword by Richard D. Lamm

UNIVERSITY PRESS OF COLORADO

First edition

World Resources and Environmental Issues Series
Publication of this book was made possible, in part, by a grant from the Tell Ertl
Family Trust.

The University Press of Colorado is a cooperative publishing enterprise supported,
in part, by Adams State College, Colorado State University, Fort Lewis College,
Mesa State College, Metropolitan State College, University of Colorado, University
of Northern Colorado, University of Southern Colorado, and Western State College.

The paper used in this publication meets the minimum requirements of the American
National Standard for Information Sciences—Permanence of Paper for Printed
Library Materials.
ANSI Z39.48–1984

Library of Congress Cataloging-in-Publication Data

Gulliford, Andrew.
    Boomtown blues: Colorado oil shale / Andrew Gulliford; foreword by
Richard Lamm.
    p. cm.—(World resources and environmental issues series)
    Includes bibliographical references
1. Oil-shale industry—Colorado—History. I. Title. II. Series.
HD9567.C6G85 1989   338.2'7283'09788—dc20   89-28004
ISBN 0-87081-178-9

Printed in the United States of America

for all the Garfield County "Survivors"
wherever they may be
and for my mother who did not live to read it
and for my two sons who someday will

Contents

Foreword

The history of the West is the history of boom and bust. More than any other region of the United States, the West has found it difficult to find a happy average. We seem almost inevitably to have too much or too little. Today's boomtowns are too often tomorrow's ghost towns.

The West, in fact, has always been a place of extremes — in its topography, in its climate, and, alas, in its economy. We have the highest mountains and we have the lowest valleys. We have the hottest weather and the coldest weather, some of the most scenic areas, and some of the most monotonous. But over the history of the West, one of the hardest extremes to adjust to is the seemingly endless cycle of boom and bust. First too much growth and then too little. Time after time the West has seen bright, excited hopes turning almost overnight into ruined nightmares. The boomtown is almost a metaphor for the West — full of hope and optimism followed by disillusionment and decay.

One of the most challenging tasks in my twelve years as governor of Colorado was how to get the state ready for energy development that we were told was coming our way.

The Rocky Mountain West has an inordinate amount of the nation's remaining resources. We have a disproportionate amount of the coal, uranium, geothermal sites, and vast reservoirs of natural gas packed into tight formations. But, however disproportionate the other energy resources are in the Rocky Mountain West, we have practically 100 percent of the usable oil shale. For better or worse, nature has placed in the West virtually all of the oil shale that has any chance of commercial development. This resource, along with the other energy resources, became a favorite topic of exploration as OPEC strengthened its hold on United States energy supplies and we started looking ever inward for our domestic energy sources.

New coal mines were opening up, new wells were drilled for oil and gas. Uranium experienced a small rejuvenation. But by far the most difficult to try to understand, anticipate, and plan for was oil shale.

It is that fascinating and instructive story that Andrew Gulliford recounts in *Boomtown Blues*. He tells the story with all its hope and despair, with all of its rich dreams and its failed enterprises. It is a tale of many parts, but always fascinating.

Planning for oil shale was like changing a tire on an automobile moving sixty miles an hour. One never knew whether one was over-reacting or underreacting. In a small area of northwestern Colorado, where in 1974 there lived under 15,000 people, we were told at various times to get ready for 100,000 people, then 250,000 people, then one-half million, and at one point even one million people. No superlative was too grand for describing what oil shale would mean to that area. All of a sudden a new breed of non-Coloradoan was seen upon the land, with polyester suits and dollar signs in their eyes. They came to Colorado to seek their fortunes. In many ways, not unlike earlier conquistadors, prospectors, or settlers, they were fueled by hopes and by dreams. They were also fueled by greed.

From an administrator's point of view, this raised many complex issues. First, most of the oil shale was on federal land, raising many legal and moral problems about the extent to which the state could and should assert its interest in the development of oil shale. Clearly this was a natural resource that appeared to be in great demand. A nation-threatening energy crisis lay before us, and obviously oil shale played some, yet unquantified, part in its solution. But more immediate was how Colorado was going to accommodate all this growth and change. Who was going to pay for the schools, sewers, water, and infrastructure that this new development would generate?

It was at this point that history came to Colorado's rescue. I had my governor's cabinet read and understand the boom and bust nature of the West. We recognized that too often today's "permanent mining activity" would tomorrow be a hole in the ground surrounded by a ghost town. We fought against local communities financing the new infrastructure and demanded that either industry or the federal government pay for the impact that was occurring. We fought for and passed a severance tax that would help compensate us for the impact that oil shale was having on the state. We insisted that energy "pay its own way."

There are few things I am prouder of than that battle. When oil shale busted, it was a tragedy but not the catastrophe that it could have been if Colorado communities had built the infrastructure with their own funds against the promise of riches. We were terribly affected but much less so than if we would have had to pay off the impact mitigation without the promised development.

There may be no way to prevent cycles in the economy of the West, but we can learn from our past and make sure that new growth pays for it impact. It is enough to live with the human tragedy without also having to live with the financial tragedy.

RICHARD D. LAMM

Acknowledgments

The idea for this book began in 1977 on a park bench in Craig, Colorado, during a conversation with photojournalist Randall Teeuwen. Randy and I had just received the first $12,000 of a $17,000 grant from the Colorado Endowment for the Humanities to produce a slide-tape program and public forums. We were to research and write "The Years Ahead: Life for the Aging in Northwest Colorado" and document energy development and its impact on the elderly. As Randy and I talked that June afternoon in Craig, the energy boom was in full swing and he regretted that we were focusing on senior citizens instead of on the boom. I argued that we had to proceed with our initial project and he finally concurred. Many of those interviews conducted twelve years ago are excerpted in this book, and almost all of the old-timers we interviewed have since passed on.

Our humanities project was one of the most successful ever funded in Colorado, and while acting as co-director, I learned a great deal about the awesome energy impact overtaking the Western Slope and the attempts by local government to deal with unprecedented growth. I finished "The Years Ahead" and then researched one-room schools for another humanities project and a book titled *America's Country Schools*. The energy boom busted: My friends started to lose their jobs, their houses, and their marriages, and after seven years teaching elementary school and community college courses in Silt and Rifle, Colorado, my wife and I moved to Ohio for graduate school. It was there I finally decided to write about oil shale and boomtown blues.

When I came back to Colorado on a research trip, local government bureaucracies and corporate oil shale divisions had collapsed. I went looking for files, records, and documents, and secretaries willingly told me to take whatever I wanted; oil shale was dead, and professional staffs on the Western Slope had been cut by 60 percent. In October of 1985, I filled my Volkswagen camper with box after box of oil shale information and outdated reports. With depressed and disillusioned people, I conducted some of the most poignant and intimate oral histories I have ever recorded, and then I returned to Bowling Green, Ohio, and began to write.

The first version of *Boomtown Blues* was written as a dissertation in American Culture that I completed in August of 1986 at Bowling Green State University. The dissertation has since been carefully edited, revised, and, where necessary, updated. Debts incurred in writing this book are many yet only a few can be specifically acknowledged here. I am particularly indebted to Professor William E. Grant, director of the American Culture Program at Bowling Green State University, because he helped to shape my thinking and gave me the intellectual freedom to research and to synthesize this interdisciplinary subject. I also enjoyed working with Dr. Kendall Baker, Dr. Edmund E. Danziger, Dr. Leslie H. Fishel, Jr., and Dr. Arthur G. Neal.

I am grateful for a twelve-month Non-Service Research Fellowship from the Graduate College at Bowling Green State University that provided me the time and opportunity so essential to complete this project. I was also privileged to receive Graduate College Dissertation Research Support funds that enabled me to conduct important oral history interviews in Houston and Denver.

To my wife, Stephanie Bruce Moran, a former boomtown teacher, I am indebted not only for her superior editing skills and her patience while I monopolized the computer keyboard, but also for her willingness to stay home with our four-month-old son when I took a six-week research trip to Colorado in the fall of 1985 and returned again in January and March 1986. She also stayed home with Tristan David for three weeks in April of 1986 while I completed a fellowship at the Smithsonian Institution's National Museum of American History. I studied with curators there while conducting additional interviews in Washington, D.C., and I examined oil shale files in former U. S. Senator Gary Hart's office. Recently, Stephanie provided me with the essential solitude I needed as I edited the dissertation into a book, but this time she had both Tristan David and Duncan Jewett to contend with.

To the dozens of people I interviewed who shared with me their lives and their dreams, their achievements and their failures, I can only say thank you. First and foremost, I am indebted to Patrick

O'Neill, the intrepid *Rifle Tribune* reporter/editor and co-owner of Liam O'Leary's Pub, who has the rare personal quality of being able to stare financial disaster in the face and to grin back; to Jim Sullivan of the *Grand Junction Daily Sentinel*; Reverend Lynn Evans, formerly of the Rifle United Methodist-Presbyterian Church; Joe Fox of the Tell Ertl Family Trust; Charles Pence, former president of Battlement Mesa, Inc.; Gary Schmitz of the *Denver Post*; Roger Ludwig, Garfield County administrator; Ralph Freedman, former Parachute town administrator; Robert Nuffer, associate director, Sopris Mental Health Center; Joyce Illian, social worker; Frank Barrow, former project director of the Colony Oil Shale Project; Sonja Fritzlan, a Garfield County native; and Rhonda Atchetee of Exxon, U.S.A. in Houston. A special word of thanks goes to Jo Mahoney, who conscientiously transcribed hours of oral history interviews.

For local history sources on Garfield County, Colorado, I wish to thank Nina McNeel and and the staff at the Garfield County Public Library in New Castle, Larry McClue of Silt, Louis and Carol Dodo of West Elk Creek, Laura Van Dyne of Missouri Heights, Rifle attorney John W. Savage, Jr., and the Boultons — John, Alice, and Owen — from Silt and Rifle who shared their original edition of F. V. Hayden's *Tenth Annual Report of the United States Geological and Geographical Survey of the Territories Embracing Colorado and Parts of Adjacent Territories (1878)*. After being carried in a saddlebag during countless prospecting trips by R. E. Boulton eighty years ago, the volume became a vital addition to my research shelf.

For contemporary sources, I am indebted to Dave Norman of the Associated Governments of Northwest Colorado; Ronald Elving, United States Senate Committee on Environment and Public Works, Minority Staff; Dr. Frederic J. Athearn, historian with the Denver office of the Bureau of Land Management; Dr. Arthur M. Hartstein, deputy director, Office of Oil, Gas & Shale Technology in the U.S. Department of Energy; Judy A. Prosser, archivist and registrar at the Museum of Western Colorado; Dr. William R. Freudenburg, Department of Rural Sociology, University of Wisconsin-Madison; John S. Gilmore, senior research fellow at the Denver Research Institute, University of Denver; Constance Albrecht and L. Geoffrey Webb of Friends of the Earth; Eleanor Gehres of the Western History Department at the Denver Public Library; K. James Cook, publisher of the *Rifle Tribune* and the *Meeker Herald;* Paul Petzrick of the Oil Shale Association in Washington, D.C.; and Judy Gasset, Penny Grigsby, Herb McGrath, and Leslie Trich of the inter-library loan and reference staff of Miller Library at Western New Mexico University.

I also want to thank Luther Wilson and his staff at the University Press of Colorado for their enthusiasm and attention to detail. Ms. Joan Sherman is to be commended for her careful copyediting, and D. J. Gulliford for his critical reading of the page proofs. Assistance in publishing this book came from the Tell Ertl Family Trust. For two decades the Ertl Family has believed in oil shale and actively supported oil shale research.

ANDREW GULLIFORD
SILVER CITY, NEW MEXICO

Boomtown Blues

Introduction

Of all the mining booms that built and shaped the American West, beginning with the California and Nevada "rushes" of the nineteenth century and progressing through the booms in Idaho, Montana, Colorado, Arizona, and New Mexico, none can compare in intensity to the energy boom of the 1970s.

The initial booms of the last century were stimulated by an appetite for hardrock minerals, but it was an international thirst for oil that created the most recent energy boom. One of the epicenters of that boom was in western Colorado, where, by 1974 estimates, the richest oil shale deposits in the world are located in one small area — the Piceance Creek Basin — containing 500 billion barrels of recoverable oil in seams at least 5 feet thick.[1] Though hardly as glamorous as gold or silver, oil shale is definitely attractive to a nation that consumes millions of barrels of oil each year.[2]

The recent boom and subsequent bust stretched across the entire length of the Rocky Mountains in New Mexico, Colorado, Utah, Wyoming, Idaho, and Montana, and included strippable coal reserves in the Dakotas as well. This region's response to the energy crisis of the mid-1970s produced 200 boomtowns, including 25 in Colorado. Small towns boomed because they were adjacent to oil shale, coal, uranium, oil, natural, gas, or even underground reservoirs of carbon dioxide.[3]

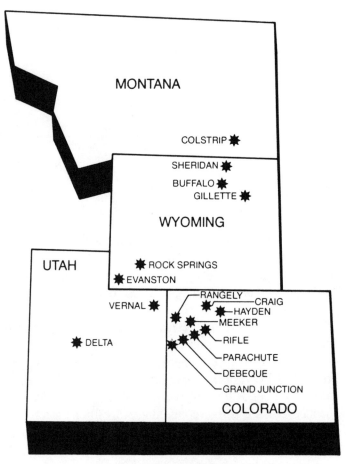

BOOMTOWNS

The mid-1970s and early 1980s produced over 200 boomtowns in the Rocky Mountain states, but the center of the boom was in the oil shale region of western Colorado. *From Lamm and McCarthy,* The Angry West (1982). *Copyright © 1982 by Richard D. Lamm and Michael McCarthy. By permission of Houghton Mifflin Company.*

These Rocky Mountain boomtowns are characterized by physical isolation, rapid urbanization, dependence upon the extraction of a natural resource, and a swift community decline when the price of the natural resource falls. This cycle produces profound effects upon boomtown inhabitants, who are frequently victimized by these episodic changes in fortune.

In many respects, contemporary boomtowns replicated their predecessors in their adaptation to both the boom and the bust economies. Gillette, Wyoming, for example, has been noted for its "drunkenness, anomie, mental discord, suicide attempts and teenage rebellion," and the "Gillette Syndrome" of social unrest and population impact became a generic label applied to western boomtowns by social scientists.[4] Hardrock miners from the previous century would have felt right at home in Gillette.

The major difference between Rocky Mountain boomtowns in the 1870s and the 1970s was the makeup of the resident population. A century ago, most of the residents were scattered bands of Native Americans who were quickly forced from their ancestral lands, and the nineteenth-century gold and silver camps sprang up on the sides of mountains far removed from civilization. In contrast, the late twentieth-century boomtowns rapidly evolved from quiet communities of third-generation farmers and ranchers who were not at all prepared for the influx of newcomers and the demands they placed on antiquated and overtaxed municipal systems. Thus, rural communities previously characterized by the relative stability of farming and ranching economies encountered the disruptive elements of boomtown growth: drunkenness, depression, delinquency, and divorce. Then, just when city planners, school teachers, social workers, and county sheriffs had begun to stabilize and improve local life, the boomtowns became bust towns, and thousands of the newcomers left as quickly as they had arrived. As the value of oil declined, so, too, did the market value of other forms of energy, such as coal and uranium.

Historians have delighted in describing the ephemeral life of mining camps of the past, and they have placed mining camp successes and failures into regional and national perspective. But little attention has been paid to these mining camps as communities within a broad social and cultural context. The larger questions of what constitutes a community and how communities are formed, sustained, and changed over time have not been applied to modern mining camps because the questions themselves address social and cultural issues rather than historical ones.

During the 1970s, numerous sociologists studied the unsettled atmosphere of western boomtowns, but few are studying the more recent economic downswing and its social impact. In particular, few scholars have studied oil shale development and the aftermath of the largest localized mining boom and quickest bust in western history. Historians and sociologists should find common ground with a topic that is as old as the mining frontier in the United States and as new as the latest coal, gas, oil, or uranium strike. Yet, despite a plethora of recent community studies, cultural historians have not concerned themselves with small, isolated Rocky Mountain communities in the throes of rapid urbanization, nor have sociologists bothered to return to those depressed western communities they first studied when the towns were booming and state, federal, and corporate research dollars were plentiful. This study is the first thorough social and community history of a recent Rocky Mountain boom. Its focus is oil shale development in Colorado from 1885 to 1985 and the impact of this development on communities in the Colorado River Valley, specifically the towns of New Castle, Silt, Rifle, Parachute, and Grand Junction.

Now that those communities have suffered the pangs of shrinking budgets, vacant housing, unemployment, and bank foreclosures, sociologists remain in their academic enclaves and historians wait for time to pass. The historians saw no reason to study the boom's upswing, and the sociologists and economists have lost interest in the downward spiral. Yet the damage has been done, and the opportunity to reflect and gain perspective is *now* — not at some distant point in the future when the cycle begins to repeat itself.

Boom-and-bust cycles have perennially plagued the resource-rich West, which has depended upon eastern capital to finance expansion, industrialization, and community settlement. A century ago, eastern money flowed in to develop the Comstock Lode in Virginia City, the Independence Mine in Cripple Creek, and dozens of other booms throughout the West. But the profits flowed east, leaving communities destitute when the paying ore was gone. Wallace Stegner writes that, then as now, the mining camps "went out like blown matches."[5] The physical decimation of a mining region like Appalachia is well known, but equally significant, though harder to identify, are the social and cultural effects of boom-and-bust cycles that may leave the environment relatively unscathed but have profound effects on local residents nonetheless.

Historically, boomtowns were mining camps and tent cities perched precariously on some of the highest mountains in North America. The 1882 boomtown of Carbonate, Colorado, for example, at 10,783 feet was relatively inacessible in summer; in winter, stakes driven into the ground to mark boundaries for town lots lay buried under 12 feet of snow. Thus, a key factor in any analysis of boom-and-bust cycles in the Rockies is physical isolation. As sociologist William Freudenburg wrote in 1984, "The communities experiencing rapid growth are among the most geographically isolated in the nation."[6]

Because of this isolation and the homogeneity of the farmers and ranchers whose families have lived for two or three generations on the same land, rapid development by outsiders created community conflict. The isolation of ranching communities led to the establishment over time of rural attitudes, traits, folkways, and values that ran deep and often counter to the heady boomtown atmosphere of financial speculation on leveraged real estate options and investments. Yet many long-timers did enjoy what I term "boomtown euphoria," and today they miss the hustle and excitement. The appeal of a quickened boomtown pace to rural westerners has not been described in the social science literature, though it was a definite and interesting phenomenon.

Unlike social scientists who spent a few months visiting the boomtowns of their choice, I moved to Silt, Colorado, in the late summer of 1976 and stayed through the summer of 1983. My role as a "participant-observer" lasted seven years. I have also repeatedly returned to locate sources, update interviews, and take the changing pulse of the communities I describe.[7] My study illustrates some unique boomtown impacts not previously described, including "boomtown euphoria" and "the crucible effect" that forced white collar workers to develop their professional expertise under stressful conditions. I also describe the step-by-step phases of a boomtown bust, just as John S. Gilmore described the boom phases in his seminal article published in *Science*.[8]

With the energy boom of the 1970s, small towns were changed overnight by rapid growth. The feeling of excitement, of being part of a larger whole, was an urban attitude new to long-time rural residents. From the family practice physician to the grade school janitor, in a boomtown situation everyone works hard just to keep up. In Parachute, Colorado, during the height of the boom, one gas station proprietor pumped more gasoline in a week than he normally pumped in two months. Residents enjoyed the commotion, and everyone with a job felt needed — though often overworked and overwhelmed. Even Danny the Bum, who slept in the alleys of Parachute, made a daily dollar by sweeping out O'Leary's Pub.

The Rocky Mountain communities that expanded and girded for growth have recently faced economic woes similar to those experienced by their industrial kin in Akron, Detroit, and Youngstown, but western boomtowns lack the occupational infrastructure of eastern regions to help absorb unemployment. Ironically, the western boomtowns have new city halls, sewer systems, schools, churches, and paved streets, but few residents.

The oil shale boom of the 1970s was not the nation's first. As war clouds loomed in 1914, the nation took stock of its strategic resources, and experts announced that the country had only a nine-year supply of oil reserves. Three years later, President Woodrow Wilson withdrew 45,444 acres of Colorado oil shale lands and 86,584 acres of shale lands in Utah to establish a permanent Naval Oil Shale Reserve. From 1919 to 1920, prospectors filed 30,000 oil shale claims on 4 million acres. Yet no technology emerged to process this shale, which was nicknamed "rubber rock" because, once heated, it flows for a short time and then solidifies in shale retorts.

The first oil shale boom also went bust. With the discovery of millions of gallons of crude oil in the Permian Basin of Texas and Oklahoma, this first boom came to an abrupt halt in the early 1920s, but not before substantial changes occurred in land ownership. Corporations consolidated their holdings up and down Parachute Creek, then put up a few fences, stocked the pastures with cattle, and waited.

The story of Parachute pioneer Mike Callahan (for whom a prominent peak north of the Colorado River is named) is an apt local parable. According to legend, Mike settled near Parachute in the early 1880s and built a log cabin from indigenous materials. When he was finished, he invited all his friends over for a housewarming. Whites and Indians alike complimented Mike on the new cabin and warmed their backsides by the fireplace until the housewarming got too hot. The fireplace Mike had built out of shale rock started to drip and catch fire, and the cabin burned to the ground. Like Mike's cabin, the first oil shale boom flamed brightly, then turned to ashes almost as quickly. When the cycle recurred in the 1970s, however, it caused significant community and social impact.

Nearly half a century after Mike built his ill-fated cabin, price fixing by the Organization of Petroleum Exporting Countries (OPEC) in 1973 precipitated a worldwide energy crisis. A host of political scientists, economists, and national defense experts predicted dire consequences caused by our dependence on foreign crude. The international hoopla over rising oil prices and a national panic over the depletion of a finite resource finally changed the consumer habits of Americans who were furious at waiting in line to buy gas. Smaller cars successfully competed in the marketplace, and Americans explored alternative energy sources as a major shift in energy conservation occurred. Nineteenth-century gold and silver booms may have pumped millions of dollars into the U.S. economy and helped to fuel a young nation's expansion, but the energy crisis of the 1970s had a worldwide ripple effect that toppled governments, shifted billions in assets around the globe, and rearranged U.S. political constituencies.

Three different presidents contended with the energy crisis in the 1970s: Richard Nixon, Gerald Ford, and Jimmy Carter. In response, Nixon began Project Independence, and Ford endorsed and expanded Nixon's plans. But Carter, who pronounced that energy self-sufficiency for the United States was "the moral equivalent of war," called for nothing less than an $88 billion outlay — more money than had been spent on both the space program and the interstate highway system. Under Carter, Congress established the Synthetic Fuels Corporation and allocated $12 billion for seed money. While grade school students learned to turn down thermostats and turn off lights, the West — from Texas to Montana — boomed as development capital poured in for the extraction of energy resources.

In a decade characterized by double-digit inflation and rising unemployment, residents of western Colorado had no worries about layoffs. "The nation needs oil," they were told; "America's dependence on foreign oil must stop," the experts said.[9] Boomers on Colorado's Western Slope knew they lived near a "black gold mine" of shale oil, and they took comfort in those vast reserves.

Though oil shale is distributed throughout the globe and constitutes a major hydrocarbon resource, our country's most important deposits are located in Colorado, Utah, and Wyoming. Best of all, oil shale deposits are on federal lands available for long-term lease under the Mineral Leasing Act of 1920. These deposits, located in the heart of the American West, seemed the perfect answer to high oil prices from the unstable Middle East. The national mood called for action, and prospects of high profits whetted the oil companies' appetites for major, crash development of synthetic fuels. Healthy federal subsidies only sweetened the pot. Consequently, companies bought oil shale leases worth $210 million in 1974. Soon, roads needed to be built, apartment buildings constructed, schools enlarged, and telephones installed. Industrial giants roared into rural western Colorado to begin heavy construction, and thousands of workers from Michigan, Illinois, North and South Carolina, and every depressed state in the nation began to flood into Garfield County. The unemployed came to put in applications with The Industrial Company, Daniels Construction, and Gilbert-Western.

Then, in mid-1980, the largest company in the world, Exxon, U.S.A., a division of Exxon Corporation, bought out the oil shale interests of Atlantic Richfield Company (Arco) and, in partnership with The Oil Shale Company (Tosco), set out to aggressively develop the Colony Oil Shale Project. Exxon planned to spend $5 billion in a 100-mile-long valley with fewer than 100,000 people. Brown & Root, the second-largest contracting firm in the nation, was hired to do the construction work. By 1981, in addition to Exxon's Colony Project, oil shale development included ventures or joint ventures by Union,

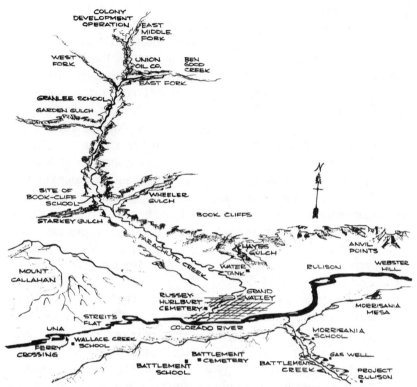

The locations of historic communities near the oil shale boomtown of Parachute are shown in this illustration from Erlene Durrant Murray, *Lest We Forget: A Short History of Early Grand Valley, Colorado, originally called Parachute, Colorado* (1981).

Chevron, Mobil, Tenneco, and Occidental, as well as smaller firms like Equity, Paraho, and Rio Blanco Oil Shale Company. The economic, environmental, and social impacts were unparalleled.

In Colorado, on the western side of the Continental Divide, some 200 miles from the Denver metropolitan area, the oil shale impact fell on the small towns of Parachute (pop. 300); Rifle (pop. 2,200); Silt (pop. 900); and New Castle (pop. 700). Exxon planned to build an entirely new community on Battlement Mesa, just south of Parachute, on land that was only marginal cattle range. Population for the town of Battlement Mesa was expected to reach 25,000 by the 1990s — equal to the existing population of the entire county! Planners anticipated that Parachute's population would swell to 15,000, and the other small towns in the valley would also mushroom.

But the limitless West is a land of limitations. Despite the lure of magnificent scenery and soaring mountain peaks, the Rockies have remained sparsely settled and largely devoid of manufacturing and industry — for good reason. As John Wesley Powell made clear in his 1878 *Report on the Arid Region of the United States*, only an "oasis civilization" could survive in the West, for beyond the 100th meridian, precipitation averages less than 20 inches a year.[10] Water has historically been a limiting factor, yet the oil companies proceeded with oil shale development on the premise that ample water supplies existed. Developers felt that water was being wasted on agriculture, and fortunes were made by farmers and ranchers who retained title to their land but sold their senior water rights for shale oil processes that required a barrel of water to produce each barrel of oil. Exxon officials even planned to pipe water from the Missouri River basin to Piceance Creek.

Exxon's infamous "white paper" titled "The Role of Synthetic Fuels in the United States Energy Future" (1980) stunned scientists and journalists alike.[11] Among its other prodigious plans, the company suggested rearranging the drainage system of the North American continent to suit the energy emergency. (Officials insisted that costs could be kept to a minimum.) However, the proposals did not fully take into account the fact that water is the lifeblood of the West and the unifying factor in western economics, politics, and culture.

Such was the scope of the oil shale boom and the environmental frenzy in the late 1970s and early 1980s. Quiet Colorado River Valley towns became polarized boomtowns, and an entire city was being built to accommodate the fastest development of a new industry in the history of the United States. In late 1981 and early 1982, tremors of doubt began to filter through the boomtown euphoria, and there were warning signals within the industry. But western Colorado continued to enjoy the boom that business people had dreamed about. Few speculators wanted to listen to reason, despite the warnings of environmental activists like Edward Abbey.

In a speech given in 1976 at The Vail Symposium VI, Abbey urged westerners to stop planning for growth and, instead, send "those

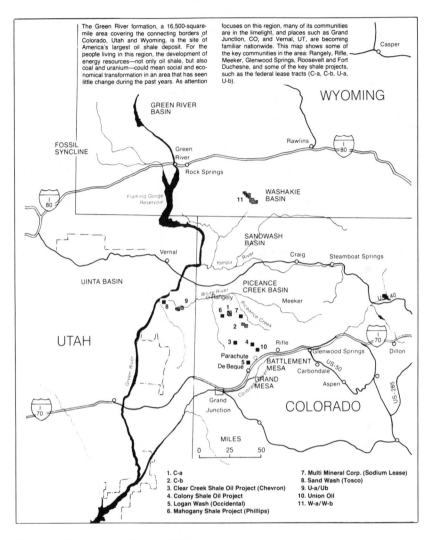

The Green River formation, a 16,500-square-mile area covering the connecting borders of Colorado, Utah and Wyoming, is the site of America's largest oil shale deposit. For the people living in this region, the development of energy resources—not only oil shale, but also coal and uranium—could mean social and economical transformation in an area that has seen little change during the past years. As attention focuses on this region, many of its communities are in the limelight, and places such as Grand Junction, CO, and Vernal, UT, are becoming familiar nationwide. This map shows some of the key communities in the area: Rangely, Rifle, Meeker, Glenwood Springs, Roosevelt and Fort Duchesne, and some of the key shale projects, such as the federal lease tracts (C-a, C-b, U-a, U-b).

1. C-a
2. C-b
3. Clear Creek Shale Oil Project (Chevron)
4. Colony Shale Oil Project
5. Logan Wash (Occidental)
6. Mahogany Shale Project (Phillips)
7. Multi Mineral Corp. (Sodium Lease)
8. Sand Wash (Tosco)
9. U-a/Ub
10. Union Oil
11. W-a/W-b

Courtesy of Shale Country *(January 1982).*

iron crocodiles" crawling back to where they came from — the Caterpillar and heavy equipment factories in the Midwest. He suggested that "wherever you go in your auto travels among the wonders of our Rocky Mountain West," always carry "a gallon or two of shellac with you, and a bucketful of fine clean sand." The shellac was intended "for the fuel tank and the sand for the crank-case" of offensive, interloping heavy construction equipment.[12] A prominent environmental group, Friends of the Earth, proclaimed oil shale and massive synthetic fuels development as its primary concern in the United States.

Many local people in the oil shale region thought differently. Although they felt overwhelmed and fatalistic about the impending energy development, many older residents saw opportunity as well. They resigned themselves to the demise of their way of life, but hoped for employment for the young. Retired Rifle schoolteacher Robert Wamsley succinctly expressed the views of most area senior citizens when he said, "Oil shale is here to stay. When you have companies which have committed a good many millions to development programs, they're not in here for fun. They're here for real." He expressed the patriotic sentiments of many Coloradans when he explained that oil shale is "badly needed by the nation. I have mixed emotions about what'll happen to the countryside, and you know they'll tear up the mountains and add pollution, but on the other hand we need the economic stimulus of industry."[13]

But it was neither Edward Abbey's shellac-toting eco-activists nor recalcitrant ranchers fearful of losing their water rights that stopped the heavy equipment. It was pure economics and a decline in the price of oil. On Sunday, May 2, 1982, Exxon announced it was closing down the Colony Project. The day of the announcement is known locally as "Black Sunday," and almost everyone in Garfield County remembers what he or she was doing when the news broke. By Monday morning, 2,100 people knew they were immediately unemployed, for when they reported to work, they found the gates locked; they were not even allowed to retrieve their lunch pails and coats. For workers who had moved hundreds of miles to the Exxon site, severance pay was only two hours extra wages and mileage to and from the job site.

Despite twenty-one months of intensive development on a project estimated to cost $5 billion, Exxon stopped all work on the Colony Project in one day. In eighteen months, a brush-covered pasture had become a town of 1,700 people, but on the day Exxon ceased spending $1 million a week on Battlement Mesa, 400 apartments and condominium units were under construction, as were 46 single-family homes.

Memories, both good and bad, are still fresh. Residents faced foreclosures, bankruptcies, and divorces caused by emotional and financial stress. In twenty years, they will have made their adjustments, and their attitudes will have mellowed. At present, however, the pain is real, for these people acted in concert with what they felt were national needs and priorities, investing time and money in projects that rarely succeeded. As greed became a prominent factor in the boomtown equation, financial security for these once prudent people vanished. Local newspapers have written about returning to a "pre-boom" economy, but that is not possible. Congress voted in December 1985, to abolish the Synthetic Fuels Corporation, effectively dampening any immediate hope for a viable oil shale industry.

For local residents, shock often gave way to deepening depression. Just as individuals must go through a grief process when faced with extensive personal loss, so, too, must communities grieve. The few newcomers who have stayed consider themselves "survivors" exactly as if they had endured a natural catastrophe.[14]

After seven years, there is finally emotional acceptance in Garfield County, but the stasis achieved is uneasy. Local employment is limited, and because of large debts and hefty mortgages assumed during the boom, many residents must now commute to work over ninety miles on roads that are snow-packed in the winter. Some men even stay all week at their worksites, making "weekday widows" of their wives. Senior citizens who once looked forward to their children living nearby have adjusted to their departure. Traditional patterns of rural life have been irrevocably altered.

As happened in the nineteenth-century exploitation, rural westerners in the late twentieth century found themselves powerless to control the external economic forces dictating development. In 1936, Bernard DeVoto published his famous essay calling the West a "plundered province,"[15] and revisionist historians such as Patricia Nelson Limerick and William G. Robbins have enumerated similar patterns in recent years.[16] Gene M. Gressley has also made it clear that westerners are perfectly capable of complaining loudly about government intervention and corporate largesse while stretching a hand behind their backs and seeking fistfuls of dollars.[17] If there are lessons to be learned from boom-and-bust cycles in the West, the oil shale saga is more than just an excellent case study. It is *the* case study.

Now, seven years after the most recent collapse, eagles are returning to their nesting areas and the salinity of the Colorado River is unaltered by leaching from spent shale. Yet fossil fuels will always be a nonrenewable — and therefore precious — resource. The recent energy bust is only a truce — not a lasting peace. An oil shale boom may come again, for the economies of the world are still fueled by enormous appetites for energy, and the rock that burns lies deep in dark layers of shale.

1

Exploration and Settlement in the Valley of the Colorado

Such was the nature of this particular valley; its history would be unique and different from all earlier migrations of men into Colorado. There were no minerals to attract those who might gamble on a wild get-rich-quick existence. Emigrants would choose this valley for a piece of good earth in which they could put down roots to produce a home.

Reading Club of Rifle
Rifle Shots

Any history of the Colorado River Valley and its small towns must begin with a description of the landscape, for it is the majestic mountains, mesas, and valleys that have shaped the course of the region's history and set it apart as one of the last areas to be settled in the United States. The north side of the Colorado River near Rifle and Parachute is characterized by high cliffs marking the upper boundary of the valley. There, the oil shale forms very steep walls, below which are concave talus slopes molded from weathered shales. This wall of cliffs is pierced by the canyons of Rifle Creek to the northeast, Parachute Creek to the north, and Roan Creek to the northwest. These canyons penetrate far back into the cliffs, and their bottomland resembles that of the valley floor, a fairly level alluvial flood plain. On the south side of the river, the mesas are ancient alluvial fans of lighter-weight, highly fertile volcanic materials. In the valleys of creeks and streams, and in the bottomlands, the alluvial soils are organically rich. Above the mesas stand uplands, and over them the North and South Mamm peaks rise an additional 6,000 feet above the valley floor to a total elevation of nearly 11,000 feet.

On the valley floor grow willows and cottonwoods. Higher on the mesas, native plants include blue-gray sage, greasewood, piñon, juniper, and scrub oak, extending up to timberline. The high mountain terrain is heavily forested with Colorado blue spruce, Douglas fir, Ponderosa pine, and large stands of aspen trees. The Western Slope of Colorado, so named because all waters here drain to the Pacific Ocean and not the Gulf of Mexico, has thousands of acres of national forests that were set aside in 1891. The White River National Forest and the Battlement National Forest are huge reserves; of all the national forests and parks, only Yellowstone was set aside earlier. One section of the White River National Forest, the Flat Tops, is a unique range of mountains 10,000 feet high, but level on top, that contains dozens of accessible alpine lakes. Less than 5 percent of all national forest qualifies as wilderness worthy of preservation "for all time for people of the nation and the world" — the intent of the National Wilderness Act of 1964 — yet the Flat Tops is an area so pristine and remote that 235,035 acres have been withdrawn as the Flat Tops Wilderness — one of the largest tracts of primitive land to receive that national designation. All motorized vehicles are banned and access is limited to travelers on horseback or on foot.[1] The world's richest oil shale deposits lie within 100 miles of the Flat Tops.

From the eastern end of the upper Colorado River Valley near Glenwood Springs, where the river roars out of narrow and precipitous Glenwood Canyon, to the fruit-growing regions of Palisade and Grand Junction 80 miles west, the valley has a moderate, four-season climate without excessive temperature variation. In some years, winter has been severe enough to freeze the Colorado River solid, occasionally giving pioneers the luxury of walking across it. In summer, temperatures rarely exceed 90 degrees. Clear skies, dry air, and a lack of violent thunderstorms produce uniform daily weather. The best season is autumn, when the aspen trees near timberline turn to brilliant golds and reds. In those crisp fall days, hunters track some of the largest deer and elk herds in the continental United States. Former residents often return for the hunt, which is frequently a family reunion as well.

The conclusions of the first explorers and surveyors in this area are as valid now as then: the unifying force in the region — geologically, geographically, culturally, and economically — has always been the Colorado River. As the mountains moved and the Rockies thrust upward, only the river remained constant — the river that men would call Rio de San Rafael, the Grand River, and, finally, the Colorado or Rio Colorado, the great red river of the West that drains 246,000 square miles.[2]

As the snows melt on the Flat Tops and the Cline Tops, on Storm King Mountain and the Mamm Peaks and the Book Cliffs, dozens of creeks flow with precious rivulets of water. The creeks begin in shallow mountain pools beneath stands of aspen and Engelmann spruce. For centuries, beavers have tried to stop that annual flow, but the water cascades anyway, cutting magnificent gorges like the Deep Creek and Glenwood canyons. Bighorn sheep have grazed on top of the canyon cliffs, and squawfish up to 120 pounds have swum in the muddy spring runoff of the Colorado.

The river neatly bisects Garfield County, and settlement occurred in valleys that were only a day's ride from the river's course. But before white men cut timbers for the first log cabins, Ute Indians, who were skilled horsemen, lived in the valley and regularly followed deer, elk, and an extinct species of mountain bison up narrow mountain trails to luxuriant summer meadows on the Flat Tops.

The Ute Indians in the Colorado Rockies were made up of seven groups, but it is unknown which band assisted the first white men in crossing the river — Franciscan friars Silvestre Velez de Escalante and Francisco Dominguez. In 1776, these adventurous Spanish fathers left Santa Fe seeking a shorter route to California. They came into the Colorado River Valley from the south by traveling up from the Gunnison River Valley and along the summit of the Elk Mountain Range. (Years later, hundreds of miners and prospectors would take the same route as they abandoned the frenetic pace of the boomtowns of Leadville and Aspen in search of quieter country and new opportunities.) The fathers descended from the Elk Mountains to the head of San Antonio Martir, now known as Divide Creek. They followed the creek to the Colorado and named it Rio de San Rafael. For several days, they looked for a place to cross, finally choosing a site west of Parachute at a river bend known as Streits Flat, where the channel is narrow and the water is relatively calm.[3] The friars crossed the Colorado in September and rode north to the White River Valley, then journeyed west from a campsite that was later named Powell Flats after Major John Wesley Powell. Dominguez and Escalante never made it to California. They became hopelessly lost, backtracked, and finally found themselves staring into an awesome chasm — the Grand Canyon. Confronted with this insurmountable barrier, they aborted their mission and returned to Santa Fe.

Nearly a century later, Major Powell would also see the Grand Canyon, but not from the top on horseback, as the friars had, but from the bottom as he led the first expedition to run the Colorado River through mile after mile of whitewater rapids. Powell initially conceived of running the Colorado while he was head of the United States Geological Survey (USGS) and stationed at his winter camp on the White River, less than sixty miles from the Colorado River and the Book Cliff formation of oil shale mountains. The winter Major Powell spent along the White River in 1868–1869 was to be the first of over thirty seasons he dedicated to studying the Colorado Plateau. He wrote that, after establishing winter quarters, he "intended to occupy the cold season . . . in exploring the adjacent country." He seized every opportunity to study the nearby canyons. Not one to limit himself or his fields of interest, he explained that although his job had "begun originally as an exploration, the work was finally developed into a survey, embracing the geography, geology, ethnography, and natural history" of the surrounding area.[4]

Soon his work would encompass the entire West, and in an extraordinary nineteenth-century career, the one-armed Shiloh veteran would run the roughest of the Colorado rapids, begin the USGS, become the first director of the Bureau of Ethnology, and administer the first institutions under the U.S. government that applied science to the haphazard process of settlement and development of the remaining frontier. His illustrious career, however, was almost over before it began, for Ute tribesmen of the Grand River Band came close to scalping Powell when he pounded in his first survey stakes. He discreetly removed them and spent five peaceful months at Powell Park.

With the publication of his *Report on the Lands West of the Arid Region of the United States* in 1878, Powell distinctly spelled out a plan of settlement for the West that would have prevented the major trauma and dislocation caused by naive homesteaders trying to settle regions with inadequate rainfall.[5] Powell's report was taken seriously in Colorado, if not in other states west of the hundredth meridian. One year later, in 1879, Colorado became the first state to provide for equitable distribution of water by dividing its land into irrigation districts. Settlers filing on Western Slope homesteads in the Colorado River Valley also filed on water rights, because precipitation in the valley seldom exceeds 12 inches annually. Most of that moisture comes in the winter and spring in the form of snow, which can get several feet deep in the high country but seldom more than 6 inches on the valley floor. Therefore, settlement patterns in the Colorado River Valley duplicated plans set forth by Powell, even to the shape of the county, which follows the course of the river. Settlers built their homesteads near creeks and streambeds, for irrigation played a vital role in settlement up and down the valley. However, it was not Powell's report that enticed homesteaders to western Colorado. Rather, it was F. V. Hayden's finding of area minerals, accompanied by his accurate maps. Powell wanted to survey the plateau country, study its geological history, and devise water laws that would be equitable to settlers, but Hayden was the quintessential "businessman's geologist" whose agenda was not just mapping the West but also uncovering its mineral wealth. He saw the region as the "resource West" and, in keeping with the political tenor of the times, devoted himself, in historian William Goetzman's words, to "the pursuit of practical prospecting in the public interest."[6] By 1876, mineral wealth had catapulted Colorado to statehood, and Hayden augmented that wealth by discovering coal deposits and iron ore in sufficient quantity to make Colorado the "Pittsburgh of the West." He made a fortune for knowledgeable entrepreneurs who had missed the silver strikes but found resource potential in the thick seams of undeveloped coal.

F. V. Hayden's team commenced work on the Western Slope in 1873, five years before Powell's seminal publication. They were headquartered at Agency Park near the White River Agency, an area established for Ute Indians just east of Powell Park, where Major Powell had spent the winter of 1869. Hayden's surveyors wintered there in 1876, exactly a century after Dominguez and Escalante had crossed the same valley.

Hayden's survey found "croppings of Cretaceous shales" locked in "rugged and often impassable cliffs" though noting that adjoining mesas were "well-stocked with grass." In his letter to the secretary of the interior, published as a preface to the 1878 report, Hayden describes the Grand River Valley as having "an average width of twelve miles." He explains that the valley is "limited on the north and west by the Roan or Book Cliffs," which "rise from the valley in a succession of steps to a height of about 4,000 feet above it, or 8,000 to 8,500 feet above the sea."[7]

Oddly enough, the Hayden survey made no mention of kerogen or the oil content in the "Cretaceous shales," despite instructions to evaluate mineral resources. By the 1850s, a sizable shale industry had developed in the eastern United States, effectively replacing wood as the nation's industrial fuel and whale oil as its choice of lamp fuels. At the end of that decade, at least fifty commercial facilities operated on the Atlantic Coast prior to the drilling of "Colonel" Edwin Drake's commercial oil well in Titusville, Pennsylvania.[8] Why the USGS geologists did not identify the "Cretaceous shales" as oil-bearing remains a mystery, for the Ute Indians could readily identify "the rock that burns."

Although the survey did describe agricultural opportunities in limited detail, Hayden never saw the potential for irrigation that Powell did, for Hayden was strictly a mineral geologist. He described the Grand River Valley as "for the most part a desert covered with a sparse growth of stunted sagebrush, which grows in a stiff alkaline soil." Yet he also noted groves of cottonwoods and stated that a portion of the valley "may be reclaimed by irrigation." He named three streams the "Muddy, Alkali and Desert Creeks . . . as an indication of the kind of country through which they flow"[9] and concluded that the valley to the west of the present town of Parachute "is not

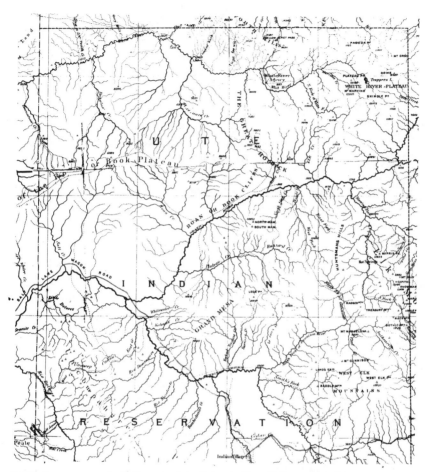

Hayden's survey crew in 1876 traversed the Colorado River Valley and found numerous mountains, canyons, and chasms but only one road — a wagon road to Salt Lake City. *From F. V. Hayden,* Tenth Annual Report of the United States Geological and Geographical Survey of the Territories Embracing Colorado and Parts of Adjacent Territories *(1878).*

adapted for agricultural purposes, and much less for grazing." Throughout the 3,000-square-mile region, his men encountered only one road, a wagon road to Salt Lake City, because "the cañon of the Grand appears to be impassable, and the road makes a detour around it."[10] He also noted that "the country has heretofore been almost entirely unexplored and was described by the nearest settlers as a broken cañon country, extremely dry."[11] Yet he indicated that the

Grand River, west of the present site of Glenwood Springs, enters a broad valley "of which a very considerable part, about 72 square miles, can be irrigated and made productive."[12]

The region would remain isolated and remote. Settlers moved into the country and homesteaded, but travel was never easy. Farmers and ranchers followed the path of least resistance up and down the creeks, but at the river itself, passage was frequently blocked by cliffs; it had been for the original surveyors. The first settlers at Parachute had a journey of two weeks to buy winter supplies at Grand Junction — a trip that now takes only forty minutes on a four-lane freeway following the river's course.[13]

Exploring north of the town of Silt, George B. Chittendon, official topographer of the White River Division, named the area between the river and the Grand Hogback "Cactus Valley" for "its thick carpeting of prickly-pears and other low-growing cacti." He stated, "[I]t can be readily irrigated, and from the mild climate which it must possess in the winter . . . it will prove available for agricultural purposes" and "will produce many crops that it is impossible to raise in the valley of the White River."[14] To the south of Cactus Valley is the river; to the north the highest point along the Hogback Range is 9,311 feet. Above that rise the Flat Tops and Cline Tops, where the survey found "freshwater lakes and timber." Hayden concluded that on the Western Slope the country is nearly all inhabitable, both winter and summer, and considerable portions of it valuable . . . though three-quarters of it is within the Ute Indian reservation."[15]

The Utes' tribal rights would soon be voided. Major Powell had wisely pulled up his stakes when they offended the Ute Indians, but sanctimonious Nathan Meeker lost his life over a Ute horse racetrack that he insisted on plowing up. He wanted the Indians, who had always hunted and lived nomadically, to become farmers. Because of deep misunderstandings between Meeker and the Indians at the White River Agency, violence erupted in 1879. Meeker sent an emergency dispatch to Fort Steele, Wyoming, for support from the Fourth U.S. Calvalry. The troops were two days from the agency when they were ambushed in a narrow canyon along Milk Creek. While some Utes maintained the siege, others returned to the agency and killed Meeker and ten other white males. Women were taken captive, though later released unharmed. Sensational newspaper headlines described the slaughter and mutilation of the corpses.

Despite Meeker's obvious error in judgment, Colorado Governor Frederick Pitkin demanded reprisals against the Utes and insisted that the Northern Ute tribes be removed from the state. Congress concurred. The Utes were then forced onto a new reservation in the desert country of eastern Utah. Eleven million acres of vacated Ute lands were officially opened for settlement on June 1, 1882, although miners and farmers had moved into Garfield County even earlier. The accuracy of Major Hayden's report and the prophecies of Powell would soon be made manifest.

The situation in Colorado was unlike the Oklahoma land rush for the difficult mountain terrain and desert-like conditions discouraged an immediate influx of land-hungry settlers. Homesteaders drifted into the area, but they did so in handfuls. The real impact came not from settlers, but from miners who sought bonanza strikes like those at Leadville and Aspen, which had transformed high mountain valleys into bustling boomtowns. Miners initially stampeded into Garfield County for the boom of Carbonate, the first county seat, located high on the Flat Tops at an elevation of 10,783 feet.

One notorious citizen, Scarface Bill Case, encouraged otherwise sane men to prospect at Carbonate, despite the fact that annual snows were "two Utes deep" and travel could only be accomplished in the bitter cold of early morning or late evening when the snow had a firm crust. Scarface had graduated from an earlier career of horse-stealing to the more lucrative business of salting mines. Having found a ninety-foot shaft and a two-room cabin vacated by a previous prospector, he went to Leadville to locate partners and secure a few hundred pounds of precious "lead float." If the ore at Carbonate showed no trace of silver, Scarface was determined to bring in his own.

By the spring of 1879, Leadville's population included thousands of miners, and Scarface had no problem finding partners among the riffraff on the street. According to local legend he did, indeed, return with Leadville ore for his Carbonate mine and sprinkled samples throughout the mine shaft. Around February 1, 1880, Scarface came down out of the mountains with the Leadville ore and had it assayed. It appeared that he had struck pay dirt, although Hayden's men could have confirmed the absence of silver-bearing ores north of the Colorado River. Nonetheless, news of the rich ore strike was published in Leadville newspapers, and hundreds of people begged Scarface to lead them back to Carbonate. Another ore sample was taken to Red Cliff, and the assay test again showed silver.

Only heavy snows kept miners from rushing up the Ute trail into the boomtown of Carbonate, whose population reached 5,000 residents within eighteen months. By April 5, 1883, a full square mile of town had been laid out with lots, city blocks, and even named streets. Mining claims sold for $1,000 and were resold by syndicates for as much as $125,000.[16] However, most miners were not as lucky as the corporate swindlers. Joseph Elam, for example, was murdered in August 1883 with only 65 cents in his pocket. As for Scarface, he stayed around camp until mining experts arrived to inspect the ores. Then Scarface headed west.

Carbonate struggled on, but the winter of 1884 proved to be one of the hardest in western history. Deep snows caused the post office to pack up and move to Glenwood Springs, a tent town on the banks of the Colorado River. Legend has it that county records were carried out by a large, white mule whose owner prudently decided to leave in the middle of the night rather than risk opposition from irate miners and town promoters. Today, nothing remains of the townsite, and it would be ten years before any community in the county boomed again. Meanwhile, miners and their families came down from the higher elevations at Leadville and Aspen by cutting wagon roads through the aspen, spruce, and pine. At lower elevations, they were slowed by mile after mile of oakbrush, piñon trees, greasewood, and sagebrush securely rooted in the alkaline soil.

However great the difficulties, here was a land of opportunity — unspoiled, unfenced and unirrigated — a land where late nineteenth-century pioneers and their families could gain title to free land. As Wallace Stegner wrote about the frontier, "Here everybody was his own boss, here was a wide open and unskimmed country where a man could hew his own line and not suffer for his independence."[17]

In 1879, at the mouth of Divide Creek, Bill Gant squatted on land and waited for government surveys to verify his claims. So did James Porter in 1881, and C. B. Larson and W. L. Smith a year later.

Early settlers constantly worked to improve their homesteads in the valleys that drained into the Colorado River. This pioneer family had a duck pond, a fenced-in garden, and a large cabin. *Courtesy of the Grand River Museum Alliance.*

James Ewers also "located" on Divide Creek in 1883.[18] At the confluence of Elk Creek and the Colorado River, Jasper Ward homesteaded in 1882; his homestead title in the Ute Series Land Grant #23 would become the townsite for New Castle. In the same year, Abraham Maxfield and Charles Marshall settled where Rifle Creek flows into the Colorado at the present townsite of Rifle. The day Congress threw open the Ute lands, June 1, 1882, A. B. Hurlburt left the Fall River Valley in northern California with 2,000 head of yearling ewes. By October 4, he had arrived at the point where Parachute Creek and the Colorado River Valley meet and for $100 bought the cabin and claim of a prospector known only as Hungry Mike. Hurlburt and his family spent the winter at the former White River Agency, now the town of Meeker, and in the spring they came south to farm and graze sheep where the town of Parachute was later platted.[19]

Unlike the raucous gold and silver boomtowns of the mining frontier, the quiet communities of Silt, Rifle, and Parachute in the upper Colorado River Valley were developed by homesteaders who became ranchers, farmers, and fruit growers. The exception was the coal mining town of New Castle, which boomed in the early 1890s only to recede after serious union strife and two of the worst mining disasters in the state's history. Tracing the historical lineage of the people who settled in the valley — where they came from, what they did, and why they stayed — is essential to understanding the impacts that their descendants faced during the oil shale boom of the late 1970s and the subsequent bust in the early 1980s.

Men and their families came to Garfield County from dozens of European countries, and eastern states such as Iowa, Ohio, Oklahoma, Kansas, New Jersey, Tennessee, Michigan, Missouri, Wisconsin, New York, and Maine. From Denmark came the Claussens and the Nedricksons; from Scotland came the McPhersons, Dows, and Yules. German settlers included the Nurnbergs and Seivers. The Walds came from Switzerland, the Rosenbergs from Austria, the Waters from Ireland, and the Larsons from Sweden.[20] These families did not leave their homes specifically to settle in Garfield County, Colorado. Many simply moved westward with the nineteenth-century flow of migration. The Hoffmans, Clines, Alpins, O'Tooles, and Werhonigs arrived at Parachute via the bustling boomtown of Leadville. With the repeal of the Sherman Silver Purchase Act in 1893, hundreds of miners also left the boomtown of Aspen to homestead in the lower valleys, for plenty of land remained available. As late as June 15, 1913, Jacob Hess filed Desert Land Entry Serial #07395 at the land office in Glenwood Springs. In the higher valleys, remote parcels of land remained unclaimed and available for homesteading until 1934.[21]

The early settlers grew only enough crops for their own use because water was scarce. A few tried growing wheat with the new techniques of "dry farming," and many had gardens. The settlers raised cattle, which required only a small amount of deeded land because excellent forage was available in the timber and alpine meadows of the high country. Therefore, these early ranchers initially homesteaded, preempted or bought a relatively small acreage, and let

Abe and John Boulton homesteaded on Mamm Creek in 1883 near the same watershed that Dominguez and Escalante descended on their route to the Colorado River. By 1902, Robert E. Boulton had homesteaded on Dry Hollow where this photo was taken in the 1920s. *Courtesy of John and Alice Boulton.*

the cattle run "out the back door" on what would become national forest.

The beginnings of community in the valley can be traced to those seasonal activities that are a part of ranching life. Unlike autonomous boomtown prospectors searching for the mother lode, ranchers had to work in teams. Men worked together during the vast spring roundups to brand yearling calves, and in the fall they culled beef for market. Though few historical sources document these communal activities, cowboys recorded them in their own vernacular poetry.[22]

Roundups testify to the solid bonds of the ranching community in Garfield County at the turn of the century, where families grew up with the shared experiences of spring and fall roundups. The hospitality of cow camps is legend. Ranchers kept these cow camps or line camps stocked with wood, water, bedding, and canned goods that could be used by any cowboy on the range. The only requirement was to replace the wood and water, and ranchers knew they would get their grub back when they found themselves in time of need and had to stay in someone else's cabin. In addition to the shared work values of

Cowboys herded thousands of cattle on the Western Slope before homesteaders began to fence their 160 acres. The large annual roundups held south of Rifle are described in John Grigor's folk poem "Rounding Up the Strays" from an unpublished manuscript, dated January 17, 1921, in the Rifle Public Library. *Courtesy of the Grand River Museum Alliance.*

branding cattle, mending fence, and riding herd in a vast, mountainous country, community was also defined by large get-togethers and dances that the whole neighborhood attended.

Pioneer settlers had to be self-sufficient and often bought grocery staples for six months at a time. This self-sufficiency also applied within the family, where the hard, demanding labor was shared equally, regardless of sex. Women were an integral part of the ranch community and worked beside their husbands. They contributed to the family unit not only by raising a garden, preparing meals, and attending to the young children, but also by riding the range and spending long, cold nights at a cow's side during difficult periods of calving, for they had experienced the pains of childbirth and knew best how to pull calves. Members of the ranch family functioned individually and collectively, with each assigned specific daily and seasonal chores.

One of the few original buildings on Battlement Mesa is the stone schoolhouse completed in 1897. At such pioneer schools in the Colorado River Valley, box socials and dancing often lasted all night. *Photograph by the author.*

As the pioneers defined it, in this "new country" they constantly "improved" their places by putting up corrals, barns, and double-walled log cabins chinked with a mud mixture in which deer hair served as a binding agent. Early settlers made do with available materials in building their homes. Aspen trees, or "quakies," were used for fence and corral posts. Spruce logs went into log cabins, and cedars or junipers roofed many a potato cellar because the wood is hard, durable, and almost impervious to rot. South of the Colorado River, ranch families built solid, hand-cut stone houses 33-feet square with walls 28-inches thick. One of the houses had rooms approximately 15-by-13-feet, rising a full 40 feet from the hand-poured basement floor to the top of the chimney. The Banta Ranch had a two-story stone barn that still stands.

School buildings like the Battlement Mesa School (1897) were also built of stone. As more land went under cultivation and local families prospered, a stone addition was added to the school in 1904.[23] Other one-room schools on Elk, Divide, Canyon, and Wallace creeks were wooden structures that served the community well. Built by farm and ranch families, these school buildings helped define the community by giving it boundaries — the same as those of the school district — and names such as Dry Hollow, Fairview, and Blue Goose.

It was at one of these small, one-room schools that the president of the United States addressed a Sunday congregation during a bear-hunting trip up Mamm Creek in 1905. In *Outdoor Pastimes of an American Hunter* (1908), Theodore Roosevelt wrote, "Some twenty good-natured, hard-riding young fellows from the ranches within a radius of a dozen miles had joined our party to 'see the President kill a bear.'" Teddy described them as "a cheerful and eagerly friendly young crowd, as hardy as so many young moose, and utterly fearless horsemen."[24] In his book, Roosevelt also wrote about Garfield County as "very steep and rugged; the mountainsides were greasy and slippery from the melting snow."[25] As T. R. noted, "It was a great, wild country. In the creek bottoms there were a good many ranches; but we only occasionally passed by these, on our way to our hunting grounds in the wilderness along the edge of the snowline. The mountains crowded close together in chain, peak, and tableland; all the higher ones were wrapped in an unrent shroud of snow."[26]

The president was accurate in describing "a good many ranches" in the creek bottoms. Garfield County has never had any exceptionally large landowners, because only a small percentage of the county is privately owned. (The designation of the White River and Battlement Forest reserves in 1891 had begun local opposition to federal regulation of timberlands.) But Roosevelt's descriptions of Garfield County mountains and ranches reveal only part of what he saw. He also saw extensive overgrazing.

After hunting on Mamm Creek in 1905, Roosevelt never again hunted in the West. Perhaps that is just as well, for he would not have been welcome because after his hunt in May, he returned to Washington and in collaboration with his chief forester, Gifford Pinchot, drew up statutes calling for grazing fees on the national forests. On January 1, 1906, a new law went into effect charging "from twenty to thirty-five cents per head for the regular grazing season and from thirty-five to fifty per head for the entire year."[27] Throughout the West, cattlemen were furious. What the Forest Service called "a reasonable fee" cattlemen called "the fight for free grass." Just as there had been intense local opposition to the formation of the White River Reserve in 1891 and the "locking up" of potential homestead land, ranchers who had supported Roosevelt now blasphemed him for the necessary beginnings of range regulation. The new regulations sought to correct those rangeland abuses Roosevelt must have seen while hunting on Mamm Creek. Gifford Pinchot even traveled from Washington, D.C., to Glenwood Springs in December 1905 to explain the regulations to local ranchers and assuage their anger, but it was not until 1911, when the Fred Light case had failed on appeal to the United States Supreme Court, that ranchers reluctantly paid their fees.[28] Thus, in the early 1900s the pattern of strong family and community roots in ranching was set in Garfield County, as were bitter feelings of impotence and anger toward distant government bureaucrats who made decisions with far-reaching local consequences.

The community of ranchers excluded those who raised sheep, just as immigrants were excluded from social life in the coal-mining boomtown of New Castle. The ranching communities formed along the creeks, as Powell had said they would. Families wrested a living from the land and coped with the ups and downs of cattle prices. Some went broke trying to exist on a meager diet of cull potatoes and deer taken during "farmer's season" — any time a homesteader needed fresh meat. Failure at farming and ranching also limited community size and served to make community membership self-selective. Of the pioneer families who survived, their descendants earned clear title to their ranches and set down deep roots in the dry, alkaline soil that Hayden had said was unfit even for grazing.

Where creeks meet the river in Garfield County, towns grew up at Parachute and Rifle. The small town of Silt developed between Rifle and New Castle because it was seven miles — or an all-day trip on muddy roads in the spring — to each town on either side. New Castle grew not because of agriculture, however, but because of coal.

Community bonds in Garfield County, Colorado, were both ethnic and occupational. Northern European families migrated to the

Silt grew up as a farming community in the early 1900s and was named for the sandy, loamy soil near the Colorado River. *Courtesy of the Grand River Museum Alliance.*

Western Slope and began to ranch on the south side of the river in the Rifle and Parachute area, after false starts in Aspen and Leadville. Hispanics came into the region near Silt to work as section hands on the railroad and to find better opportunities than existed for them in southern Colorado and northern New Mexico. Italians and Austrians came as coal miners to work the rich Wheeler vein that begins just west of the town of New Castle, sinks under the Colorado River, and extends for sixty miles south to Thompson Creek and the town of Redstone on the Crystal River. The vein is one of the richest low-sulfur coal seams in the nation.

Some newcomers spoke German and had names such as Seivers and Urquhart, others spoke French (the Vagneurs) or Italian (the Dodos, Benedettis, Fazzis, Prettis, Zangs, Ruggeros, and Zarlingos). Almost all the Italian immigrants who came to mine coal stayed in the area because of its similarity to their homelands on the Italian-Austrian border and areas like the Tyrol of Austria. They came as miners because the mines paid their way as an advance against future wages, and once in Colorado, their only thought was to acquire land and succeed as they could not have done in their native villages.

Swiss and Italian immigrants first came into the Colorado River Valley in the 1890s to mine silver and coal. The Eccher family who posed for this portrait at Spring Gulch in 1894, came from the Italian Tyrol and moved from mining camp to mining camp before settling on Silt Mesa in the early 1920s. *Courtesy of Carol Dodo.*

The immigrants came to the coal mines of New Castle and other mines up and down the Roaring Fork Valley from Glenwood Springs to Aspen. At the turn of the century, these men worked ten- and twelve-hour days, and safety procedures were minimal. If they were fortunate to live long enough, these miners often contracted black lung disease. For the unfortunate ones, a pocket of dangerous methane gas could spell disaster and leave an entire town mourning the loss of husbands, fathers, and sons, as happened twice in New Castle. But of the hundreds of Italians, Swedes, Austrians, and Greeks who came to mine with the wave of late nineteenth-century immigration, only the Italian families stayed to work their way up and out of the mines and buy farms and ranches.

With the big silver strikes of the late 1870s at Leadville and Aspen, silver became king in the area. But coal was to be queen. The small mining camps of Coal Basin, Spring Gulch, and Marion began in 1881, shortly after the Meeker Massacre. Within a few years, Marion had 50 coke ovens, and dozens of miners' log cabins surrounded the mine. In 1886, the mines at Sunlight opened, and the camp at Cardiff boasted 240 coke ovens, 50 miners' cabins, 30 rental homes, and a depot for the Colorado Midland Railroad. West of Glenwood Springs, only an old steel bridge along the Colorado River remains of the busy South Canyon mines area that once held 27 cottages, a school, a church, a literary society, a 1,200-volume library, a baseball team, and a town of 300 people. The South Canyon mines were exceptional in that they employed black miners — something unheard of in the gold and silver camps — though few of the blacks remained in the county.[29]

With financial assistance from New York City, the Boston and Colorado Coal Company had bunkhouses for 100 men "furnished with neat iron bedsteads and bed clothing supplied by the Company. In fact, the building is run rather on the hotel plan with attendants to keep the place in order."[30] The promotional literature touted a comfortable camp, but health and safety precautions were routinely ignored, and working conditions were deplorable. The 1887 Bureau of Labor Statistics for the State of Colorado reported that in Garfield County "the coal miners have grievances which require some redress. The air in the mines is bad, and an inspector is needed." The report explained, "If a man makes the least kick against bad air or gas he is immediately discharged. This should be looked into as there will be loss of life here if action is not taken immediately."[31] Yet many miners were unable to protest their working conditions because the coal companies had paid their passage — and that of their relatives — to the United States.

New Castle, Colorado, possessed a typical boomtown population with urban characteristics. At the end of the day's shift, hundreds of workers from nearby mines swarmed through town, making Main Street "look much like Broadway in New York City at noon."[32] Residents squeezed their homes into a narrow valley, with the Colorado River directly to the south and a massive rock ridge to the north. Houses were built close together, and streets went up the ridge as far as building conditions permitted. As early as 1888, urban amenities included direct rail connections to Denver for the shipment of passengers and coal. Within five years, the community had 1,800 people and a bustling business district that included clothing stores, grocery stores, meat markets, hardware stores, brick kilns, and cigar stores. Small businesses prospered, such as barber shops, restaurants, rooming houses, livery stables, printing shops, bakeries, and offices for bankers, lawyers, contractors, and realtors.[33] None of the other communities at the west end of Garfield County could match the population density and urban atmosphere found in New Castle, but neither did the ranching communities face intense labor conflicts, mining disasters, and bitter union strife.

Though paid in gold instead of scrip, New Castle miners worked in poorly timbered underground tunnels sometimes only 3-feet high and dripping with cold water. Each man had to furnish his own tools and oil for his lamp. Cave-ins, small explosions, and fires were frequent, but it was missed paydays that prompted the miners to strike in October 1893. The strike began over consistently missed payrolls — sometimes two or three months overdue — but other conditions soon became issues. The shot-firers, for example, wanted to be out of the mines at lunchtime after placing dynamite charges to loosen the long seams of coal. The miners also wanted only one person in the mine to set the dynamite charges, so as not to accidentally blast one shaft just as charges were being set in another. Their third request was to vacate the mine when the dynamite blew. A final issue was the Wolf Safety Lamp that had a mesh cover over the wick that collapsed in the presence of pockets of gas; although the lamp was a significant safety device, it offered poor illumination and miners refused to use it.

Under the direction of owner John C. Osgood, management ignored the strikers' demands. Conditions improved slightly at the Vulcan — one of the town's two mines — but at the Consolidated, owned by Osgood's Colorado Fuel & Iron, the miners stayed out for five months. In response, the superintendent boarded up the mine and threatened to let it fill with water and permanently close. The immigrants had little recourse, for they were starving in a strange land, and most of them had families to support. Consequently, despite bitter feelings, the miners went back to work, where they were humbled into accepting lower pay. The management hired back only 62 of the original 162 men who had gone out on strike.

In a move destined to bring violence, the Santa Fe Coal Company reduced the Vulcan miners' pay to match that of the Consolidated miners. Then, after a weary winter of strikes and painful concessions, the miners had just gone back to work when the United Mine Workers called a general strike for the nation. After so much trouble of their own, the New Castle miners very reluctantly went out on strike. Violence flared that summer when the Colorado Midland railroad bridge was burned to prevent thirty U.S. marshals from entering town. The state militia had to be called in to insure safe passage for trains.

Even after the UMW called off the general strike, a petulant John Osgood announced that the Consolidated Mine would be closed indefinitely. The Vulcan reopened immediately with three eight-hour shifts. The Consolidated then reopened two months later, in October, but in both mines wages remained at pre-strike levels, and there were no changes in working conditions. By 1896, the ten mines in Garfield County employed 457 men, 287 of whom worked in New Castle.[34] Immigrant workers struggled to make a living in the mines, while above ground, signs in New Castle business establishments proclaimed that all transactions had to be conducted in English. The original Scotch-Irish who had settled the town continued to control all its institutions, and only a few Italians owned businesses. The im-

A work crew above the entrance to the Consolidated Mine; by 1896, Garfield County had ten coal mines employing 457 men, 287 of whom worked in New Castle. *Courtesy of the Grand River Museum Alliance.*

migrants hoarded money to buy farms and survive on small acreages away from town, but their only source of income was the mines.

On February 18, 1896, the Vulcan exploded with such force that solid mine timbers were hurled 400 feet away to the banks of the Colorado. The entire town felt the explosion and saw the belching cloud of thick black smoke and poison gas as the mouth of the tunnel filled with demolished timbers, shattered rocks, and other debris. "Death came without warning," reported the *New Castle News*, and "the loud report" of the explosion was heard up and down the valley for miles.[35] The community responded at once to the disaster, and New Castle's twenty-two saloons closed their doors. Volunteers rushed across the river to the mine one-and-a-half miles east of town, though they could do nothing because poisonous gas forced everyone back from the mine's entrance.

Though the Vulcan exploded at 11:27 A.M., it was not until midnight that the first victims were found 450 feet into the shaft.

Forty-eight volunteer miners worked around the clock to re-trieve the mangled dead and those who looked like "they had just stretched out for a nap" after being killed by the explosive concussion.[36] Rumors about the disaster quickly began to circulate, including tales of how 70 men had been killed, how the rescue workers had heard the tap-tap-tapping of desperate men on the other side of a wall, and how the disaster had been planned by pro-union men to gain sympathy for the union's cause.

On Wednesday afternoon, a special train arrived in New Castle carrying State Mine Inspector David Griffith and several of the mine owners. Though Griffith took charge of the search, by Friday only 13 bodies had been recovered. Family and friends of the 49 miners still trapped abandoned hope. Almost every family in town was affected in some way, from the little children who would vividly recall strange bodies laid out on the dining room table, to wives who had lost husbands and sons.[37] Over the next several weeks, horse-drawn farm wagons hauled bodies from the Vulcan to a temporary morgue set up in town, but by March 7, two-and-a-half weeks after the explosion, only 36 of the 49 missing miners had been located. As the coroner's inquest began on March 19, the last body was recovered. Because they were all Italians, the Italian government officially protested and demanded compensation, but no funds were ever obtained. [38]

Constant strife, dangerous working conditions, and an uneasy social climate in town led Italians to homestead farms and small ranches up Main Elk, West Elk, and East Elk creeks, north of New Castle. The families settled on the dry sagebrush in what Hayden's surveyors had labeled "Cactus Valley." Among these homesteaders were Michael Dodo and Irene Coniglia. Michael was born in Rog-lione, Italy, in 1868 and had run way from home before emigrating to the United States to work in the Vulcan mine at New Castle. The day of the explosion, he had not gone to work. Irene Coniglia's husband had; he was killed in the disaster, and she was left destitute after being in this country only fifty days. After an appropriate period of mourn-ing, Irene married Michael Dodo in 1899, and they began ranching just west of New Castle. Dodo was one of the first permittees on the White River National Forest.

Mining has always been a hazardous occupation. On their way to the graveyard these mourners, probably miners, posed for a final portrait with their companion. Some of the men wear black silk armbands; the whiskey bottle is for the wake after the internment. *Courtesy of the Grand River Museum Alliance.*

Rather than return to the poverty of their native villages, those Italian immigrants who could not afford to farm after the 1896 Vulcan disaster kept working in the mines to earn cash to homestead or buy land. But in 1913, because of continued corporate negligence and excessive coal dust in the mine, the Vulcan again exploded, this time killing 37 men. The new owner of the Rocky Mountain Fuel Company caused much local disgust when he offered only $75 per man for funeral expenses.[39] In response, Italians worked even harder to become property owners, particularly of available farm and ranch land lying just below the Flat Tops in the valley between New Castle and Rifle. New Castle ceased to boom as the population spread out from the compact boundaries of town to settle on these farms and ranches. A steady decline was inevitable after the second Vulcan explosion on December 16, 1913. The mine was closed forever, yet the legacy of coal mining will remain in New Castle. Fires were frequent occurren-

Many Italian miners are buried in the New Castle cemetery, and their descendants live in the Colorado River Valley. The ridge in the distance is known as Coal Ridge, where a seam of coal is still on fire from the last Vulcan Mine explosion in 1913. *Photograph by the author.*

ces in the mines, but one fire was never extinguished. Today, a large expanse of Ward's Peak directly south of town is treeless and blackened due to the fire that swept through the vein, under the river, and across to Roderick's Ridge (now known as Coal Ridge). New Castle annually celebrates Burning Mountain Days as a tribute to the coal miners who died and to the mountain that is still on fire.

The immigrant miners who stayed despite the hardships eventually became farmers and ranchers and settled into an equilibrium of planting and harvesting, branding and butchering, with irrigation water key to their agricultural survival. And like the history of ranching and coal mining in Garfield County, the history of irrigation is essential to an understanding of the community makeup. During the recent oil shale boom and over the last twenty years, large oil companies quietly purchased ranches primarily to acquire the water rights. Families readily sold their places, particularly on Parachute Creek; but they continued living on the ranches as tenants. By doing so, they changed long-standing cultural patterns of family land ownership.

As both Powell and Hayden had predicted, the immigrants who turned to farming needed water to survive. Irrigation projects first got under way west of New Castle in 1887 with the Grass Valley Land & Water Corporation, financed by English investors. After the silver mines closed in Colorado following the devastating panic of 1893, miners and their families were encouraged to move to the tiny community of Antlers, situated in the valley between Silt and Rifle; to provide water, the corporation built the Grass Valley Reservoir at the site of Harvey Gap. John Harvey had homesteaded the gap, and his rights were purchased to build the reservoir, which was constructed with mule teams and fresnos, or large metal scoop shovels.

Chittenden wrote that "on both sides of the Grand Hogback, along its entire extent, there is good pasturage, but the amount of arable land is limited." [40] The reservoir would change all that. It was completed in 1894 but washed out in April 1895. The English corporation did not have funds to rebuild the reservoir, and their development project soon failed, but enough farmers had settled in the valley to build the Cactus Valley Ditch between 1890 and 1898. Five years later, the Farmer's Irrigation Company incorporated to rebuild the reservoir. Using horses and hand tools, the company could make the reservoir only 28-feet deep; however, that was a vital beginning.

Fruit grown in Garfield County within the next ten years included plums, strawberries, apples, grapes, and pears. Peaches were so successful west of New Castle that the small valley became known as Peach Valley. At the St. Louis World's Fair in 1904, W. S. Parks from Silt took first place with prize peaches and apples. The Coe and Fleming Ranch won prizes for its fruit, and William Johnson won for his potatoes. John Hasley grew the largest sugar beet exhibited in St. Louis.

Other investors purchased the failed Grass Valley Land & Water Corporation, and in 1907, the Antlers Orchard and Development Company enlarged the dam with Japanese labor. When it was finished and water was released through the ditch, alfalfa hay bloomed where there had once been only sagebrush. Land under the ditch began to blossom with vegetables and fruit, and German-Russian families like the Kirstens and Ecchers came to work in 3,000 acres of irrigated beet fields between New Castle and Rifle. In 1919, land was sold to Weiss,

Fech, Heitz, Rohrig, Kaufman, and Horst, and in the next decade, German, Austrian, and Russian farmers included Becker, Rinehart, Lind, Linker, Kline, and Mickeal.[41] These families eventually inter-married with the Italian immigrants to form strong attachments to the soil, as well as interconnected kin relationships among their children and grandchildren.

Wallace Stegner writes of "the abiding aridity of the West" and the fact that "Indian and Spaniard and Mormon had all been ultimate-ly forced to community morality. Mutuality was a condition of sur-vival."[42] Just as reservoirs and ditches were built along the hogbacks north of the Colorado River, so, too, did settlers with common goals and needs mutually build ditches and dams on the south side. On Battlement Mesa, Holmes Mesa, and Morrisania Mesa south of Para-chute, settlers filed homestead and desert claims and carved farms and ranches out of Hayden's sagebrush. They settled on Wallace Creek, Battlement Creek, and Muddy Creek. They interlaced the valleys with hand-dug ditches that had to be kept constantly clean and free of rocks, branches, and other debris. Cattle trampled in excess dirt, and these irrigation ditches were frequently damaged by high water in the spring.

The persistent drought of the late 1880s and 1890s caused farm-ers and ranchers in Garfield County to file for water rights, but their claims were small compared to those of Arthur and Richard Have-meyer of Newport, Rhode Island, who invested a fortune to irrigate 8,000 acres between Rifle and Parachute. The Havemeyer Ditch be-gan as the Riverside and Orchard Home Association, organized by W. H. Hallett in 1891. Water was to be applied in vast quantities to the dry soil, and the desert was to bear fruit. The company had purchased the 8,000 acres for a future orchard, and on an overcast day, May 4, 1912, after years of preparation and an expenditure of $425,000, ceremonies were held west of Rifle at the headgate of the 27-mile-long ditch. The engineer who was master of ceremonies boasted that the new irrigation district was "the first and foremost in this valley" and traced the history of irrigation from Biblical times. He spoke of canals in Egypt and described how Cortez and Pizarro "found well devised and constructed means of irrigation in Central and South America." In his opinion, the Havemeyer Ditch was of equal importance to the Colorado River Valley. Yet, despite the speech-making, the band-playing, the bonfires, and the moonlit dancing at the dedication, a month later the weather turned hot, melting huge drifts of snow in the high mountains. The swollen creeks rushed down to the Colorado River, and the expensive headgate did not withstand its first spring thaw.[43]

What did succeed were much smaller irrigated plots of five and ten acres on Morrisania Mesa south of Parachute. Lack of frost on the mesas led to the development of an intensive fruit-growing industry, begun by E. F. Campbell and Peter H. Morris, who in the early 1890s contacted nurseries to purchase fruit trees. The irrigated orchards succeeded, and the Morrisania Orchard & Development Company incorporated in 1902 to divide their 880 acres into small parcels. In 1922, literature from the Frederick R. Ross Investment Company of Denver titled "Morrisania — the Home of Better Fruit" appealed to Kansas and Nebraska farmers tired of fighting dry winds and poor prices for crops on the Great Plains. In this brochure, men who had bought their fruit tracts between 1909 and 1915 offered vivid testimonials about profits to be made from dewberries, raspberries, and strawberries that averaged $2,500 to $3,500 in annual market value. The fruit-growing land on Morrisania Mesa attracted bankers, miners, and farmers, who now raised hay, black raspberries, beans, and "Royal Ann" and "Duke" cherries. W. B. Eames, owner of a 13-acre tract since 1910, wrote in 1922 that he "would not take $1000 an acre" for it.[44] Water had come to the desert and it had bloomed.

Dominguez and Escalante had crossed the Colorado River in 1776 and ridden north along the Book Cliffs to the White River Valley, where Major John Wesley Powell would winter in 1869. He, in turn, saw the Book Cliffs from a boat on the Green River, as he cut swiftly across the Colorado Plateau to his rendezvous with destiny in the whitewater of the Grand Canyon. Seven years later, men of the Hayden survey described the "Cretaceous shales of the Roan or Book Cliffs" but made no mention of their oil-bearing qualities. In the last quarter of the nineteenth century, the Utes were driven off their ancestral hunting grounds and the Western Slope was opened for settlement. Ranchers, coal miners, and fruit growers came to call the valley their home, and they established ties of community based on intermarriage, water rights, grazing rights, and the communality of shared work in a new and undeveloped country — a virgin land with thousands of acres of valleys, meadows, and forest.

Ranchers herded their cattle up the circuitous JQS Trail to graze on the lush grass of the Book Cliffs. Below, farmers irrigated with water that flowed from Parachute Creek and Clear Creek, and deep in the earth, seams of coal at New Castle had been mined since 1886. But the shale cliffs themselves remained "rugged and impassable." Exploration and settlement had transformed the valley of the Colorado, but it was not until World War I and a petroleum crisis that oil shale boomed and focused national attention on the rock that burns.

2

Outsiders, Insiders, and Ties That Bind:
The First Oil Shale Boom and Its Aftermath

To belong to a clan, to a tight group of people allied by blood and loyalties and the mutual ownership of closeted skeletons. . . . To know always . . . that there was one place to which you belonged and to which you would return.

Wallace Stegner
The Big Rock Candy Mountain

Children born on pioneer homesteads in the Colorado River Valley experienced the first oil shale boom from 1915 to 1925 before struggling through the Great Depression. Two decades later, they sent their sons to World War II, and they lived through the stagnant years after the war when the agricultural base of Garfield County was halved between 1950 and 1960.[1] Then, in the wake of the OPEC embargo and continued projections of dwindling national petroleum reserves in the 1970s, these men and women, as senior citizens, watched as another oil shale boom utterly transformed valley land ownership and changed the way of life their families had known for three generations. Thus, direct descendants of the first pioneers experienced boom, depression, stagnation, boom again, and a wholly unexpected bust.

The recent boom had an uncanny similarity to the first oil shale boom half a century earlier, but with one notable exception — the first boom never resulted in boomtowns, characterized by a rapid influx of newcomers and wholesale community disruption. The first boom, instead, followed the standard western motif of colonial domination by eastern corporate interests, as major oil companies quietly acquired thousands of acres of shale lands. By the end of the 1920s, residents in the western end of Garfield County had lost control of their destinies to major national oil companies through corporate acquisition of ranch land and water rights. Hundreds of acres of homesteaded land were sold, and thousands of acres of public land passed into corporate ownership. Prior to 1939, outsiders working behind the scenes for these corporations bought large blocks of land; in the post–World War II years, insiders with technical and engineering backgrounds painstakingly purchased contiguous blocks for themselves. And at least one family laid the foundation for an unrivaled oil shale empire.

To understand the local and community impact of the recent boom and devastating bust, it is essential to trace the history of the first oil shale rush and analyze the community evolution between 1915 and 1970, when pioneer settlements grew into stable small towns and farms were consolidated into larger agricultural units as the livestock business continued to demand long hours and hard work for small cash returns.

For many years, agriculture had dominated the Colorado River Valley, which was first known as the Grand River Valley. At the turn of the century, promoters in Parachute changed the town's name to Grand Valley to encourage agricultural settlement. Although the Colorado legislature voted in 1907 to change the Grand River's name to the Colorado and Congress approved the change in 1921, the town of Parachute continued to be called Grand Valley until 1978, when citizens elected to change the name back to Parachute. For consistency, this text refers to the town as Parachute, though it was known as Grand Valley during the first oil shale excitement.

The small farming community of Parachute never boomed like the coal mining town of New Castle, but both Parachute and De-Beque, the community just west along the Colorado River, became sites of frantic oil shale activity in the 1920s, as the mining rush focused on mineral claims on thousands of acres along the Book Cliffs. The towns never actually boomed, however, because the oil shale industry never emerged from the dreams of its entrepreneurs. Individual miners and investors believed they could make fortunes as easily as the forty-niners who had stormed the Sierra Nevada looking for placer gold, but oil shale mining and the retorting of kerogen into liquid crude required more capitalization than gold and silver mining had.[2] The techniques for extracting precious metal had been practiced for centuries in South America and Europe, but no proven technological precedents existed for retorting western shale. Consequently, no one knew how to mine and retort sufficient quantities of shale to produce oil at a commercially viable price.

Those technological limitations hamstrung entrepreneurs in the 1920s (and, in fact, still baffle oil companies today). Comparing rich Colorado shale and the fledgling U.S. oil shale companies at the turn of the century to the well-established Scottish oil shale industry proved of little benefit. Scottish shale had a lower yield of oil per ton, but it possessed a higher organic content, was similar to peat, and was thus much easier to heat and retort. Furthermore, the Scottish shale was not located 2,000 feet above a high mountain valley whose elevation itself is 5,000 feet. Thus, Scottish shale could be retorted and commercially refined; Colorado shale retorting could not be made profitable.

Unaware of such technological limitations, the first serious oil shale developers established the Parachute Mining District in 1890. Two years earlier, a brother of W. H. Hallett, the man who had planned the ill-fated Havemeyer Ditch, retorted a quart of oil from shale he had extracted along Parachute Creek. Other pioneers also heated shale rock to extract oil, but at that point the oil was more a novelty than anything else, though it was used to augment axle grease for farm wagons and was added to smudge pots for orchards.[3] Local settlers began the Parachute Mining District to register their own claims, but they themselves had few financial resources for this mining development. Outside funds were needed and soon arrived. Outside investors included James Doyle, a lucky miner from Maine who had made a fortune at Cripple Creek with a mine he named the

Portland, after his home town. One of the wealthiest men in Colorado, he traveled to Parachute in 1908 to gather shale samples before proposing commercial extraction of shale oil. That same year, President Theodore Roosevelt warned the nation of an impending oil shortage, and James Doyle consequently began lobbying for the first United States Geological Survey reconnaissance of northwest Colorado.

A year later, Joseph Bellis saw the Garfield County shale after arriving in the area from depressed Colorado gold camps in Gilpin and Clear Creek counties. Observing that the oil shale ran in stratified lines and varied in color from a light amber to a dark brown, Bellis named the richest and darkest of them "mahogany" shale. It was this mahogany zone that oil companies sought to mine because of its much higher yields.[4] Doyle and Bellis were the first of many prospectors to look for oil shale in Garfield County. Ultimately, however, it was the scientists, not the prospectors, who would make Colorado's oil shale famous.

As the specter of a national fuel shortage increased and diminishing petroleum reserves emerged as a national security issue, one of these scientists, chemistry professor Dr. Otto Stahlman, made a trip west to garner shale samples that he retorted in Salt Lake City before publishing his results in chemistry and mining journals.[5] At the same time, increasing numbers of prospectors pressured the USGS to send out a research team in 1913. David T. Day and Elmer G. Woodruff served as co-leaders of the first federal shale survey to conduct field tests on shale samples with a portable retort, or "still," that was loaded with 100-pound batches of shale. They estimated that Colorado's shale could produce from 16 to 61 gallons of oil per ton — an amazing discovery for a nation supposedly running short on oil. Woodruff and Day published their findings in *Oil Shale of Northwestern Colorado and Northeastern Utah* in 1914, but it was not until Dean E. Winchester published his follow-up report, *Oil Shale in Northwestern Colorado and Adjacent Areas* (1916), that the first oil shale boom really began.[6]

Woodruff and Day had confirmed the existence of the shale and made a valuable preliminary report, but Winchester was sent back into the field by the USGS to ascertain exactly where the shale was and how much oil it contained. He continued his shale research each summer from 1915 through 1918. The improved efficiency of his portable retort compared to Woodruff and Day's equipment resulted in a more accurate assessment of the huge quantity of oil locked in Colorado's shale, as well as the amount of ammonium sulphate available for use as an agricultural fertilizer. Although his equipment repeatedly clogged with residue from the retorted shale, Winchester was finally able to calculate the amount of oil in local shale. In the government's second shale bulletin, published in 1916, he wrote that Colorado shale contained an incredible 20 billion barrels of oil and noted that 300 million tons of ammonium sulphate could be extracted from the Piceance Basin just north of the Colorado River.

Concern over inadequate petroleum reserves for the armed forces in the event of war prompted President Woodrow Wilson to withdraw 45,444 acres of Colorado oil shale lands and 86,584 acres of shale lands in Utah to establish a permanent Naval Oil Shale Reserve on December 16, 1916. The oil shale boom that had been slowly percolating immediately came to a rolling boil as war engulfed Europe and the public learned that billions of barrels of oil were available on unclaimed government land.

Meanwhile, an astounded scientific community reacted to Winchester's report with skepticism, so the USGS sent him back into the field to check his calculations. His superiors who felt he had erred were proved correct: D. E. Winchester had, indeed, incorrectly estimated the number of recoverable barrels of oil. A second edition of Winchester's bulletin, published in 1917, clarified that the amount of available oil was not 20 billion barrels as originally estimated, but 40 billion barrels.[7] The rush was on. Between 1910 and 1920, prospectors filed 30,000 oil shale claims on four million acres, and over 250 companies incorporated to sell oil shale stock, with 150 corporations chartered exclusively to develop Colorado shale.

Into this oil shale frenzy stepped Doris Stratton, a young woman who had arrived in Parachute by train in 1917 to accept a teaching position in DeBeque. Earlier that year, she had graduated Phi Beta Kappa from the University of Colorado with a degree in math and science. She had not read Winchester's bulletin, and she knew nothing

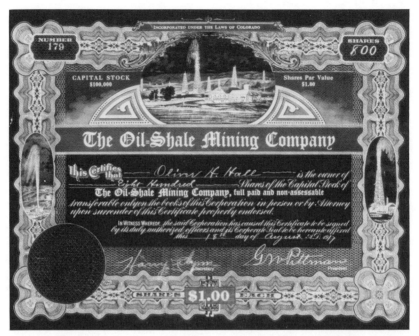

A stock certificate from The Oil Shale Mining Company shows the false symbolism of gushing oil wells. In reality, oil shale must be crushed and heated before the oil is released. None of the small companies created during the first oil shale boom from 1915 to 1925 survived. *Courtesy of the Savage Family Oil Shale History Collection.*

of oil shale. "I had never heard of oil shale until I arrived in De-Beque," Doris recalls. "The dinner topic my first night at the boarding house was oil shale. Well, I was a fair listener and a real whiz at asking questions and from that time on whenever and wherever I went — the post office, the school, the ladies' aide, the boarding house — everybody was talking oil shale. My students knew more about it than I did, and that encouraged me to start gathering information from every source."[8]

Two weeks later, Doris met Harry Flynn, who had arrived in DeBeque with his brothers Tom and Charlie to file oil shale placer mining claims in July 1916. A typical small-town boomer, Harry Flynn sold five- and ten-acre peach orchards near Palisade to farmers who had given up in the Midwest. Doris remembers, "Harry used to sell peach orchards by lantern light because the days just weren't long enough to accommodate all the people moving in." Constantly scan-

An oil shale entrepreneur poses atop his derrick, which was needlessly erected; oil does not flow from the ground. This derrick may have been built as part of an oil shale stock swindle. The large number of such frauds prompted formation of the Securities & Exchange Commission. *Courtesy of the Grand River Museum Alliance.*

ning the newspapers for news of war, the Flynns also filed oil claims, and in the spring of 1917, they consolidated their claims on several hundred acres along Roan Creek, twenty miles northwest of De-Beque. Flynn and his brothers then incorporated The Oil Shale Mining Company, and by July 1917, they fired the first oil shale retort in Colorado, modeled after a sketch of Scottish retorts they had found in the *Encyclopaedia Britannica*. The retort looked like a very large outdoor barbecue made of stone. After draining off the first batch of oil, Harry was confident enough to begin selling stock.[9]

The Oil Shale Mining Company seriously sought investors for the huge capitalization needed to develop a commercial oil shale plant, but other stock companies chose merely to peddle paper. In one of the last large, national frauds before the establishment of the Securities and Exchange Commission, dozens of bogus oil shale companies began hustling stock to unsuspecting corporate investors. Promoters argued, "Why drill for oil? We have mountains of it for sale at a penny a share!" Instead of costly searches for hidden reservoirs of liquid black gold, here was the opportunity to make a fortune on a proven and visible resource. Like pushcart vendors hawking sandwiches, dapper salesmen on Larimer Street in Denver and State Street in Chicago erected small portable retorts that puffed thick, black clouds of smoke as they heated shale rock to drain off oil. When the sooty smoke plumes attracted a crowd, salesmen hustled stock at a few dollars a share; the certificates themselves bore pictures of miniature oil wells gushing upwards in false symbolism.[10]

Stock changed hands quickly. One corporation, The Western Oil Land Validating Company, contended that oil shale resources in the West were so vast that each American was entitled to twenty acres. For a modest $100 fee, the company promised to file shale claims for its clients. However, Western Oil Land actually filed few claims, but it did collect $200,000 from naive customers. Another shale swindle was perpetrated by the Colorado Shale and Metals Company, a Denver firm. It invented a retort capable of processing a ton of shale daily that allegedly would yield 2 barrels of oil, $85 worth of gold, $14 worth of silver, $85 worth of platinum, $9 worth of zinc, $6 worth of potash, and $4 worth of ammonium sulphate. F. V. Hayden's surveyors would have been astounded at finding such rich mineral content in the "Cretaceous shales" they had assessed in the 1870s.[11] Other unscrupulous firms did not even go through the pretense of establishing a Colorado office. Articles of incorporation of the Colorado Oil, Shale and Refining Corporation, for example, stated that the "principal business of this corporation shall be transacted in Pierre, in the County of Hughes, in the State of South Dakota, but a business office may be located at Chicago, Illinois." Of the company's seven corporate directors, only one lived in South Dakota; the others all hailed from Chicago.[12]

Such rampant fraud led geologists with the Bureau of Mines to lament, "It is to be regretted that a few companies, judging by the extravagant promises of impossible profits and other preposterous statements made in their prospectuses, bear all the ear-marks of absolute fakes."[13] This cautionary note on "absolute fakes" appeared in

A variety of inventors tried numerous devices to get oil from "the rock that burns." None of the attempts were commercially successful, and almost all of the steel and piping from the early oil shale plants went for scrap during World War II. *Courtesy of the Colorado Historical Society.*

a bulletin titled *The Oil Shales of Northwestern Colorado*, published in August 1919. Its release may well have been prompted by the sensational article "Billions of Barrels of Oil Locked Up in Rocks" that appeared in the February 1918 *National Geographic*. As the country marshalled its resources to fight World War I, writer Guy Elliott Mitchell asked, "Is the United States facing a gasoline famine? Shall we be required to forego automobiling except to meet the stern necessities of war and of utilitarian traffic?" He then explained that Americans would not need to make such sacrifices because "one of our greatest mineral resources" had just been located — a resource that "for generations to come will enable the United States to maintain its supremacy over the rest of the world as a producer of crude oil and gasoline." Mitchell's hyperbole rose to an even higher crescendo in a photo caption that stated, "As the great creator, through his servants

The first oil shale retort in Colorado resembled a large outdoor barbecue. Harry Flynn designed the retort from an illustration on oil shale in Scotland that he saw in the *Encyclopaedia Britannica*. This photograph, taken by the U.S. Geological Survey, was first published in *National Geographic* in a 1918 article titled "Billions of Barrels of Oil Locked Up in Rocks."

After a *Saturday Evening Post* columnist wrote in 1920 that "never were conditions so favorable for the building of a great new industry," Parachute, then called Grand Valley, expected oil shale to bring prosperity. But the first shale boom was short-lived. The local railroad station shipped very few barrels of oil, and none were produced at competitive prices. In the distance, the oil shale cliffs are covered with snow. *Courtesy of the Grand River Museum Alliance.*

of old, caused water to flow from rock in the wilderness, so through twentieth century science, He is causing oil, for ages locked up in the shales of America, to be released for the relief of human necessity."[14] Mitchell argued that "the potential value of this immense oil resource of America is almost beyond comprehension" and as for "the establishment of a new industry . . . this time is now at hand." Among the photographs that illustrated the article was one of the Flynns' experimental oil retort, or "still," near DeBeque; they were delighted with the effusive publicity in *National Geographic*.

Soon, other magazines followed suit. Explaining that "in the decade ending in 1918 . . . the total oil reserve of the nation was increased by less than an amount equal to three years consumption," the *Saturday Evening Post* warned of a petroleum shortage as it cheered the new oil shale finds in Colorado. In his March 1920 *Post* column titled "Everybody's Business: Oil from Shale," Floyd W. Parsons exclaimed that "practically one-half of all our underground pools of petroleum have been drained" and even added that not only were there abundant shale reserves but "shale gasoline will have more power per gallon." The lubricating oils made from shale, he stated, "are of splendid quality" and sulphate of ammonia produced in the shale process would add "to the productivity of farm lands of the country." Parsons declared that "never were conditions so favorable for the building of a great new industry."[15]

Harry Flynn also felt conditions were favorable. He married Doris Stratton in 1919, and she quit teaching school to do product research for their company. Unable to commercially retort oil, they experimented with other uses for shale. Doris developed a shale oil stock dip to kill livestock parasites on sheep and cattle. "We sold the dip all over western Colorado," she says. It was also tried on humans during an emergency. As Doris relates, "One afternoon the workmen were firing the retort and one of them caught his sleeve on fire and soon his whole arm was aflame. We were out beyond the creek where there wasn't much anyone could do but throw dirt on him." One of the other workers grabbed the man's arm and stuck it into a barrel of shale oil to prevent blistering. Later, Doris continued treating the man's arm with shale oil, and it healed "remarkably well in a short time." Using her chemistry degree, she concocted an oil shale ointment with an herbal base, and husband Harry, ever the optimistic salesman, began marketing it and other "Shalo" products on the Western Slope. [16]

The Flynns were not the only local entrepreneurs to experiment with shale oil by-products, as a cottage industry developed in Parachute and DeBeque. Prospectors Mike Boyle and Joseph Bellis, for example, formed a company to manufacture table tops and bowling pins using these by-products and even considered producing self-oiling ball bearings from oil shale. Parachute resident Si Herwick offered a mail-order remedy for dandruff and falling hair — pulverized shale that was briskly rubbed into the scalp; for half a dollar, he promised to send enough shale to "treat every head in a family."[17] Harry L. Brown, founder of the Index Shale Oil Company in 1918, began to market patent medicines derived from shale to Western Slope residents, through the C. D. Smith Drug Company.[18] A Los Angeles newspaper quoted one enthusiast as stating that over 250 different products could be made from oil shale[19] including paraffin wax, carbon black for printer's ink, paints, alcohols, asphalt, cement, road oil, varnishes, dyes, explosives, and soft rubber. In an article published in *Scientific Monthly*, chemists even stated they believed they could process edible fats from oil shale.[20]

Despite the plethora of potential by-products, only 500 barrels of oil had actually been produced by 1920, although over 30,000 claims had been filed in the Parachute Creek and DeBeque region. The lack of petroleum production resulted from poor capitalization of the oil shale plants and woefully inadequate retort technology.

The record of minutes of the Mt. Logan Oil Shale Mining & Refining Company of DeBeque stated that shareholders started the business with only $8,000 of capital stock "to be divided into eight hundred thousand (800,000) shares of one cent each for each share and cumulative voting thereof shall be allowed."[21] In 1920, the company issued a circular "after two years of actual field work, for the purpose of raising capital to increase the capacity of its present plant." According to the brochure, company assets included 1,120 acres of land estimated to contain 108,900 barrels of oil. Employees needed daily for processing the shale were four men on a Cushman drill, two men on a steel sharpener, tramway operators, a jaw-crusher operator, a pulverizer operator, a mechanic, a general superintendent, and retort operators working on 24-hour shifts. With retorts sufficient to handle a 100-ton plant, the company expected to make $80,300 per year. The last paragraph in the prospectus stated, "You can get an interest in this proposition by helping finance a larger retorting plant. The treasury stock is offered for that purpose, at the present time, at $1.00 per share. Send remittance direct to Company, at DeBeque, Colorado."[22]

Selling stock capitalized at a penny per share for $1 seemed an excellent idea to the owners, but the real money in oil shale lay not in selling worthless stock, promoting exotic by-products, or developing functional oil shale plants. The real money lay in selling oil shale claims to large, established oil companies, for those claims increased in value exponentially after the 1920 passage of the Mineral Leasing Act. Prior to that, oil shale claims had been filed as placer mining claims in accordance with the 1872 Mining Law that had been forced through the House and Senate by Nevada Senator William M. Stewart. At its passage, critics complained that the law was inadequate, but by 1920 it was still the only law on the books, and though applicable for gold and silver, it did not accurately define oil shale deposits.

John W. Savage, Jr., a practicing attorney in Rifle, Colorado, whose grandfather H. K. Savage helped stake and survey some of the early shale claims, explains, "The problem is that oil shale and many other massive mineral deposits do not fit into the two categories of mining claims either as a lode claim or as a placer claim. Lodes are primarily rock in place veins," and placer claims are "gravel [deposits] in which gold and silver have been washed out of the vein. Oil shale isn't either one."[23] Yet the Parachute Mining District was formed in 1890 to stake association placer claims that enabled eight people to join their 20-acre claims together into one aggregate holding of 160 acres. Any number of claims could be filed within a given district. The intent of the law was to prevent individuals from monopolizing the mineral wealth of a specific region, but under the association concept, the same eight men could claim up to 1,280 acres and control surface discoveries of most precious minerals. In addition, the same individuals could file any number of claims and rule them by proxy votes. However, domination of oil shale resources by single individuals was not a problem because the shale region extended some fifty miles from Garfield County, Colorado, to the Utah border, with the Green River formation shale in northeastern Utah of poorer quality. The sheer size of the oil deposits meant their value lay in massive processing and retorting. Even though thousands of claims were filed, prospectors had to spend $100 annually for five years on assessments and make on-site physical improvements to actually receive a deeded patent on their claims. During the oil shale boom, most prospectors simply filed their claims and made little or no assessments until 1920, when the law changed.

Because of pressure from politically active Progressives and the growing strength of the conservation movement in the United States, Congress finally passed new mineral legislation in 1920 that forever limited private ownership of valuable minerals found on public lands. The Teapot Dome scandal in Wyoming had created a public fear that millions of barrels of potential oil from Colorado shale would fall into private hands. Consequently, the 1920 Mineral Leasing Act stated that *some* minerals on federal lands were leasable, but coal, gas, phosphates, and oil shale would no longer be considered in the public domain. In the mad scramble to patent oil shale lands before the law

The DeBeque plant typifies the steep and dangerous oil shale slopes. On July 30, 1921, a steel cable snapped on an oil shale tram; seven men died as the tram plunged down the 70 percent grade along Parachute Creek. *Courtesy of the Colorado Historical Society.*

went into effect, one prospector reportedly spent all day on horseback in his rush to sink his survey stakes. The origins of claims filed before passage of the law became a matter of serious dispute.

Residents in Parachute and DeBeque who felt that the new legislation severely limited their economic opportunities were angered just as area ranchers had been outraged by the introduction of Forest Service grazing permits and even earlier settlers had been upset when thousands of acres were reserved for the White River National Forest in 1891. In his dissertation titled "Colorado's First Oil Shale Rush, 1910–1930," William Edward Beilke writes, "Government agents were criticized for using every method at their disposal to hinder and prevent oil shale claims from being patented." Residents complained that officials from the Department of the Interior used "capricious and punitive methods" to foil local prospectors, and newspapers in Parachute and DeBeque "published stories and editorials condemning General Land Office Agents as malicious bureaucrats who had little to do on the Western Slope except intimidate and obstruct the efforts of honest people." [24]

While Parachute and DeBeque residents argued with government officials in Glenwood Springs and mailed out packets of oil shale hair restorer and bottles of herbal ointment, a serious accident in Wheeler Gulch, a year after passage of the Mineral Leasing Act, proved the inability of small-scale oil shale companies to actually create an oil shale industry. All the companies had mines high in the upper ridges of the Book Cliffs, on ledges that the Hayden surveyors had deemed "rugged and impassable." There, the shale rock was mined, then placed in large tram buckets that descended to the crusher before the shale was retorted. The top tramway bin at the entrance to the Mount Logan Oil Shale Mine was 3,000 feet above the valley floor. Tram buckets held 1,000 pounds of shale and were suspended in midair by steel cables; men rode the buckets up the mile-long tramway and spent the day filling them with extracted shale. On July 30, 1921, five miles up Parachute Creek, a cable gave way on the temporary Doyle-Reed-Schuyler Mine tram at 5 P.M., just as men were coming off work. When the cable snapped, men died instantly as they were thrown from the tram car or they died seconds later when the car crashed to the bottom of the slope. Three workers were injured and seven died. One of the casualties was a man who, believing the tram was too dangerous, decided to walk down the steep slope; moments later, the whipping cable severed his body at the waist.[25] Local oil shale companies suffered from publicity about the tramway accident.

By 1921, the maximum annual oil shale output was just 225 barrels, marketed by a dozen companies. Despite 141 patent certificates issued for oil shale retorts between 1915 and 1927, the minimal production figures were a direct result of inadequate technology and retorts which failed to work over an extended period of time. The heated "rubber rock," as Parachute's first settlers dubbed oil shale, clogged retort pipes and prevented consistent flows of oil. Half a century later, the same problems would stymie the major oil companies.[26]

In the 1920s, with the discovery of fabulously rich pools of west Texas crude — still the benchmark for American oil prices — the value of oil plummeted from $3.50 to $.40 per barrel. Consequently, the oil shale industry ceased before it even truly began. Visible evidence of the mines and tramways disappeared during World War II with the campaign to salvage scrap metal, and no boomtowns resulted from the first oil shale boom. However, thousands of acres of prime oil shale land passed from the public domain into corporate hands, for the real money was made not in retorting shale, but in selling land. Shale land that had sold for $.75 per acre brought $5 in 1923 after passage of the Mineral Leasing Act, and $75 in 1926. Sales promotions included special trains that left Denver for DeBeque, where the local chamber of commerce offered excursion trips "through the Shale Fields" together with a free lunch of barbecued venison.

By 1928, 50,000 claims had been filed within the Parachute Mining District alone. Of the smaller companies with oil shale claims not necessarily patented, the Federal Oil Shale Company, controlled by attorney D. D. Potter, claimed 20,000 acres. Potter started the company in 1917, and a year later conferred with the prestigious engineering firm of Ford, Bacon and Davis on the construction of an oil shale processing plant. Upon learning its projected cost, Potter decided to sell his properties, but in his lifetime he patented almost 100,000 acres of oil shale lands. Other small corporations with oil shale claims included the Midwest Oil Company, which claimed 15,000 acres, and the Ventura-Colorado Oil Company, which claimed 10,000 acres; Continental Oil acquired claims on 11,000 acres. By the end of the 1920s, 82 patents had been issued for 533 claims on 89,893 acres.[27]

Attorney Potter made a fortune selling out to Union Oil of California, which bought 20,000 acres near Parachute Creek. In the mid-1920s, Standard Oil of New Jersey — later to become Exxon, U.S.A. — purchased 24,000 acres, which were sold in 1941 for $5 per acre or less. The ante was considerably higher when Exxon re-entered the oil shale game in 1980 and bought out Atlantic Richfield. As William Beilke notes, "Private acquisition of presumably rich tracts of land became the paramount historical feature of Colorado's first oil shale rush."[28] By 1960, some 168,000 acres of shale lands had been patented, and two decades later, those lands were owned by Union Oil of California, Exxon, U.S.A., Mobil Oil Corporation, Superior Oil

Rifle in the early 1920s, looking west to the Book Cliffs and mountains of oil shale. In 1925, the town's citizens held a big oil shale bonfire and street dance on Railroad Avenue to celebrate the already waning boom. *Courtesy of the Grand River Museum Alliance.*

Corporation, and subsidiaries of Chevron Corporation, Conoco Inc., Cities Service Oil and Gas Company, and Getty Oil Company. Huge additional tracts are in private hands controlled by estate lawyers and investors. John Savage, Jr., still has numerous claims in litigation, and his family has a deeded interest in 230 claims on 30,000 acres. Among the claims purchased by his father were those filed by the Mt. Logan Oil Shale Mining & Refining Company, which never turned a profit and ceased operations in 1924.[29]

In the summer of 1925, one year after the Mt. Logan corporation failed, the U.S. Bureau of Mines announced plans to build a prototype oil shale plant. The facility was erected on the Naval Oil Shale Reserve five miles north of the community of Rulison, a town known for its orchards, where farm families had moved to buy small plots and raise fruit trees as they had done on Morrisania Mesa. Just as Rifle citizens had celebrated the Havemeyer Ditch in 1912, so did the Rifle and Rulison citizens welcome the prototype oil shale plant with a big hoopla and street party in Rifle. A morning parade, noon picnic,

THE AWAKENING

A 1930 decision by the U.S. Supreme Court validated oil shale claims, even as abundant liquid petroleum from Texas and Oklahoma oil fields restricted shale development. Political cartoon from the *Rocky Mountain News* January 8, 1930. *Reprinted with permission from the* Rocky Mountain News.

afternoon band concert, and twilight street dance were held on July 23, 1925, to bring the community together in celebration of the first oil shale boom. The town council even planned a colossal bonfire — fueled by oil shale instead of wood. But the boom was already beginning to wane. The fortunes of local oil shale entrepreneurs declined as huge petroleum reserves were found in Texas, California, and Oklahoma. The Oil Shale Mining Company started by Harry Flynn in 1917 was one of the casualties. Doris Flynn recalls, "We came to the conclusion that it was going to take more than a husband-and-wife team to develop an oil shale industry. Any second thoughts we might have had about sticking it out were taken care of by the discovery of oil in Texas and Oklahoma." She adds, "The oil was flowing out of the ground with no sign of letup and the going rate was $1 a barrel. Well, we couldn't even mine oil shale for a dollar a ton let alone refine it."[30] In an interview a few years before her death, she described her feelings about oil shale during those boom times:

There was something magnificent about going up into the hills and driving onto your own place where everything you surveyed was yours. There was solitude, yet you were near enough to the neighbors that you could get to them if you wanted them or needed them. There was a solitude and grandeur for the individual homes or farms or shale camps. That's all gone. We had the whole valley to ourselves. At that time we were sure the oil shale was going to develop. There was a [petroleum] shortage and everybody needed it, and it was to be an overnight sensation. But you're always going to have some things that go backwards — like the shale. We put our hearts into it and stayed there for ten years and held on a lot longer than that hoping and praying that it would develop. The hope has long since vanished. I'm perfectly honest when I tell you that I don't think it'll ever go until the government puts up all the money and the big oil companies do it. It won't be any small man's deal — ever. But my years spent in the shale and the things that we learned to do with it and the way we learned to exist were very valuable. In some years we had $30 a month to live on. We didn't have any new clothes for ten years, but nobody else had any. The only thing you bought was shoes.[31]

Doris Flynn stayed in the Colorado River Valley because it had become her home and she found a strong sense of community there — a sense shared by ranchers who kept trailing their cattle up Roan

Creek, Parachute Creek, and Divide Creek looking for grass to sprout when oil shale fortunes did not. Parachute Mayor Floyd McDaniels remembers that in the 1930s his father helped dismantle a shale plant just to salvage the bricks. The oil shale corporate presence remained unseen during this period. Union Oil, which had purchased almost all the farms and ranches in the twelve-mile-long Parachute Creek Valley, followed attorney D. D. Potter's advice to keep a low profile and lease the land back for ranching and hay crops.

Thus, the first oil shale boom had come and gone without enriching Garfield County citizens, whose farm income continued to decline from World War I highs. Despite numerous projections for a burgeoning shale industry, the area remained isolated and rural. Its way of life had not been altered by the boom. The sense of community and local culture also remained intact largely because of limited transportation, for aside from the one railroad line, there were no major transportation arteries and few serviceable roads in Garfield County. Through the 1920s, travel in the winter and spring was restricted to horseback and then only when a horse could walk through the deep snow or morass of springtime mud. The region's dry, alkaline soil had considerable adhesive qualities when wet that made farm wagons flounder; when dry, the mud hardened with the cohesion of concrete, freezing wagon axles and leaving deep ruts in the roads that lasted for months.

Mabel Moore Harness was born in 1903 in a stone house that her father had built in 1887. She remembers:

The roads in those days were more or less wagon ruts through the high sagebrush. Where I was born was great high sagebrush. I remember only three buildings in Silt. I attended a country school for awhile then the weather got bad and I didn't go any more. This was all open country and sagebrush land. I was born three-quarters of a mile from where I live now. I've ridden all over the base of this hogback when there wasn't a foot of fence anywhere. [32]

Mabel lived near Silt, Colorado, on the the north side of the river and south of the Grand Hogback, named by one of Hayden's surveyors ten years before her father "took up land" in the dry and barren

Cactus Valley. Her father farmed a small truck garden, providing vegetables for the boomtowns of New Castle and Leadville.

John Dwire was born across the river in 1914, and at the age of thirteen he was doing chores to assist his family when they lived south of the river up Garfield Creek. His grandfather, sheriff when New Castle boomed, died in a gunfight, and his wife's family came from Italy to work in the coal mines at Sunlight. John Dwire recalls:

I've been alone a lot. I used to batch when I was 16 or 17 years old, and build fences and herd sheep. Come out of the hills one time with a broken leg riding six miles on a workhorse. I never will forget that. If we had a dollar to spend we had a lot of money. I worked for $40 a month and board on one of the biggest ranches up Garfield Creek. I worked out in the winter and run a trapline. Those days was hard. After we got through feeding 450 head of cattle, I'd ride trapline the rest of the time, and I fed the whole family. That's all the money in the world we had comin' in was what I made. My dad was always sickly; for years he was sickly. And many a night I rode my horse in a blizzard [and returned with] maybe a coyote, maybe a weasel, or muskrat or something. But in those days you could get $15 or $16 out of a coyote hide or weasel and that was a lot of money. I kept groceries on the table for the whole family. We never saw a chunk of coal. We skidded logs and chopped wood.

John Dwire and young men of his generation worked hard to help their families survive. Harsh conditions prevailed, yet families were self-sufficient. As Dwire says,

Everybody made a living. On Garfield Creek and Divide Creek there was a family on every little ranch. They had a few cows. They had a few hogs. They didn't have no money but they made a living. My dad would butcher a little calf for veal and take it down to the store and trade it for groceries. We didn't have no way to get around except by horses. There were a few cars, but no roads. I'd ride down off Garfield Creek to get a sack of flour or a sack of sugar, but I've been up on that creek six months at a time and never gone to town.[33]

Despite the isolation they were born into, rural Garfield County families worked hard to prosper and transform their sagebrush homesteads into well-stocked ranches and well-watered farms. After the coal mines shut down, immigrants stayed to farm and ranch, for like the native-born Americans who came to homestead, they believed in owning land and becoming debt-free. They also believed in the sanctity of marriage and the virtues of self-sufficiency and economic independence. Their conservative attitudes evolved from lives of hard, physical work. Their sense of identity was firmly rooted in the mountains and in their family, and they placed the utmost importance on raising children and grandchildren in the valley they called home. Families might arrive in Parachute, stay for a few years, then farm up Divide Creek south of Silt or ranch near New Castle. Older sons might run the ranch, younger sons might work in Rifle or Glenwood Springs. The valley itself defined their lives, from the mountain lakes on the Flat Tops north of the river to the prominent North and South Mamm peaks on the other side of the Colorado River. Totally familiar with the landscape, they drew careful distinctions between different areas and would speak of the Divide Creek or the Morrisania "country" as if they were separate worlds. Identity and status came not from having and spending money, but from knowing the creeks and the game trails, knowing where the biggest bucks could be found in the gray hours of dawn on the first day of hunting season, and in having stout barbed wire fences, healthy Hereford cattle, and tall stacks of fresh-cut hay.

Older couples eventually retired to one of the small towns in the valley and left their land to their children. Highlights of their year included family reunions when children, grandchildren, and great-grandchildren gathered around these original pioneers. Grandmothers presented handmade afghans or quilts to their offspring, and the elderly women became models for younger farm wives, teaching them to raise gardens of rhubarb, asparagus, winter onions, tomatoes, peppers, carrots, and cucumbers — gardens with colorful borders of four-o'clocks, asters, and petunias. Older women taught younger ones how to can vegetables and venison and to raise children with a minimum of injury from the numerous homestead hazards. Men taught their sons to ride horseback and brand cattle; they initiated them into the rituals of big-game hunting by teaching them how to track, kill, and butcher large mule deer and even larger elk that can weigh up to a thousand pounds and feed a family all winter. The family itself extended beyond blood and kin to take in hired hands who were treated as "one of the boys" and fondly remembered for making wooden toys for the children or teaching them to walk.

The years of the Great Depression solidified the isolated ranch communities, though bitter feuds over sheep- and cattle-grazing rights persisted. Yet, the abundance of wild game and wood, the open seams of coal, and large gardens enabled families to survive. Beef cattle were generally raised for sale, not for family consumption. Instead, mountain folk ate the wild game that they shot either in regular hunting season, according to game laws, or during "farmer's season," — any time they needed meat and saw deer or elk in their hayfields.

Folktales abound concerning hunting season and its rituals; one story from the Depression illustrates a local game warden's compassion:

A rancher had gone up into the forest to cut wood and had taken his rifle with him. Before cutting any timber he shot and gutted a buck and placed it in his wagon. Though he did not expect to see the game warden, he took precautions and covered the buck with split cord wood. Just as he was ready to leave, the game warden arrived and asked the rancher if he had heard any rifle shots. The rancher said no and that he had to be going before it got dark. "Well," said the game warden with a long look at the wagonload of wood and the patches of moist soil underneath it, "I guess you better head home, but hurry before that pile of wood bleeds to death."[34]

Ranchers who shot wild game did so out of necessity. In 1930, the average Colorado income was $551, compared to a national average of $640.[35] As western Colorado began to feel the Depression's effects, farmers tried numerous cash crops, including attempts at growing lettuce at high altitudes. Between 1929 and 1932, income dropped 40 percent, and Garfield County families worked doubly hard to make ends meet.

Deyoe Green, who was born at his family's ranch along the Grand Hogbacks on Rifle Creek, had been in partnership with other men running cattle on the national forest. During the hard times, they began to abuse public lands, and when they added two bands of sheep to their already overgrazed summer pasture, Deyoe Green wanted out of the partnership. He explains:

So they bought me out and I bought a ranch and got part of their cattle and a permit on the forest so then we were on our own. That was in 1930 when we moved onto the ranch. Right away the Depression hit, but still we were our own boss. It was tough goin' and we could hardly make it. Even while we were scratchin' the hardest to hold on to things, I really believe that was the happiest time because the kids all worked in the fields and looked to me for everything, and we all worked together. We never suffered for food. We always had plenty of food, but we were pretty short on clothes during those Depression years and we had a drought in '34.

Deyoe remembers with nostalgia a trip he made to Grand Junction, Colorado, to sell hogs when his family was without shoes and he desperately needed cash, as did all Colorado farmers. He says:

I remember the time Velma, our middle daughter, said to me, "Daddy, do you think we'll be able to have some shoes when we start to school?" They'd been goin' barefoot all summer. I said, "I don't know, Velma. If I can sell these pigs that you kids've been pullin' weeds for all summer we'll buy some clothes." There was no market for hogs up here at all, but there was an outfit down in Grand Junction that was buyin' pigs to kill so one day we loaded those four pigs into the pickup. The bigger kids had to ride in the back of the pickup with the pigs. It was real hot — just before school started. Frances and I and the two little kids were in the cab and we got down there and I carried water and put water on those pigs to cool 'em off and give 'em a drink. We pulled into this place where they were buyin' pigs and this man he come out and he looked at 'em and he said, "They're nice pigs, but I don't think they're big enough — heavy enough. They won't take anything at the slaughterhouse that doesn't weigh 180 pounds — otherwise they're feeder pigs. I don't think your pigs are big enough."
  Oh, I thought they would weigh 180 pounds, and of course the kids were all standin' around lookin' real disappointed, and I said, "Well, is there any place else I can sell feeder pigs?" "Well, I don't know of any," he said, "but I'll tell ya if you'll take 'em out of the pickup and put 'em on the scales we'll know how much they weigh." So we herded 'em out of the pickup and on to the scales. They had to weigh 900 pounds. Anyway we put 'em on there. Frances and the two little kids were still in the cab of the pickup, but the

other three and I were standin' there — and he put that scale at 900 and he said, "Now, they'll have to lift that up to weigh it."

I believe the Lord must have put his hand on there. Pretty soon it lifted up. "By golly," he said, "they do weigh it." And those kids just brightened up. And that's all those pigs weighed. They just barely balanced.[36]

With his family depending upon him, Deyoe Green would have been a poor provider if forced to take the pigs home from Grand Junction because of insufficient weight. For that reason he had chosen a hot day to make the trip and watering the hogs well before putting them on the scales not only increased their weight, but saved his self-respect. A story from the hard times of the 1930s has now passed into family folklore for the Greens, but other ranchers were not so lucky. Many families went broke despite their hard work; for them, there is no nostalgia, only bitterness.

Feeding weeds to fatten hogs as the Greens had done was a direct result of the 1934 drought, exacerbated in the West by extensive overgrazing. In *The New Deal and the West* (1984), Richard Lowitt writes, "The West by the 1930s was for all intents and purposes not far removed from a pioneering stage of development in the way it utilized its grass, its soil, its timber, and its watersheds." He adds, "All were exploited; some were seriously deteriorated . . . people debated the historic questions of just who exploited the region: eastern corporations, local residents, or both ?"[3] Lowitt describes the New Deal and "strenuous efforts to manage the arid environment" so that local residents could live with their natural resources "without substantially depleting them from one generation to the next."[38] The problem had become acute on the nation's rangeland.

When Deyoe Green dissolved his partnership interest in the HLH outfit, he did so because "the senior partners thought the sheep were movin' into the country real bad and crowdin' in on the public domain." Rather than react in a rational way to the overgrazing, "they got the idea we had to buy sheep to protect ourselves." Deyoe explains, "I was very much against it, but they bought two bands of sheep [each band is 2,000 head] and started to runnin' 'em right with the cattle. We were already short of range. It was terrible." What had been prime grazing land was now in such poor shape that HLH cattle "were just goin' around eatin' the brush that the sheep couldn't reach."[39]

These local conditions were well known to Congressman Edward P. Taylor, a Democrat from Glenwood Springs who served thirty-four years in the House and chaired the important Appropriations Committee throughout the Depression. Taylor knew the need to limit overgrazing. In 1934, in the midst of one of the century's worst droughts, Congress rallied to pass the Taylor Grazing Act, effectively closing the public domain to further homesteading and individual proprietorship. This act was pivotal legislation because it placed all unclaimed lands under federal jurisdiction. Some lands that had been homesteaded on the forest reverted to the public domain because of Depression-caused nonpayment of taxes, and those lands not in national parks or under control of the Forest Service became the purview of the Bureau of Land Management. Altogether, millions of acres were involved. The act was necessary, because as Taylor explained, "On the western slope of Colorado and in nearby states I saw waste, competition, overuse and abuse of valuable range lands and watersheds eating into the very heart of western economy. Farms and ranches everywhere in the range country were suffering," he asserted. "The basic economy of entire communities was threatened. There was terrific strife and bloodshed between the cattle and sheep men over the use of the range."[40]

Actually, most of the strife in Garfield County had already taken place, but the depressed national economy had forced cattlemen to increase their herd size and damage the carrying capacity of the land. Animosity did exist between sheep- and cattlemen, yet wholesale community disruption did not occur. Community roots were strong enough that there was very little out-migration from Garfield County, unlike parts of eastern Colorado and the Great Plains states where one in every four families left during the Depression.[41] Of all the mountain counties in northwest Colorado, only Rio Blanco lost population in the 1930s. During this arduous period, residents remained dedicated to raising hay, cattle, and fruit in a natural equilibrium based on summer livestock grazing on forest service lands and cattle and sheep shipments in the fall.

Community life was characterized by frequent person-to-person contacts, and people acted in a neighborly fashion. Country school-teacher Esma Lewis, for example, brought clothing for the German-Russian children whose families had settled on Silt Mesa in the defunct Orchard Development. When the value of beets dropped sharply and the immigrant and Hispanic children of beet-harvesting families had little to wear, others came to their aid. Esma, who taught three generations of Garfield County children and retired after sixty years, explained that the community thrived during the hard times of the Depression:

I taught through the Depression and we had to help each other. Anybody that I ever did anything for did much more for me in many ways. I have always said I cast my bread upon the waters and it came back cake. Forty years later a man came to do a day's job for me and said with a twinkle in his eye, "No, I won't take any money from you. I remember what you did for us once."

"Oh," I said. "That was forty years ago and you've restored my faith in human nature, but you have to take this money for the work you did."[42]

Doris Flynn, who had left her oil shale dreams behind to operate two drugstores — one in New Castle and the other in Silt — also affirmed community neighborliness:

We took bankrupt drugstores, in a time when we needed to make money, we needed very badly, and with our bootstraps pulled ourselves up to where they became paying stores. It was a very nice feeling when you knew everybody you were dealing with and didn't hesitate to give anybody credit. Any time there was sickness or tragedy in the community a town without a doctor had a druggist which was the nearest thing. You became a very vital link in the community. During the Depression we took care of our customers whose income was their cream check. An average five gallon can of cream brought from $1.56 to $4.39 and that was their [the farmwives'] spending money. They bought their groceries, kids' shoes, and medicines all out of that.

[In diagnosing children] I've said, "Johnny has a cold and a cough." So I'd put out five cents worth of Epsom salts in a paper sack, and I'd give them some turpentine. I would probably charge them five cents — maybe ten cents, but it was a ten cent bottle. We went behind every day, but in either store we never turned anybody away without medicine. That's how you get

Steady work on the railroad continued to bring immigrants into the Colorado River Valley, including Italians and Hispanics, many of whom stayed to raise families and become farmers. *Courtesy of the Grand River Museum Alliance.*

close to your community. It's doing for somebody else and they were doing for us. [43]

During these years, New Mexico had the lowest per capita income of any state in the nation, and farmworkers and laborers migrated north into Colorado by the thousands. (At one point, Colorado Governor Ed Johnson declared martial law and called out the National Guard to post roadblocks and patrols at the state line, but New Mexico's governor vowed to boycott Colorado goods if the border remained patrolled.)[44] Many Hispanics migrated into Garfield Country from New Mexico and southern Colorado during the Depression to work in the beetfields or as section hands and maintenance men on the railroads. Eventually, they bought houses and town lots in Silt and Rifle and settled unobtrusively into the farm and ranch communities, while maintaining their language and customs. To the county's vernacular building traditions of stone houses, log cabins,

A local legend in the Silt and Rifle area, Jim Farris farmed with horses all his life. Jim expertly handled his team; with large, heavy draft animals he could "turn a corner on a dime and leave you a nickel in change." *Photograph by the author.*

and dugout potato cellars roofed with cedar and sod, the Hispanics added adobe houses and garages built from solid frame-works of discarded railroad ties. One member of this community, Juanita Ulibarri, remembers:

In the olden days we had to dry everything. We dried the meat. We dried vegetables, chiles, peas, beans, everything green we used to dry. This is the way we did it to store it for the wintertime. Our soap, we used to make our soap, too. The root of the yucca, we call it "amole," and you get that and you smash it really good and put it in a tub of water. It would make all these beautiful suds and you can wash your hair in it. This is what we used to do because we didn't have the money. God gave us things so that we could survive if we really know how to use them. Medicine is a part of our culture. We used a lot of herbs. We didn't run to a doctor. In fact we didn't have a doctor where I was raised. So we gathered herbs we knew were good from our ancestors. This is the way we took care of ourselves.[45]

Salomon Estrada, born in New Mexico, moved north to work as a horse wrangler, sheepherder, and railroad hand. Over time, he bought ten lots in Silt below the Cactus Valley Ditch, where he and his wife irrigated and cultivated a huge garden of lettuce, radishes, onions, turnips, cabbages, corn, hot chili peppers, potatoes, green beans, cantaloupe, sweet peas, early peas, and squash. One of his greatest delights was giving away his produce in the true spirit of community. As he aged, Salomon no longer spaded his garden but had Jim Farris turn the soil over each spring with his plow and team of horses.

Farris had ranched south of the river on Mamm Creek and was known far and wide for his powerful horse teams that could "turn a corner on a dime and leave you a nickel in change." He recalls:

I never had a tractor on the place, just five head of good workhorses. Anybody that was farming, thirty, forty acres could farm it so damn much cheaper with stock. It'd take you three head of horses to do it. If that's all you had, that's all you'd need around. Stack your hay instead of bailing it. Get you an old buckrake and you ain't out no money to speak of — just a man to stack it, you know. Everybody used to laugh about it and talk about it up there on that creek. They'd say, "Those damn fellas that do it all with horses, they're the first ones through and going to help everyone else finish up!"[46]

When Jim finished his own work, he often helped his neighbors, especially in the summer when tall cumulus clouds gathered over the mountains and threatened rain on hay that was ready to cut. Years later, when he moved to Silt to semi-retire, he erected a mailbox in front of his house and set it inside the handles of a horse-drawn plow that he painted chrome silver. The mailbox thus became an enduring pioneer motif and a symbol of one man's strong ties to horses and the soil.[47]

Among the local legends are stories of the wampus kitty, a large, mischievous cat with long whiskers and a multicolored fur coat who left gates open, let cattle out, spilled milk, knocked down fences, and generally took the blame for all human error. A friend of the wampus kitty was the sidehill gouger, a speedy animal with a prominent snout who sped around the mountaintops and never lost his footing because one set of legs was appreciably longer than the other, giving him added traction on steep slopes.[48] Neighbors also talked about Sadie Connors, a woman with penetrating blue eyes who lived alone on her

Divide Creek homestead that bordered the national forest. Long past World War II, she had been known to snowshoe over the top of the mountains into Glenwood Springs to get her mail. A reclusive woman, she died of natural causes one winter; when her body was found outside her log cabin late that spring, it was obvious that her hungry housecats had gnawed her flesh. Another notable character was Cedar Post Bill, who grew up barefoot in the woods, cut fenceposts for a living, and claimed to have calluses "like a mule." John Dwire even told stories about a mountain lion that chased him to his pickup and turned his hair white overnight. Local culture and folktales helped community and kin sustain one another despite isolation and the hard years of the Great Depression.

Though the Civilian Conservation Corps brought jobs into the area and young men built mountain trails and campsites, the region was still removed from larger events and social change after the first oil shale rush. Like other areas of the West (which in 1940 covered fully one-half of the continental United States but had only 14 percent of the population), Garfield County, Colorado, remained rural and remote.[49] Many county roads were not graveled until 1935, and electricity did not come until 1948. After World War II, native sons joined the steady flow of Americans moving to urban and suburban areas, and daughters married men who took them far from the valley and the mountains they had known as children. Yet the ties that bind kept the small communities together. County population remained constant and actually grew 3.4 percent between 1950 and 1960, to a total of 14,821. For those who stayed, jobs were few and opportunities limited, but family ties gave meaning and texture to life.

The mountains of oil shale had not been forgotten. Union Oil kept experimenting with a commercial shale plant, and well-educated private investors quietly purchased shale claims, knowing that petroleum was a nonrenewable resource and, sooner or later, another oil shortage would occur. The big oil companies offered no obstacles to private entrepreneurs who purchased large blocks of defunct shale claims.

In this netherworld of abandoned claims and bright prospects for an eventual industry, two family names stand out — the Savages and the Ertls. The Savage family lived in Parachute before moving to

Born in 1914, Tell Ertl graduated with a B.S. from the University of Washington and worked as an underground miner in five states before earning a doctorate in philosophy and pure science from Columbia University in 1946. His interest in oil shale grew out of his position as chief of the mining section, Bureau of Mines, at the Oil Shale Mine in Rifle. When this photograph was taken in the early 1950s, he was professor of mining and petroleum engineering and chair of the department at Ohio State University. In his spare time he staked innumerable oil shale claims in the Colorado River Valley. *Courtesy of the Tell Ertl family.*

Rifle. John W. Savage, Sr., a Stanford graduate with a chemical engineering degree, formed the JoJo Oil Shale Company on February 1, 1956, and began to purchase property and oil shale claims and make astute investments in ranchland. The Ertls also lived in Parachute, and Dr. Tell Ertl served on both the Rifle and Parachute school boards. He had earned an M.S. in mining engineering (1941) and a Ph.D. in philosophy and pure science (1946) from Columbia University. From 1944 to 1948, he was chief of the mining section at the Bureau of Mines' Oil Shale Mine in Rifle; later, he headed Union Oil's oil shale department. Tell Ertl continually promoted oil shale and began purchasing shale claims in 1951, as well as property near Parachute. Wearing khaki pants and construction boots and driving old pickup trucks, Ertl and Savage drove the dusty backroads looking for survey stakes or following ruts and trails where no roads existed. They tediously proved up on claims and tracked down descendants of the original prospectors, certain that oil shale would make a comeback. Time and the nation's energy appetite were on their side.

Tell Ertl advocated oil shale at every opportunity. In a speech on August 5, 1957, he declared, "Colorado's ace-in-the-hole is energy resources," and claimed, "We can and will produce more oil in Western Colorado from oil shale than the entire world will produce from petroleum." In December of the same year, he spoke in Las Vegas, Nevada, noting, "The Colorado [River] drains the largest concentration of energy that occurs anywhere on earth." He added that "the trillion barrels [of oil from shale] guarantee to you and me, to our children, to our grandchildren and to their grandchildren fine liquid fuel at low prices." In a similar address before the National Western Mining and Energy Conference in 1960, Ertl concluded that an oil shale industry would yield "nearly limitless amounts of cheap energy for a greater and better United States." [50]

Although commercial interest in oil shale remained minimal, Tell Ertl continued to believe in it and systematically acquired more claims. Theo Ertl, one of his sons, remembers riding in an old truck with a flatbed full of surveying stakes. "Dad and I used to come up [to the mining claims] when the roads were so rough Dad would have to keep his hand pushed against the ceiling of the truck, bracing himself to keep from bouncing so much." He adds, "The most vivid memories I have of that time are running around this acreage looking for corner stakes marking our claim." [51] To pay for the fifty acres Tell bought west of Parachute, and numerous mining claim options, he spent winters teaching at universities in the Midwest and once headed the mining engineering department at Ohio State University. He even moved his family to Brazil to help develop a shale plant there.

Other oil shale entrepreneurs had valuable national contacts. J. H. Smith, heir to the Smith cough drop fortune, was a Renaissance man who had been an Olympic Gold Medal winner, naval submarine expert, and special assistant to the secretary of the Navy during President Eisenhower's administration. His diverse interests included oil shale. Unlike Savage and Ertl, Smith did not live in the Colorado River Valley, but in 1959 he bought the North Star Ranch near Aspen. It was there that a top-secret team developed the Polaris missile system.

As the nation moved into a postwar boom and petroleum use increased astronomically, shrewd investors like Smith, Savage, and Ertl kept acquiring claims or adjacent property. New York attorney and investment advisor Allan Stroock encouraged his clients to invest in oil shale, including the wealthy Loeb family of New York City and Huntington Hartford, heir to the A & P grocery chain. Investors saw an opportunity to make money on oil shale and to encourage development of American energy resources to reduce our dependence on oil from Middle Eastern countries.

In 1957, the Loeb family invested $300,000 in Savage's JoJo Shale Company. The Loebs were also initial investors in Tosco (The Oil Shale Company) providing the young corporation with more than a million dollars in investment capital. That same year, Union Oil's $8 million plant supposedly produced 30,000 gallons of oil daily (a fraction of the possible output of oil from shale) and earned valuable national publicity in a *Newsweek* article "Riches in Rock," that was published May 27, 1957, and a similar article in *Reader's Digest*, printed in June of 1957.[52]

As industry experts once again predicted a rosy future for oil shale, Smith, Savage, and an investor named Irvin Nielson decided that such an industry would need a large municipality to accommodate the necessary workers. They then formed the Valley Land Owners Association as a public interest group, but the name was a misnomer because the association represented only the interests of its three founders. Through his contacts, Smith convinced the planning department at Cornell University to draw up a comprehensive plan for a new town to be built south of the Colorado River, adjacent to Parachute. The preface of the report included acknowledgments to

"Dr. Tell Ertl, Mining Engineer, Grand Valley, Colorado" and "Mr. James Hopkins Smith, Director, International Cooperation Administration."

"Grand Valley, Colorado: A Plan for the Development of the Grand Valley of the Colorado River — Proposed by Graduate Students of City and Regional Planning, Cornell University, Ithaca, New York" is an extraordinary document that was completed in the autumn of 1958. Under the direction of the dean and two faculty advisors, twenty-four students from the United States, South Vietnam, Scotland, India, and England produced an incredibly detailed plan that would be the forerunner to all the massive oil shale studies and environmental impact statements undertaken in the early 1970s. The students looked at every aspect of the valley, from its history, topography, geography, and geology to its weather patterns, growing seasons, and drainage conditions. They produced a masterwork in designing a comprehensive plan for a city of 350,000.

The Cornell report noted that "although the U.S. accounts for 57% of the world demand for petroleum, it has only 15% of the estimated world reserves" and stressed, "Dependence upon overseas sources is hazardous."[53]

In 1957, the year the Grand Valley Plan was being researched, the town's only permanent doctor retired. The Grand Valley Bank, closed in 1933, had never reopened its doors. Over the years, fire had destroyed stores, stables, hotels, and an entire block of business buildings that had faced First Street between Parachute and Hallett streets, and what remained of the business district was closed and boarded up. And in 1950, only 814 people were employed in man-ufacturing on the entire Western Slope. Yet, in dramatic contrast to the physical reality of Parachute, the graduate students waxed enthusiastic on the topic of oil shale's future.

In the preface to the report, they stated, "The development of processes by which petroleum may be economically extracted from rock . . . opens a new era of industrial and urban development in the region." They wrote of vast shale reserves so huge "that it would take 300 years at the present rate of consumption to exhaust the supply in the Green River Formation" and expressed the belief that "scientists have developed methods of extracting oil from shale at a cost low enough to make development of a new oil industry possible." However, they warned that this development "naturally creates problems of housing and services on a metropolitan scale for the tremendous immigration of population anticipated in connection with this industry." [54]

Cornell's planning students must have relished the opportunity to design a new city where none existed. In the preface, they explained, "Unbridled by the usual restrictions of an existing pattern and the incorrigible mistakes of . . . the past, it is clearly our duty to design the world's most modern city." [55] The oil shale city the graduate students were designing would be unprecedented.

They argued that the new community had to be well enough integrated with the area to keep it "free of industrial blight" and "planned so as not to encroach upon the grandeur of mountains, forests and streams." They also wanted it so "sufficiently diversified that it need never become another ghost town." [56] The Cornell report accurately cautioned that the light breezes in the valley that had been a boon to the fruit growers would spread the dust and smoke pollution of an oil shale industry producing one million barrels per day. The report also predicted both major water shortages and mammoth power needs. The existing two-lane roads, only 13 feet wide, would be inadequate as transportation corridors. And the insufficient ground water supplies meant that the new oil shale industry's huge water needs would have to be satisfied via limited appropriations on the Colorado River.

Yet, environmental effects were minimized in the report. The fact that sulfur and other chemicals from spent shale would leach into the 250,000-square-mile Colorado River drainage system was only casually mentioned. And as for the spent shale, the report suggested it could be "dumped into neighboring canyons" after it had been retorted.

The Cornell report argued that "the great mining boom will make the Grand Valley increase in population many times . . . this pattern will last 30 years or more." [57] To accommodate such growth, they suggested a monorail system for transportation, shopping centers in a high-rise urban environment, and a stunning cultural center, for this would be a young city peopled with young couples. The Cornell plan also called for "varying the population densities and housing types," as well as a variety of greenbelts and a central business district with a city hall that would have both a civic and governmental cultural center for "theatre audiences." This civic center would have an ideal site "expressed through an imposing group of buildings set dramatically upon a bluff, commanding the superb view up and down the Colorado River Valley, and across it to the Roan Cliffs, wherein lies the oil shale — the sine qua non of the region."[56] The students suggested "as little bulldozing and regrading as possible" because they felt "the frontier heritage . . . to be a tradition worth preserving in the valley." They concluded, "The introduction of a large-scale oil industry to Western Colorado will bring about urban development" and offered their plan "in the belief that it is a valid basis on which to prepare for the imminent growth of the region."[59]

Unfortunately, Garfield County had no planning department. There were no planners to make use of the Cornell design nor was there a technical staff to implement its recommendations. Members of the Valley Land Owners Association, however, did make use of the plan. They had bought land in the 1950s when the Cornell Plan was being drafted. This core group of entrepreneurs had already purchased the site where the town would be built. John Savage held 15 percent of the land ownership with Allan Strook and Huntington Hartford as additional owners. Original association members and other shrewd investors sold 3,000 acres on Battlement Mesa — the proposed site for the oil shale city — to Tosco. Individual members of the Valley Land Owners Association even hedged their bets by retaining small tracts of adjacent acreage that would mushroom in value once development occurred. Tosco sold its interest in the site to Atlantic Richfield which in turn sold the Colony Project to Exxon, U.S.A. The ranch purchased by James Smith, one of the original members of the Valley Land Owners Association, is now the east end of the Battlement Mesa golf course.

The first boom had gone bust in the 1920s, but three decades later, entrepreneurs were already maneuvering for the second boom. Even the Atomic Energy Commission had a plan of its own. Rather than mine shale, they suggested detonating a 50-kiloton underground bomb — the size of the bomb that leveled Hiroshima — to fracture shale in place. The plans for this Project Bronco were the beginning of shale shock in the late 1960s; fortunately, they were never implemented.[59]

By 1980, Exxon, U.S.A., a subsidiary of Exxon Corporation, the largest corporation in the world, would declare its intent to spend $5 billion developing oil shale in the region. On the surface, the Colorado River Valley appeared quiet and unchanging. All evidence of the first oil shale boom was gone. Timbers and trams had been salvaged, and any loose metal or iron had been removed for the war effort during World War II. Only small mine holes, barely visible on the Book Cliffs, remained. In local communities, cattlemen saw to the needs of their herds, and sleepy small towns saw to the needs of the cattlemen. But national and international events would soon change the valley's history and make it the setting for the fastest development of a new mining industry in the history of the United States.

3

Shale Shock

The roaring current of change . . . overturns institutions, shifts our values and shrivels our roots. Change is the process by which the future invades our lives, and it is important to look at it closely, not merely from the grand perspectives of history, but also from the vantage point of the living, breathing individuals who experience it.

Alvin Toffler
Future Shock

In 1979, a dramatic upsurge of prostitution and drug abuse in the boomtown of Rock Springs, Wyoming, led the Federal Bureau of Investigation to launch an undercover probe without notifying the local sheriff. In an altercation later defined as self-defense, the sheriff shot an undercover Brooklyn police officer between the eyes as they sat together in the sheriff's patrol car. Similarly, in Gillette, Wyoming, on May 1, 1981, a local youth took a bulldozer on a million-dollar joyride, ripping up streets, crashing into buildings, and crunching seventeen cars. Police fired at the rampaging bulldozer, but it was not until the youth had smashed the vehicle into an apartment building that his escapade ended. These events are representative of "the roaring current of change" that impacted small western communities and turned them into raucous energy boomtowns overnight.[1]

Impacts in Wyoming and Montana offered valuable lessons that were learned by local government officials and city planners from Garfield County, Colorado. There, major oil companies, including Exxon, U.S.A., a subsidiary of the largest corporation in the world, found themselves negotiating with county commissioners who had the power to restrict mining activities by approving or denying special-use mining permits. Of the three commissioners, all were Garfield County natives and only one had attended college for a few years. Though they were inundated with slick plans and projections by a dozen oil companies, whose proposals had been carefully crafted by consulting firms and whose contracts had been reviewed by prestigious law firms, in the quiet granite and marble chambers of the Garfield County Courthouse, the commissioners held their own and did a remarkable job of preparing the county for all contingencies except one. And that contingency, the possibility of a shutdown that would cripple the region's boomtown economies and bring the Western Slope's people to their knees, was not even a consideration. After all, the president of the United States had declared energy self-sufficiency "the moral equivalent of war" and within 120 miles of Garfield's county seat lay over 500 billion barrels of recoverable oil locked in shale.

Although the search for and extraction of coal, oil, natural gas, and uranium resulted in numerous energy impacts throughout the West, the fledgling oil shale industry and its accompanying development placed all other energy-related activities into low relief. Contradictory forces focused on Garfield County, as the quiet communities in the Colorado River Valley found themselves confronted by social, political, economic, and environmental change second to none in the West.[2] Other western communities may have grown faster and far more haphazardly, but none experienced a rapid boom and bust of such epic proportions.

Running absolutely counter to the fast track development of an oil shale industry was the critical environmental legislation that conservationists had urged for years and that had become national law in the late 1960s and early 1970s. Americans were angered at soaring gas pump prices, but significant environmental legislation also reflected U.S. attitudes toward natural resources and the important values of conservation and protection of the few remaining wilderness landscapes. In Garfield County, the Flat Tops had been designated a National Wilderness Area and consequently had Class I air standards under the Clean Air Act of 1970. Visibility in western Colorado averages 179 miles and ranges from 150 to 200 miles. But Terry P. Thoem, regional representative of the Environmental Protection Agency, stated that visibility under Exxon's scenario for oil shale development would drop to only 12 miles. Western Slope air could become twice as bad as the New York/New Jersey/Connecticut corridor. Two hundred miles to the east, Denver's pollution would increase fifteen times.[3]

While local citizens were stunned by socioeconomic impacts and concerned with immediate problems like the shortage and expense of housing, the environmental ethos encouraged the Environmental Defense Fund and international groups like Friends of the Earth to actively oppose oil shale development. Though headquartered in Washington, D.C., Friends of the Earth even opened a Western Slope office in Grand Junction because they deemed the abolition of oil shale development and the Synthetic Fuels Corporation one of their top environmental priorities.

The experience level of the new energy executives created another contradiction. The oil industry is composed of managers who have been baptized in west Texas crude. Admittance to upper-echelon management circles usually requires an early career stint in a major oil refinery. These men are experts at drilling for oil anywhere in the world, whether it is under the South China Sea or the Alaskan tundra; if it's black and liquid, and the reserves are there in sufficient quantity to warrant the expense, they'll get it out. But they know little about mining, and oil shale is found in kerogen, a marlstone. Thus, despite the fact that the immensity of oil shale reserves was proved by Dean Winchester in 1916, there had never been a viable oil shale industry because the petroleum business was dominated by men with little experience in mining.

The first shale boom failed because of inadequate capitalization and technology. With the recent energy boom, investment capital was plentiful, but there was still no technological breakthrough. Yet, although no commercially proven process existed for retorting oil shale, by the spring of 1980, a dozen companies were planning oil shale plants capable of producing thousands of barrels of oil daily. Most major U.S. companies were directly involved through their subsidiaries or joint ventures. The only exception was Exxon, U.S.A. Then, in an incredible display of one-upmanship, Exxon formally entered the shale game in August 1980, with a development scenario that stunned scientists, journalists, and state and local government officials, who were given no advance warning. The largest oil company in the world would show everyone else how to do it. Exxon proposed to have a 50,000-barrel-per-day oil shale plant operating by 1985; eight million barrels per day were forecast by the year 2000. Senate hearings were soon held in the city hall in Rifle, Colorado. Before long, the unemployed began to arrive by the hundreds, and land speculators descended upon Garfield County like the proverbial swarm of locusts.

The risk-reward corporate culture and its energetic entrepreneurial spirit collided head-on with family values inherent in the small communities of New Castle, Silt, Rifle, and Parachute where most families had lived for generations. Though wages were agriculturally based and characteristically low, newcomers who had moved in over the previous twenty years enjoyed the magnificent scenery, the closeness of friends and neighbors, and the high quality of life. Whatever else they had or did not have, Garfield County residents had strong networks of family and friends, but, like other rural residents in the West, they soon found that their community assets had become liabilities, for where there are fewer people, there is less political clout.

Meanwhile, throughout the West, intricate plans called for energy resources to be extracted and utilized on site. Shale would be mined and retorted, spewing tons of sulfur dioxide into the pristine air. Coal would be strip-mined and burned in nearby, coal-fired power plants. The energy would be extracted, and the pollution would remain — all in the name of an ever-expanding economy and wholly erroneous projections of national energy needs.

The OPEC oil embargo of 1973–1974 shifted the search for new energy development sources into high gear, for it supposedly posed serious threats to all energy-consuming nations. In the United States, daily consumption of oil had risen from 11 million barrels in 1964 to

17 million barrels in 1974 and showed no prospect of abating. In an address given at the Vail Symposium V, Dr. Noel J. Brown, director of the New York Liaison Office of the United Nations Environment Programme, explained that the oil crisis was causing one of the largest transfers of wealth in history. The U.S. was exporting $246 million per day to pay for its energy consumption, resulting in a weekly capital crisis of between $2 and $3 billion. The Oil Petroleum Exporting Countries rivaled the wealth of most corporations on the New York Stock Exchange. Brown proclaimed, "OPEC members could very well become the largest holders of gold and foreign exchange reserves in the world."[4]

As the nation pondered its limited energy alternatives, the United States Department of the Interior in 1974 accepted sealed bids to lease oil shale lands that had been restricted for development since the Mineral Leasing Act of 1920. As the oil embargo intensified, bids came in at a whopping $327 million for 20-year leases on the 5,200-acre tracts C-a and C-b in Colorado. Other bids were accepted for federal oil shale lands in Utah. President Ford signed the Energy Independence Act of 1975, and Project Independence was initiated to free the United States from dependence on foreign oil and an escalating trade imbalance. But despite the carefully reasoned and environmentally sound conclusions reached in the Ford Foundation Energy Policy Project's *A Time to Choose: America's Energy Future*, energy legislation epitomized the philosophy that growth was good and rising energy consumption should be met by increased energy production, not conservation.[5]

Scientists added to this climate of fear and emergency by predicting that the nation's oil, gas, and uranium reserves would be exhausted within two to three decades. Ralph W. Richardson of the Rockefeller Foundation spoke of regional environmental management as a national imperative because of massive energy development. Even the water resources were endangered; as Wallace Johnson, assistant attorney general of the United States, explained, "The Justice Department recognizes that the development of the energy resources in this area . . . will put new burdens on the already scarce water supplies located here."[6]

Although gasoline prices rose at the pump, oil shale activity remained minimal through the mid- to late 1970s. In fact, by 1976, oil shale development had been temporarily suspended and both Atlantic Richfield Corporation (Arco) and The Oil Shale Company (Tosco) withdrew from the federal leasing program. But in other parts of the West, the boom had just begun as oil men from Texas, Louisiana, and Oklahoma placed millions of dollars worth of orders for new drilling rigs. Across the United States, power plants and factories switched to coal for fuel, and giant metal buckets began to strip native grasses on rangeland in the Powder River Basin of Wyoming and Montana. Coal-development proposals encompassed 250,000 square miles and included low-sulfur lignite deposits in North and South Dakota. The favorite strip-mining machine was a GEM — giant earth mover — with a 60-cubic-yard bucket big enough to lift two Greyhound buses.

In the Southwest, the Peabody Coal Company began a massive strip mine on Black Mesa, in the heart of the Navajo Reservation, where, in Edward Abbey's words, "Blasters shatter the coal seam underneath [and] power shovels scoop the coal into trucks bigger than a house, trucks that look like stegosauruses on wheels."[7] In south central Utah, power plants to be built at Warner Valley, Escalante, and Caineville were expected to annually spew pollution in "magnitudes greater than those that now profane the Los Angeles Basin."[8] The completed Four Corners Power Plant near Shiprock, New Mexico, became one of the worst industrial polluters in the world, leading Abbey to remark that smog from the Four Corners power plant "was the sole human artifact visible from the moon."[9] Denver quickly became a regional energy center with headquarters for over 2,000 energy companies. In the rural West, overnight development occurred near Forsyth, Montana, at a major power plant and strip-mining complex called Colstrip. In Wyoming, boomtowns included Buffalo, Evanston, Gillette, Rock Springs, and Wheatland, and in Colorado, new strip mines and coal-generated power plants were constructed at Craig and Hayden.

The social costs of such "progress" were great. Craig, Colorado, for example, has been the subject of extensive social science research that showed family disturbances rose 352 percent between 1973 and

1976, child abuse and neglect jumped 130 percent, substance abuse shot up 632 percent, and crimes against persons soared 900 percent. Craig had expected a labor force of 1,000; instead, the power plant work force peaked at 1,700.[10] Similarly, Farmington, New Mexico, saw increased alcohol abuse and spouse abuse. Rugged construction workers there wore T-shirts that proclaimed "I'm Oil Field Trash and Goddam Proud Of It."[11]

One of the reasons why boomtowns present enormous social problems is because construction occurs in phases. There is a constant turnover in the work force as skilled tradesmen leave after one phase of construction is finished and a new group supplants them; pipefitters replace welders, electricians replace pipefitters, and so on. Problems also exist with local ranchers, because despite the abundance of energy resources like coal, those resources may not be available to local consumers. Energy development also radically inflates wages, and newcomers frequently trespass on grazing lands, angering long-time residents. At the Hat Ranch west of Craig, Colorado, Art Brannan explained:

It is an awful job for us to get coal to burn here in our house to keep us warm. Of all the millions of tons they're hauling out of here, they won't sell it to local people. It's all under contract going somewheres. And as far as livestock operators are concerned, all these people that they're bringing in and all the big wages and all, it's not gonna do us much good. We could no more pay even $20 a day to hired help. You can't put out more than what [the stock] can bring back. No way can any man pay $48 a day [the going construction rate in Craig].[12]

Brannan sympathized with the construction workers who trespassed on his land but wished they used more common sense:

People come out in the country, and I don't blame them for wanting to get out in the country. I like it out here too, but they run across your land; they disrupt your livestock. They won't leave them alone. We got a windmill up here. It's got a water tank where the animals water. [Newcomers] set up to picnic there and those animals aren't used to people, strangers especially. And they won't come in and water. During sage grouse season my wife went up there and saw three guys setting on the edge of the tank shooting, and there were cows anywhere from a quarter to a half mile away standing out there wishing they could get a drink of water. One of the hunters said, "They can come drink if they want to. We ain't bothering them. They can come right over here between us." Well, you explain that to a cow.[13]

Embittered ranchers were only one reflection of the cultural chaos appearing in rural regions of the West. John S. Gilmore and Mary K. Duff describe other difficulties that fell upon Wyoming communities. In Rock Springs, for example, the mental health case-load multiplied nine times, and calls to police rose from 8,000 to 36,000 as Sweetwater County increased from 18,000 people in 1970 to 37,000 in 1974. Professional planners were not hired until un-restricted growth was well under way. Gilmore and Duff describe a "problem triangle" in which the quality of life deteriorated, industrial productivity declined 25–40 percent — resulting in enormous cor-porate cost overruns — and the local service sector failed to meet local needs. Companies responded to lower productivity by bringing in more people, which in turn only created more problems.[14] In a frequently cited article in *Science*, Gilmore defined the four stages of boomtown impact on local communities — enthusiasm, uncertainty, near-panic, and problem-solving. Unbridled growth in Sweetwater County, Wyoming, dramatically demonstrated each stage.[15]

By the late 1970s, two important conclusions had been reached concerning energy impacts in modern boomtowns in the West. The first was that unmanaged boomtown impacts cost corporate dollars — a poor quality of life for construction workers who were housed in unappealing trailer camps led to high absenteeism and job turnover, ultimately resulting in poor output. The second conclusion was that boomtown problems create swift political backlash. John Gilmore predicted that locally elected boomtown officials could not last five years. Boom impacts and increased stress radically altered local po-litical patterns, and on the state level, they resulted in significant impact legislation. In Wyoming, the severance tax more than doubled in five years, and the state passed the innovative Wyoming Industrial Siting Act that required rigorous corporate compliance with zoning laws and land use planning. Coal strip mines and community disrup-tion in Montana, a state long dominated by Anaconda Copper, re-sulted in the highest severance tax in the United States — 30 percent — and equally stringent industrial plant siting legislation. In North

Dakota, the announcement of plans to build coal gasification plants triggered plant siting legislation, a coal severance tax, and an excise tax on the outputs from coal conversion.

These regional impacts and subsequent responses were not lost on local government officials in Colorado, where discretionary permitting powers are decentralized to county levels. In December 1974, the Colorado governor's office released *IMPACT: An Assessment of the Impact of Oil Shale Development* in five lengthy volumes.[16] As oil shale development seemed imminent, the Colorado State Department of Local Affairs even flew the Garfield County commissioners to Gillette, Wyoming, for an eye-opening tour of boomtown conditions. The commissioners vowed not to make the same mistakes.

However, they could not have anticipated President Carter's proposed energy policy, which would totally redesign the Energy Independence Act of 1975 and its related tax proposals. Carter had a broad vision. In a television and radio address to the American people on April 18, 1977, he proposed his energy policy, stating that, "with the exception of preventing war, this is the greatest challenge our country will face during our lifetimes. The energy crisis has not yet overwhelmed us, but it will if we do not act quickly." Energy self-sufficiency would, he said, "test the character of the American people" and "this difficult effort will be the 'moral equivalent of war'" because the "oil and natural gas we rely on for 75 percent of our energy are running out." The president explained, "During the 1950s, people used twice as much oil as during the 1940s. During the 1960s, we used twice as much as during the 1950s." Such increases could result in "$550 billion for imported oil by 1985." He affirmed, "Now we have a choice. But if we wait, we will live in fear of embargoes. We could endanger our freedom as a sovereign nation to act in foreign affairs." Bringing energy independence to prominence as a national crusade, Carter said, "If we fail to act soon, we will face an economic, social and political crisis that will threaten our free institutions." He added, "We must start now to develop the new, unconventional sources of energy we will rely on in the next century."[17]

Two days later, he addressed a joint session of the United States Congress and reiterated his stand on a "comprehensive national energy policy" to create a Department of Energy and foster solar and synthetic fuel development and effective conservation efforts to "protect our jobs, our environment, our national independence, our standard of living and our future."[18] In response, energy companies rushed to lease petroleum reserves and to locate additional oil supplies. Interest in oil shale, which had waned slightly in 1976, rapidly increased. The first oil shale boom between 1915 and 1925 would pale in comparison to what was coming.

While President Carter sought legislation to implement his national energy policy, other legislation had already been passed by Congress and the Senate to protect the nation's air, water, and wilderness. In 1964, the year that investors from Colorado, Ohio, and New York formed the Colony Oil Shale Project (and named it using initials from their respective states), the National Wilderness Act was passed. Three years later, the Atomic Energy Commission proposed Project Bronco to fracture oil shale in place with a 50-kiloton nuclear blast. The Bronco Oil Shale Study, prepared by the Atomic Energy Commission, the Department of the Interior, CER Geonuclear Corporation, and the Lawrence Radiation Laboratory, admitted that "conceivably, the shale oil could be contaminated with radionuclides at several points in the process" and "minor release of radioactive effluent cannot be ruled out. In such a case, the major radionuclides should be xenon, krypton, and iodine and their decay products," that would become airborne and drift into the Flat Tops Wilderness Area. Yet the report concluded, "No serious problem areas are foreseen in the selection of this site." The authors came to the astounding conclusion that "the event is not in a region of high ground water supply or usage." How the Atomic Energy Commission managed to ignore the Colorado River and its downstream users, which include half of the western United States, remains a bureaucratic mystery. In the final event, Project Bronco was never permitted to buck.[19]

A similar underground atomic blast, however, did occur two years after the Project Bronco report was issued. Across the river along Morrisania Mesa, near the small community of Rulison that had been settled by fruit growers before World War I, the Atomic Energy Commission successfully detonated a 40-kiloton blast in an effort to release greater quantities of natural gas. Project Rulison took place near the Battlement National Forest and appeared to have little effect.

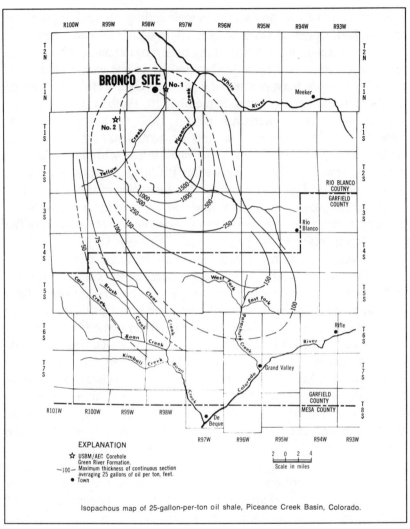

Isopachous map of 25-gallon-per-ton oil shale, Piceance Creek Basin, Colorado.

In 1967 the Atomic Energy Commission planned to fracture oil shale underground with a 50-kiloton atomic bomb — the size of the bomb that leveled Hiroshima. Despite close proximity to the Colorado River Valley and the knowledge that "minor release of radioactive effluent cannot be ruled out," the authors of the AEC report concluded "the event is not in a region of high ground water supply or usage." *From* The Bronco Oil Shale Study.

Because they were entitled to do so, residents in Parachute filed claims with the Atomic Energy Commission to repair cracks in the walls of their houses and damage to their ceilings, though most of the damage had happened years before. The state of Colorado, however, passed a referendum forever banning underground nuclear blasts, and recently a lawsuit has been filed on behalf of gas well owners who claim the Rulison blast polluted the gas from their wells. The date of the Project Rulison explosion, September 10, 1969, is significant, for less than four months later, on January 1, 1970, the National Environmental Policy Act became law; this act would have prevented any such detonation adjacent to a national forest without significant public review. The NEPA legislation included provisions of great importance for Garfield County, because henceforth any major development projects on federal lands would require an environmental impact statement, together with a socioeconomic assessment of the project's impacts.

Subsequent environmental legislation included the strengthening of the Clean Air Act in 1970 and passage of the Clean Water Act in 1972 — the same year that Occidental Oil Corporation began field tests on its 4,000-acre site west of Parachute near DeBeque. Because thousands of acres of oil shale land are federally owned, the Piceance Creek Basin, which contains the richest shale deposits, became one of the most comprehensively studied ecosystems in the world. The Bureau of Land Management set aside 750 acres in Garfield and Mesa counties as a management area of "critical environmental concern." Five computer-generated and color-coded maps were prepared to illustrate management and development alternatives for the Piceance Basin, in the first full-scale use of automated systems for compilation and color separation of a map series published by the United States government.[20] Satellite reconnaissance aided in determining soil erosion patterns, and plant specialists identified a threatened species of small barrel cactus, the Uintah basin hookless cactus (*sclero cactus*), at the mouth of Roan Creek near DeBeque. Wildlife biologists monitored mule deer movements in the basin, and a highway sign on Colorado 64 accurately proclaimed:

CAUTION. You are entering the winter range of the largest migratory deer herd in the U.S.A. Deer and livestock on highway. Vehicles kill over 100 deer each year on this road. PLEASE DRIVE CAREFULLY!

The ecologically significant riparian corridor along the Colorado River conflicted with projections for massive oil shale development. The corridor is home to sensitive bird species including bald eagles and the great blue herons pictured here in eighty-five-year-old nests near Silt. *Photograph by the author.*

The herd of 20,000–25,000 deer had to adapt to intense oil shale development, as did elk, mountain lions, coyotes, bobcats, black bears, and 225 species of nongame wildlife including golden and bald eagles, prairie falcons, and 21 other birds of prey. Also found in the Piceance Basin are rare ring-tailed cats; at times, even greater sandhill cranes have stopped in the area during their annual migration.[21]

In addition to the abundance of wildlife in the Piceance Creek Basin, the Colorado River and its adjacent riparian habitat, with stretches of undisturbed water and thick groves of tall cottonwood trees, is home to herons, bald eagles, and Canada geese. Approximately 350 pair of breeding geese use the Colorado River corridor from New Castle to DeBeque. An area near Silt is a traditional nesting place or heron rookery for birds that, for 80 years in late February and early March, have returned to nests in large, mature cottonwoods found on small islands. The great blue heron has been designated a "sensitive" species by the State of Colorado, and on those quiet islands, they bred, nested, and reared their young prior to migrating south.

Of all the key wildlife species in the Colorado River riparian area, the most important is the federally protected bald eagle, an endangered species. This bird is a winter resident in Garfield County, arriving in October and leaving by early April. As many as 27 of the majestic national birds roost along the Colorado River from Glenwood Springs to DeBeque. According to a report prepared by a Colorado Division of Wildlife biologist, traditional wintering areas have been "selected by the eagles over the years because they provide the necessary components for survival." However, the report ominously concluded, "Loss of suitable habitat has been, and continues to be, the single most important factor affecting bald eagle populations."[22]

Yet just within a few miles from the Colorado River riparian corridor, massive oil shale development was planned to achieve energy self-sufficiency. Occidental Oil Corporation and Tenneco had already blasted one of the largest underground mines in the world with a shaft 34-feet in diameter (only 6 inches short of the widest mine shaft in the world).[23] Incredibly, Ralph Franklin, who directed the Department of Energy's environmental work on oil shale, stated, "There appears to be no environmental problems of overwhelming consequence." [24]

As for the small communities in the valley that lived in harmony with the wildlife, the clean air, and the unpolluted Colorado River, there were no federal laws to protect them. Environmental impact statements (EISs) are woefully inadequate in describing cultural impacts. Socioeconomic impact statements (SIAs) are generally based on computer models of economic change for capital expenditures such as the infrastructure needs for hospitals, schools, sewage plants, and so forth. And despite constant references to improved models and "state of the art" impact assessments, no social scientist really knew what the boomtown impacts would be in the West. One researcher found less than two pages devoted to "disruptions in community attitudes and lifestyles" in a 3,000-page EIS. The inevitable downside of a boom was never even considered in any of the socioeconomic impact statements.[25]

On August 2, 1977, four months after President Carter's speech, Larry Kozisek, mayor of Grand Junction, Colorado, addressed a Senate subcommittee. Kozisek, seeking impact assistance funds, argued:

We are in a unique position to assess the Bill before you. Our 14,000 square mile area (larger than nine states in the union) is abundantly rich in energy resources. We have enough oil shale under the ground to meet the nation's oil demand (at current levels) for eighty years. There is an estimated 29 billion tons of coal in reserve in the area, enough to operate almost all the power plants in the nation . . . Individual communities could grow by as much as 900% . . . A high proportion of the residents of these towns are elderly people . . . Local government is on the front lines of impact. We have to live with the day to day problems . . . You gentlemen, stand between us and disaster.[26]

Even though Colorado received 37.5 percent of the federal oil shale leasing funds, which it placed in the Oil Shale Trust Fund for use by impacted communities, replacing antiquated municipal systems remained a difficult, costly, and time-consuming problem. Small towns needed "front-end" money to make expensive repairs immediately, not at some distant point in the future when their tax base had risen and they could float municipal bonds. High growth rates in rural communities simply negated conventional solutions to infrastructure problems. The town of Silt provides a good example. In 1978, Silt still had wooden water lines beneath its dirt and gravel streets; the only paved road was the highway that ran through town. The municipal water intake from the Colorado River was entirely inadequate, and when the community's water reservoir was drained because a pump finally gave out, lizards and dead mice were found at the bottom of the holding tank. Annette Brand, a Denverite, was hired as the first town administrator in December 1978. When she arrived, Silt was being impacted by rapid growth. The wooden water pipes were literally bursting at the seams.

For many young professionals, working in boomtowns that desperately needed their services was both personally and professionally rewarding. As Annette Brand remembers:

I was hired at Silt, and it was the most exciting two years of my entire life. In order to get all the things done I had to work 60 and 70 hours a week. For the first time in Silt I could affect what was happening. It was self-actualization [for me]. We rebuilt the water system completely, got through with the first two steps of rebuilding the sewer system, got the engineering done to pave the streets. We revised the building ordinance, which was 1954 vintage. The public works crew initiated me the first day I was there. I was the first full-time female [city] administrator in Colorado.

We had at least five major water leaks waiting in line to be fixed. And those extraordinary young men were in the trenches until 12 o'clock at night. I've taken them coffee when they were still slugging away. They did not get paid overtime and the salary was only $900 per month. They did not have the best equipment. The backhoe was forever breaking down. Once they got the waterline uncovered it had been patched so many times that patches had been put on top of patches. [27]

New administrators worked under intense pressures in what this author defines as "the crucible effect," a severe test or trial of white collar adaptation to boomtown stress. That adaptation included a great deal of self-awareness and unconventional education as academically trained professionals sought help from the vernacular knowledge of local residents. For Annette Brand, help came in the form of a small, pleasant, and very friendly woman named Elsa Pyles. Annette relates:

The Town Clerk, Elsa Pyles, had been there 27 years and had cared for the town as though it had been her child. She did all of the bookkeeping. She prepared the agendas for the Board of Trustees. She also knew where all the manholes were in town. She knew where all the corporation stops for the water system were. We hadn't any maps which showed where water lines and sewer lines were. Elsa could go out and walk it. [Pace the street and find the line.] She also knew the lineage of the town. I learned very early not to mention anybody to anybody in the town because people intermarried quite a bit. I learned very quickly not to mention anyone because I might be talking to a cousin once removed or a stepson or a half-brother. [Elsa Pyles] knew where everyone was buried in the cemetery. She could take the mortician to the right spot in the cemetery and block out the next burial plot. One of the very unpleasant tasks that our public works superintendent had to do was to dig the graves. He did not like that at all, but we had the only backhoe in town, and it was one of his duties.[28]

Living and working in a boomtown is a once-in-a-lifetime experience. Change occurs so rapidly that everyone feels needed and involved. And for white collar professionals, the crucible effect of working under pressure results in definite opportunities and rewards, as Annette Brand understood. She explains:

There was just activity going all the time. For 18 months of the two years I was there I woke up every morning to that beep-beep-beep which is the backup [warning sound] of some sort of heavy equipment to lay sewer lines or water lines. Another thing that made it exciting was that the people [in Silt] are just extraordinary. They are some of the best people I'd ever met. I was their first town administrator so a lot of times I had to explain what a town administrator did as well as justifying my being there, but they welcomed me with open arms. [The sense of community] was there more than I've ever known it in my entire life. That was one of the things which made Silt so exciting. It was something I had never known before.[29]

Annette Brand worked hard to upgrade Silt's infrastructure. Over $3 million was spent on sewer lines, street improvements, renovation of a church for a community center, and construction of a new city hall. As John Gilmore's boomtown model predicted, there was also internal strife and opposition to change before the community actually began problem-solving, but boomtown living also forged strong bonds, especially as housing prices escalated dramatically and a rural, agricultural county became urbanized with new residents, new housing developments, and additional planned annexations.

International events began to affect local affairs with lightning speed. On January 17, 1979, the Shah of Iran fled for his life and rigid fundamentalists took control of Iranian oil output. On the same day, the Colorado Division of Planning released a document titled "Human Settlement Policies," dealing with rapid growth. In western Colorado, Silt's population had tripled within five years, Rifle was growing rapidly because of Occidental Oil Corporation's work on its C-b tract, and Garfield County had become a developer's dream. At the Colony Project fifteen miles north of Parachute, planners proposed spending

In 1977, Silt still retained its frontier characteristics including wooden water mains under dirt streets. Because of the oil shale boom, the two historic buildings in the foreground were irrevocably altered. The grocery store became apartments, and the large white Odd Fellows Hall was razed for a parking lot. *Photograph by the author.*

$1.2 billion to build a 66,000-ton-a-day processing plant. That April, developers announced plans for a 60- to 80-unit motel complex on four acres south of Rifle because they felt Rifle needed "a good hotel." Construction was to begin in July, the same month that President Carter proposed an Energy Mobilization Board to further hasten development of alternative fuels in the wake of reduced Iranian oil imports.

Rifle residents complained, "This town's gone plumb crazy. There's a lot of people worried about conditions, but there's few people willing to put their backs against the wall and start pushing to save what we have — our way of life."[30] At the same time, President Carter proposed an Energy Mobilization Board that would trample states' rights and ignore environmental laws. He wanted this board to have the authority to waive, with congressional consent, any state and local laws based in federal law that offered a "substantial impediment" to the development of synthetic fuels. The conference committee bill outlined a superagency with the awesome authority to set binding deadlines for all federal, state, and local government reviews after a priority project had been designated. The Energy Mobilization Board featured major constitutional infringements and was opposed by an improbable coalition of the Audubon Society, the Sierra Club, the National Governors' Association, and the National League of Cities. Ironically, President Carter's own proposal threatened the "free institutions" he sought to protect by energy self-sufficiency.

On June 30, 1980, he signed into law the Energy Security Act, authorizing an immediate $20 billion for formation of the Synthetic Fuels Corporation with provisions for additional funding up to $88 billion. The Synthetic Fuels Corporation was to have a board of directors, composed of a chairman and six members appointed by the president, that would provide loans, loan guarantees, purchase agreements, joint ventures, acquisition and lease back of synthetic fuel projects, and price guarantees to oil companies engaged in synthetic fuel production. A dozen companies immediately applied for such loans to support their shale projects.

The legislation recommended totally unrealistic production levels of a 500,000 barrel-per-day (bpd) synthetic fuel output by 1987 and a 2,000,000 bpd output by 1992. Wyoming's Governor Ed Herschler stated that to meet the president's goals a new synfuels plant would need to become operational every two to three months between 1981 and 1986.[31] Nonetheless, the president was openly enthusiastic about passage of the synfuels bill. As he signed the bill, he exclaimed, "This is a proud day for America. The keystone of our national energy policy is at last being put into place." He said the synfuels bill "will launch this decade with the greatest outpouring of capital investment, technology, manpower and resources since the space program. Its scope, in fact, will dwarf the combined programs that led us to the moon and built our interstate highway system."[32]

Perceived energy shortages and strong federal action increased the large oil companies' interest in Colorado shale. And years of patiently updating mining claims paid off in a big way for the region's two premiere oil shale families, the Ertls and the Savages. The Oil

Shale Company (Tosco) had optioned 14,800 acres from Tell Ertl as early as 1964, but the purchase price remained conservative and did not reflect the urgency of the energy crisis in the late 1970s. By 1980, the situation was radically different. Oil shale land was no longer for sale, but it could be leased. Phillips Petroleum estimated it would utilize all its oil reserves within five years, and it desperately needed another proven supply. Therefore, it began to negotiate with the Ertl Family Trust for a long-term lease on 21,000 acres. At that time, the Ertls controlled 67 percent of the privately owned oil shale lands and the Savages 13 percent, with additional claims divided among numerous individuals. None of the shale mining claims were patented pending a United States Supreme Court decision on their validity. Nevertheless, Phillips Petroleum entered into a multimillion-dollar lease agreement on April 4, 1980. They paid all fees and legal bills, provided an immediate cash settlement, agreed to pay additional cash over a four-year period, and provided for an annual multimillion-dollar royalty payment once the fee patents were issued and oil shale production had begun. Phillips Petroleum paid a high price for the Ertl lease because all of their 21,000 acres were contiguous, and massive shale mines seemed the only feasible way to process oil shale.

That same month, Exxon negotiated with Atlantic Richfield (Arco) to purchase their interest in the Colony Oil Shale Project because the Department of the Interior continued to refuse Exxon's request to swap 11,843 acres of scattered ranch and mineral resource land in the Piceance Basin for a contiguous block of 10,840 acres. Arco's interest was also attractive to Exxon because Colony had received most of the required state and federal environmental permits and was the only synfuels project with a finalized environmental impact statement.

In April 1980, A. E. Lewis from Lawrence Livermore Laboratories spoke at the 13th Annual Oil Shale Conference and suggested strip-mining oil shale in a pit eleven miles wide. While environmentalists howled, he explained, "The real problem is that we lack the national commitment that is required and we lack the institutional framework that is necessary to overcome the obstacles preventing utilization of this resource." [33] Within weeks, the national commitment Lewis spoke of would become all too real.

In a May 13, 1980, press release, Exxon announced its $400 million purchase of Arco's interest in the Colony Project. On June 2, Justice Warren Burger wrote the majority opinion for the United States Supreme Court requiring the Department of the Interior to honor oil shale claims originally filed before 1920. Thus, the Ertls and Savages were vindicated. The lengthy and time-consuming process of aquiring legal title had taken half a century, but now the oil shale claims were theirs.

Congress rejected President Carter's Energy Mobilization Board, but all three branches of the federal government had cleared the way for oil shale development. Such activity met with a mixed reaction on the Western Slope. Esma Lewis, the schoolteacher who had come into the West when the country was young and stayed to teach three generations of children, opposed land sales to developers. After retiring at the age of eighty-two, she finally sold the farm that she and her husband had grubbed out of the sagebrush in Cactus Valley — the valley that had become known as Silt Mesa, where irrigation projects had brought acre after acre of irrigated hay fields to land that Hayden's surveyors had thought would never be cultivated. Esma turned down numerous offers to sell her forty acres for thousands of dollars per acre; instead, she sold it to a local farmer. In her own words:

I didn't want it subdivided at all, and I wouldn't have sold it to a subdivider. I had opportunities to sell and could have made much more money by doing so. But I thought Jim [the new owner] would take care of it and would farm it. I think it's too bad that our good land, the land that should be farmed, is being sold for houses. There are a lot of places to build houses that you can't raise hay or grain.[34]

Esma Lewis was not the only "old-timer" who refused to sell to the developers. Among the other hold-outs were the Lindauers who began ranching on Parachute Creek before World War I. In the 1940s, the family spent an entire summer expanding their two-room log cabin. Bessie Lindauer remembers, "We went to Meeker and got logs and peeled them and oiled them and put them up." The only help they

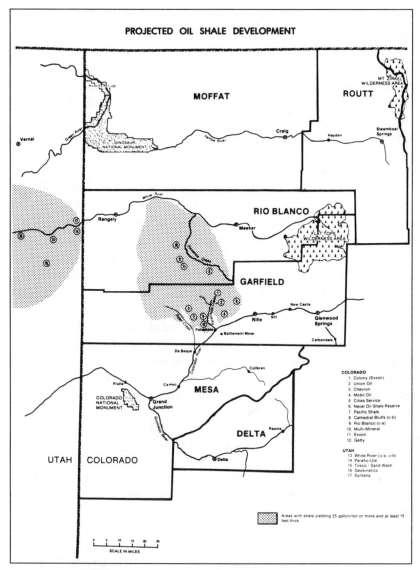

Chart from Ferraro and Nazaryk, *Assessments of the Cumulative Environmental Impacts of Energy Development in Northwestern Colorado* (Colorado Department of Health, March 1983).

had was a local carpenter living "up the creek" who "came to get us started on something . . . he'd show us how . . . and we just kept on working until we got it all done." She adds, "It took us all summer" because of interruptions to work with the cattle and irrigate hay fields, "but we got it built. Everybody enjoyed it." During the boom, land values had risen astronomically and, after her husband died, Union Oil Company sent representatives to Bessie a dozen times to encourage her to sell her ranch and prime water rights out of Parachute Creek. She consistently refused. "I couldn't sell [the house]. Paul made it — built it for me. I just couldn't find any place as nice as this."[35] But all her neighbors did sell to the oil companies. Now, only three families remain on Parachute Creek, and the Lindauers are the only private landowners.

The hundreds of people who moved into Garfield County in the mid-1970s found a sparkling world of high mountains, beautiful meadows, and thousands of acres of forest and wilderness. They also found an entire generation of farmers and ranchers who had been born in the county and had lived through the Great Depression. The values and attitudes of these natives were different. They were rooted to the soil and had a special sense of time; they lacked the urban urgency to accomplish tasks. Local residents had "time affluence" and could spend a half day "visitin'" if a neighbor or a newcomer dropped by.[36] Just as Elsa Pyles knew all the hidden manholes in the town of Silt, women like Esma Lewis and Bessie Lindauer refused on principle to sell to developers. John Cozza of Silt freely lent his tools to neighbors, and service station owner Tim Rosette would fill a gas tank for a penniless stranger and assume that the stranger would pay him back. As journalist Pat O'Neill relates, "The older folks reached out early and made friends and shared their screwdrivers and their jelly and their workbenches and their kitchen tables."[37] The Reverend Lynn Evans, who came to Rifle in 1973, recalls:

There was an awful lot of caring for each other. I remember one of the first things that happened after I got here was that there was a real tragic fire south of town at a ranch. They lost one child and a couple of others were hurt real bad. Anyway the community — the whole community — every church, every bank, every [one] pitched in and helped. They didn't have any insurance and the one kid was in a burn hospital. It was just costing them a

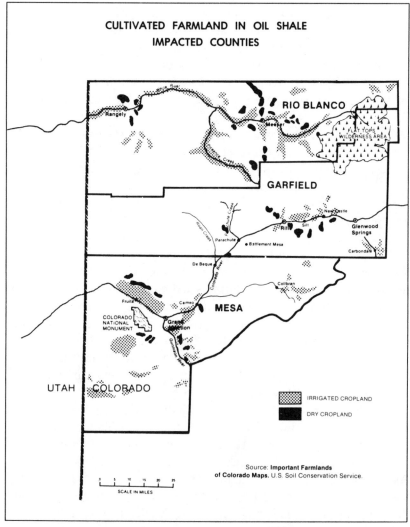

CULTIVATED FARMLAND IN OIL SHALE
IMPACTED COUNTIES

IRRIGATED CROPLAND

DRY CROPLAND

Source: **Important Farmlands
of Colorado Maps.** U.S. Soil Conservation Service.

SCALE IN MILES

Chart from Ferraro and Nazaryk, *Assessments of the Cumulative Environmental Impacts of Energy Development in Northwestern Colorado* (Colorado Department of Health, March 1983).

fortune every day and the whole town pitched in. A young couple who were members of this church had been saving up for a new kitchen. They'd been saving up for six years, living in a house that was marginally adequate, and they were within pennies of redoing their kitchen the way they wanted to do it. When this family got burned out, they gave nearly all of it — seems like they had $1,500 saved up and they gave $1,200 or something like that — and never batted an eye. Never thought anything about it. Those were the kinds of [community] values. Anything for anybody.[38]

The old-timers or long-timers — people who had lived in the county for ten or twelve years — were initially skeptical of the boom. The elderly remembered the previous boom, but they generally welcomed the hustle and bustle and the newcomers as the sleepy little towns awoke and became exciting places to live. Change was occurring at a phenomenal rate, and it could be seen daily. Past retirement and into her late seventies, Doris Flynn, who still ran the New Castle Drugstore because the community needed her, perceived the changes as threatening and cautioned:

A great many people are coming here because of the things that we had, and they're destroying the very thing they're coming to enjoy by overpopulation. As more and more people come to live along the creeks, there's no fishing and there's no place to go on a picnic. You can't have a cabin [just] anywhere. You can't hardly pitch a tent until you get clear up on top [of the Flat Tops] and it won't be long before they won't let you do that. Too many people for the amount of productive land. The wild game is getting very scarce. The cattlemen are being cut down on what cattle they can put on the forest. As I say, we're just destroying it.[39]

Farming and ranching in the semiarid climate of the Western Slope require extensive irrigation, yet the oil companies were constructing shale plants that would require two to three barrels of water — between 71 and 278 gallons — to produce each barrel of oil. As both Powell and Hayden had understood, water is a limited resource in the Colorado River Basin, making its supply and quality issues of national and international importance. But the water used in shale processes becomes highly saline and could easily be tainted with arsenic; when used in retorting shale, this water also contains high concentrations of ammonia, ammonium ions, carbonic acid, carbonate, sulfate, and solids. Suspended solids could leave a surface film on the Colorado River, as well as shoreline deposits within the ecologically delicate riparian corridors.[40] Consequently, oil shale waste water had to meet stringent state and federal standards.

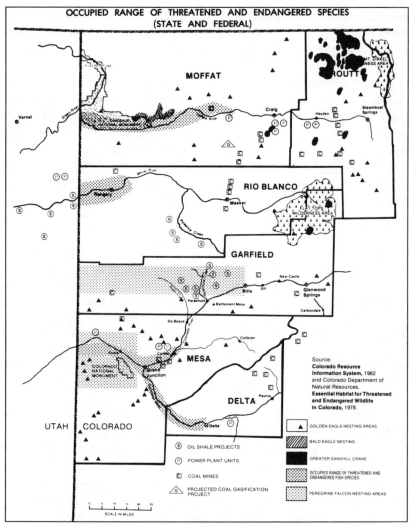

Chart from Ferraro and Nazaryk, *Assessments of the Cumulative Environmental Impacts of Energy Development in Northwestern Colorado* (Colorado Department of Health, March 1983).

Land reclamation was another major concern. Spent shale retains heat and expands to 120 percent of its unprocessed volume. Attempts at revegetation prove exceedingly difficult because seeds placed on raw shale are baked to a crisp under the western Colorado sun. Most native plants never grow extensive roots, and those that do survive can become poisonous to livestock and game animals because their roots are exposed to high quantities of boron, molybdenum, and salts found in shale. After five years of research, a twenty-person Colorado State University team with a $350,000 grant concluded that spent shale, a blackened and infertile rubble, could grow useful plants only with a gravel barrier on top of the shale and 2 feet of soil atop the gravel. In spite of these findings, however, officials of the Colony Project wanted revegetation requirements eased to permit only 18 inches of topsoil; Union Oil Company even argued that 6 inches was sufficient.[41]

Air quality standards were also a subject of contention. Rather than meet state and federal standards, companies sought a relaxation of the regulations from a set standard to use the Best Available Control Technology — a dubious request because the oil shale plants were not in operation and, therefore, the Best Available Control Technology (BACT) remained unknown. In addition, there was a real possibility that acid rain could severely damage the Flat Tops. Occidental Oil and Tenneco sought permission to emit as much as .3 pounds of sulphur dioxide per barrel of oil on their C-b tract and use up 60–80 percent of the total pollution increment of the Piceance Basin, thereby preventing other oil companies from implementing their own projects. (Pollution increments are similar in law to water rights — those who use them first can then sell or trade their "right" to pollute.)[42]

For the thousands of workers needed for oil shale development, the shale itself represents a low respiratory system hazard, but lengthy exposure can produce chronic bronchitis. Though oil shale also has a carcinogenic potential to cause skin cancer in rates higher than those for petroleum industry workers, the Occidental Oil Corporation Safety Inspector on C-b tract argued that these carcinogenic properties have "never been proven." He said, "I believe that if you rubbed Geritol in the crack of your butt long enough, you'd get cancer, I seriously do."[43] Regardless of the dangers, however, by mid-1980 the last concern of oil shale workers was potential health hazards. The United States was in an economic slump. Steel mills had shut down in the Midwest, and the auto industry had laid off hundreds of workers. Inflationary mortgage rates of 16.5 percent had stymied housing con-

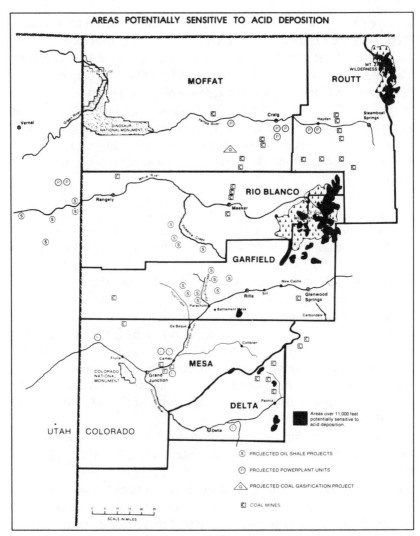

AREAS POTENTIALLY SENSITIVE TO ACID DEPOSITION

Chart from Ferraro and Nazaryk, *Assessments of the Cumulative Environmental Impacts of Energy Development in Northwestern Colorado* (Colorado Department of Health, March 1983).

struction around the country, and the lumber industry had entered a deep depression. But in western Colorado, Union Oil was paying underground workers between $12 and $13 an hour, with an additional $24 in per diem travel pay. Personnel who were "flaggers" and directed traffic earned $9 hourly, carpenters earned $16 per hour, and heavy equipment operators earned in excess of $20 per hour.

In May 1980, Exxon, U.S.A. had revealed plans to become the majority owner and operator of the Colony Oil Shale Project. One month later, the president of the United States signed the Energy Security Act, on June 30. The old-timers in Garfield County no longer had doubts — this oil shale boom was for real. Journalist Pat O' Neill remembers:

We started the *Rifle Tribune* in 1980 because of the boom. The boom was coming. Then the news came, out of the blue, that Exxon bought out Atlantic Richfield for $400 million or whatever it was. That's when all the lights on the pinball machine lit up. You could see it. Exxon was the biggest company in the world. It was bigger than 13 countries or something. It was a company that could do whatever it wanted to do. Whatever it said, it had the where-withal to do it and no reason not to. They did everything in a big Texas style way. That's when it was real, and they just jumped in.

As soon as they bought [Colony] they announced plans, they said this is what we're going to do and watch out because here comes the [impact] and it did, too. You never had any reason to doubt them because as soon as you hung up the phone from the interview after the sale, it seemed like men, young men, began to trickle in and get off the bus and stay here and ask, "Where's Parachute Creek?" That's when these funny guys in dark glasses started drifting in in Cadillacs. That's when everybody was thinking they had a future here by the balls. It was like on a train to Prosperity Junction.[44]

The boomtown expansion caused property values to skyrocket. Twelve acres that had been negotiable at $12,000 in 1974 sold for $115,000 five years later. Wealthy investors from Aspen and Vail bought out two Rifle realtors and purchased $300,000 in property between the city and outlying ranches. And that was only the beginning. Building permits in Rifle that had totaled $.5 million in construction in 1976 escalated to $2.5 million in 1977, $5.5 million in 1978, $7.3 million in 1979, and $14 million in 1980.

Change was rapid. The personal, face-to-face relationships that had characterized the small rural communities gave way to the impersonality of big business. Life in the valley had always included elements of strife and discord, but the ground rules of honesty and commitment had never been challenged. With the boom, however, everything shifted. As the Reverend Lynn Evans relates:

I went to bed one night in a sleepy little western Colorado agricultural community and it felt like the next morning when I woke up it wasn't that anymore — it was a boomtown. The first thing that went was that a person's word was [no longer] that same person's bond. And that wasn't just the outsiders. When I had decided to build a house I told a guy that I wanted him to build it. We'd been working on plans and one thing and another. That was in the height of the boom and I was having trouble finding a lot, literally. They were at a real premium. You wouldn't believe what I paid for the lot. I finally found a real estate developer here that did have a lot that he was willing to sell me, and I happened to — just by a strange set of circumstances — I happened to know what he paid for it. He was willing to sell it to me for about a $7,000 profit [which he had made] in about 30 days. But things were so crazy I was even crazy enough to pay it. But then he started, as we were working on the deal on the lot, he started to pressure me to have his builder build the house as opposed to the man I'd been talking to. I said, "No, I already told Fred that he was going to build my house." And [the developer] said, "You didn't sign anything did you?" And I said, "No, but I told Fred he was going to build my house."

Then he said, "Well, if you didn't sign anything you don't have to have Fred build your house." And that was a guy that was born and raised here in Rifle. It wasn't some [outsider]. And I think probably a few years before that he wouldn't have talked like that. That value [your word is your bond] was gone in a hurry. That way of life was gone, too. It was no longer an agricultural community and never will be again.[45]

Jim Sullivan edited the *Rifle Tribune* and saw the community change firsthand. He reflects:

I think I developed a good understanding of what a boomtown does to a community because I had to see it in every respect. In the social clubs in a small town there are fraternities. The women have their fraternities and the men have the Lions Clubs, the Kiwanis and the Rotary. Then there were new groups like the Newcomers group, and they really wanted to establish their legitimacy so they were very, very active. A nice bunch of people, a real bunch of go-getters. The oil shale boom affected the types of social clubs in the community. It affected the school population. It affected how city hall conducted its business. It affected what types of tools the hardware store inventoried. It affected the menu in local restaurants. There wasn't a thing that we covered in the *Rifle Tribune*, either editorially or in the advertisements, that wasn't somehow affected by oil shale development. I didn't write about anything except oil shale development for three years. Not directly maybe, but indirectly everything I wrote was somehow affected.[46]

Sullivan reported the local news in the *Rifle Tribune*, a small town daily newspaper that got its start as an offshoot of the more established *Meeker Herald* in Meeker, Colorado. Both Sullivan and the paper he edited were products of the boom, and he had a unique vantage point on escalating events. He explains:

Everyone was caught up in the euphoria of that boomtown economy. My colleague Pat O'Neill showed me some of Mark Twain's writings from the silver boom camps in Nevada and California. You could just close your eyes, read Twain's descriptions, and they weren't any different [here]. I had done a story on a fellow who started out as a grocery store clerk in Aspen before the boom. [He] parlayed a little money on a 3.2 beer bar in Rifle and got turned down by a number of banks before he got a loan approved to develop a small subdivision just as the boom was occurring. [He] ended up making a lot of money in real estate development. Drove a Delorean. Flew to Las Vegas to golf. Flew to California for lunch. And after the bust filed for bankruptcy claiming $33 million in liabilities.

I mean it was rags to riches to rags again. There were people making $50,000 selling real estate that, had they been in any type of normal economy, would have been stuck with a job making a third of that. [Laughter] It was something else. I can remember sitting in our little ramshackle office on Third Street, and it was ramshackle. I mean it was just a little house we had converted into an office, and these long black cars would pull up and these rather wealthy looking men would come out and say, "Tell me everything there is to know about oil shale. We want to invest some money in real estate."

These people came to be known as the sharks. They were the people who came in, made a killing on real estate, got out, had no real loyalties or allegiance to the area, but are probably a part of every boomtown scenario. There were people making profits on land that turned over six and seven times in a period of three or four years. That's a lot of people stepping on it. That's a lot of people taking a cut off it. The middle-aged people who had invested or who owned property were anxious to see the growth because they had an opportunity to make some money and nothing's wrong with that.

It won't be long now Sir!

In this political cartoon, a gas station attendant is trying to light a piece of oil shale to create oil for gasoline. The sign says "76," the corporate logo for Union Oil, which for years has had an oil shale plant. By the early 1980s, after decades of false starts, people in the Colorado River Valley assumed that a full-fledged oil shale industry was imminent. *Courtesy of* The Rifle Tribune.

It's the American Dream. They welcomed the growth and let's face it, in Rifle prior to 1978 you survived, but you didn't make a lot of money doing anything. For people on fixed incomes [the boom] was viewed as more of a threat. There were dramatic increases in things like rent, but they didn't have any more money to pay for it. Some people came in from Louisiana and North Carolina or had Okie accents, and people in Colorado didn't feel comfortable with that. They were threatened by it. And then there were the transients, and I'm not talking about the tramp miners who come with any sort of energy boom. I mean the dregs who just sort of happened on the scene. They didn't have any intentions of working. They're going to make a killing on some sort of con game. They're the human bloodsuckers. They scared people and rightfully so.[47]

Boomtowns attract all kinds of people, and the Colorado River Valley soon filled with young professionals, out-of-work auto workers, construction types quick to swing a hammer and tip a bottle, and petty thieves. The increase of drug use and abuse was astronomical.

Customers left joints of marijuana and lines of cocaine as tips at local bars. In Jim Sullivan's words:

When people are making a lot of money, drugs and alcohol are a part of it. Alcohol is part of every boomtown. What has replaced alcohol is drugs. So there were drug peddlers. Not that there weren't drug peddlers there anyway, but these weren't local and they were asking top dollar because they could get top dollar. That was their way of capitalizing on the American Dream. It was an otherwise staid, quiet community just getting shocked by growth. The social fabric was just getting torn apart.[48]

Up to this point, if the oil shale boom created community havoc, it was at least a decentralized, free-wheeling type of western brawl. The good times were rolling without any particular focus. Most local residents had jumped on the bandwagon and were enjoying the ride. But then, in the spring of 1980, Exxon, U.S.A. entered the shale game, and small communities in the Colorado River Valley changed overnight. The largest oil company in the world was going to demonstrate to all the others just how to get the job done.

4

Exxon and the Big Boom

Limitation [and] deprivation are words we must keep in mind when speaking of the reputedly limitless West . . . the social and economic character of the West has always been tentative, uncertain, and shifting.

Wallace Stegner
The Sound of Mountain Water

The Rocky Mountain West reverberated with the energy boom from southern Texas to northern Montana, but in western Colorado the boom took on epic proportions. Cafes flooded with out-of-town job-seekers, white collar professionals, bikers wearing black leather and chains, and young, single men looking for a good job and a good time in the Rockies. Restaurants that had always closed at 8 P.M. now stayed open until one in the morning. School districts hired extra bus drivers to accommodate the hundreds of new school children whose parents worked time-and-a-half and double time. Vacant spaces for house trailers evaporated. Rents for houses doubled. Liquor stores had empty shelves. Traffic and crime increased, yet so did the boom-town euphoria and the feeling of excitement — of being in the right place at the right time. The Old West had come alive again. It was "belly up to the bar" and a chance to meet new friends who had probably arrived just the week before. A strong sense of belonging, of being part of a great undertaking, revived the old-timers, stimulated

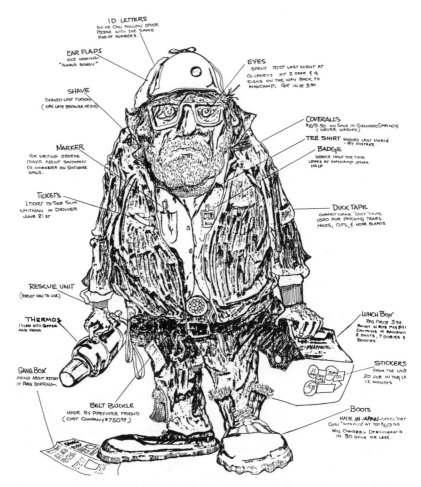

ID LETTERS
So he can follow other people with the same kind of numbers.

EAR FLAPS
Nice looking "always soggy"

SHAVE
Shaved last Tuesday (was late because he did)

MARKER
For writing obscene things about southern co-workers on shithouse walls.

TICKETS
1 ticket to see Slim Whitman in Denver June 21st

RESCUE UNIT
(forgot how to use)

THERMOS
Filled with coffee and vodka

GANG BOX
Nothing about retort or pahn borring.

BELT BUCKLE
Made by pipefitter friend (cost company $750⁰⁰)

EYES
Spent 70⁰⁰ last night at Ol-Leary's. Hit 2 deer & 4 signs on the way back to mancamp. Got in at 3:30

COVERALLS
$69.50 on sale in Glenwood Springs (never washed)

TEE SHIRT washed last March - by mistake

BADGE
Works half the time. Lives at mancamp other half

DUCK TAPE
Correct name "duct tape." Used for patching tears, holes, cuts, & nose bleeds

LUNCH BOX
Reg price 3.95. Bought in Rifle for $24. Contains 4 sandwich, 2 donuts, 7 dubies & bennies.

STICKERS
From the last 20 job in the la 12 months

BOOTS
Made in Japan - steel toed. Cost with fuzz at top $69.95. Will completely disintegrate in 30 days or less.

The typical oil shale worker is caricatured in this 1982 drawing. The caption for his lunch box states, "Reg. price $3.95. Bought in Rifle for $24.95. Contains 4 sandwiches, 2 donuts, 7 dubies & 12 bennies." The boom brought large quantities of drugs into the Colorado River Valley, and recreational drug use was commonplace. *Courtesy of Pat O'Neill.*

the newcomers, caused considerable controversy, occasional confrontation, and a great deal of unbridled, unfocused enthusiasm.

As local nurses, teachers, policemen, city planners, bartenders, and social workers all tried to adjust their personal and professional lives to a frenetic boomtown pace, grandparents saw their grandchildren bring home more money in a week than they themselves had once earned in a year.

Then Exxon extended its energy outlook and assessments to the year 2050. In July 1980, the corporation released an important industry statement, or "white paper," titled "The Role of Synthetic Fuels in the United States Energy Future" that clearly indicated that the future of the petroleum industry lay in synthetic fuels. Colorado's Senator Gary Hart commented, "Even the strongest advocates of an aggressive oil shale industry have never envisioned an industry of this magnitude and impact." Exxon's "white paper" has since become known as one of the most serious corporate faux pas of the decade and for good reason.[1]

Exxon projected an oil shale industry in Colorado beyond all measure of economical, environmental, or political sanity. An international corporation known worldwide for its ability to locate and extract liquid petroleum reserves, a corporation that ranked first in 1980 among the Fortune 500's top twenty companies with sales totaling $103.14 billion, knew little of extracting or processing shale and even less about the lead time it takes to actually get a shale plant in operation. However expert Exxon's engineers were at drilling for oil, crushing and heating rocks presents wholly different technological challenges. Yet the company blithely charged ahead with absurd projections of its corporate capacity to produce oil from shale, in wanton disregard of sensitive environmental issues and obvious resource limitations. Nor did company officials seem to understand the community chaos they were about to create. Sociologist Elizabeth W. Moen has referred to Exxon's scenario as "voodoo forecasting."[2]

The "white paper" projected a $500 billion investment in synthetic fuels and the construction of 150 oil shale plants over a 20-to-30-year period. Six massive strip mines, each larger than the Bingham Canyon Copper pit in Utah — the largest open pit mine in the world — would be 3.5-miles long, 1.75-miles wide, and a 1/2-mile deep and each mine would progress 650 feet per year. This "extreme scenario" would require 22,000 workers at each mine and 8,000 workers at each processing plant to produce 8 million oil shale barrels per day (bpd) by the year 2010, and a total of 15 million bpd from all synfuels. Exxon, U.S.A President Randall Meyer believed that 15 million bpd

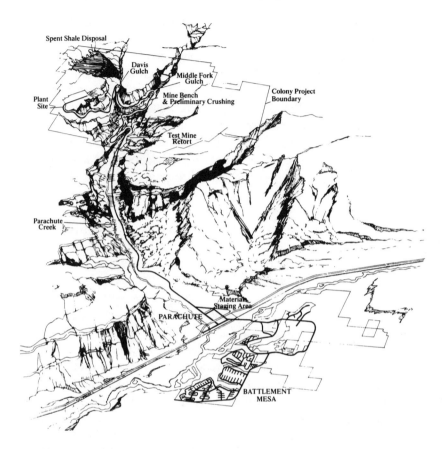

This artist's conception shows Exxon's Colony plant site, the historic town of Parachute, and the new development of Battlement Mesa. *From the author's collection.*

"by the end of the first decade of the 21st century, while it would be highly ambitious, is certainly not beyond achievement by a determined America."[3]

Syndicated *Washington Post* columnist Neal Pierce said that "total excavation" under Exxon's scenario "would equal a Panama Canal a day," and an 8-million-bpd industry would generate "15 times the amount of air pollution that already casts a brown cloud over Denver." He asked, "Is Exxon's shale scenario the ultimate technological example of the giant technological fix, an idea bound to self-destruct on all-but-inevitable cost overruns, environmental disputes, and bitter fights over Western water rights?" Or was it "fair warning of an oil shale scenario that would reshape western Colorado and — by virtue of the eventual $1.5 trillion cost — send inflationary shock waves through the entire U.S. economy?"[4]

On the morning of August 1, 1980, when Exxon finalized its agreement with Arco, bulldozers sat poised and ready to begin constructing roads on Battlement Mesa, across from the small town of Parachute. Exxon was going to build a town whose projected population would equal the entire population of Garfield County. The shale city first outlined in the Cornell University report of 1958 was about to become reality. For the next eighteen months, construction of oil shale plants and related facilities in Garfield County would represent the largest concentration of construction activity anywhere in the world.[5]

In testimony offered before the Senate Budget Committee on July 17 in Denver and again on August 29 in Rifle, Exxon Senior Vice-President William T. Slick expressed corporate views on the subject of synthetic fuels. In Rifle, he began by saying, "We're looking forward to a long and positive relationship with the people of western Colorado." He explained that "we are pleased our [white] paper has stimulated the process of public debate" although he cautioned that the report "does not constitute 'Exxon's Plan' . . . for solving the country's energy problem. . . . It is, quite simply, our assessment of the extent of this country's future energy needs and what we believe is possible should the country choose to take advantage of its tremendous potential for synthetic fuels."[6] Four days earlier, Exxon officials had presented the "white paper" in Grand Junction to an overflow crowd at a meeting sponsored by Club 20. Businessmen, government officials, and journalists left dazed and incredulous.

The Colorado West Area Council of Governments was expecting an output of 200,000 barrels per day by 1990 from the dozen oil companies involved, but Exxon sought to achieve 600,000 bpd by 1990, building to 1 million bpd in 1995 and 8 million bpd in 2010. To accommodate only a million bpd by 1990, the region would require a total of 700 schools, 3,000 teachers and staff, 700 new police and firemen with 140 vehicles, 200 new doctors, and 75,000 new housing

The following table compares the magnitude of growth associated with the Colorado West Area Council of Governments probable scenario at 200,000 barrels per day by 1990 with the Exxon scenario of 600,000 barrels per day in 1990 building to 1.5 million bpd in 1995 and 8.0 million bpd in 2010.

	CWACOG Scenario	Exxon Scenario
Population increase per year	7018	50,000
New housing units required/year	2611	18,000
Acres of land converted to residential usage/year	326	2,250
New policemen required each year	28	200
New schools/year	3	20
10 acre parks/year	2	13
	Equivalent to adding a Glenwood Springs and its service area each year.	Equivalent to adding a Grand Junction and its service area each year.

From Senator Gary Hart's Oil Shale Hearings, Rifle, Colorado.

Exxon expected to increase the population of western Colorado by fifty thousand people a year from 1980 to the end of the twentieth century. Trailers such as these were rented furnished from Exxon for up to $650 per month. *Photograph by the author.*

units. Population in the Colorado River Valley would swell to 1.5 million people. As Roger Ludwig, Garfield County administrator, noted, "It would have been one strip city certainly from New Castle to Parachute, going back as far as the valley carried, and then into the forest lands. This valley is so narrow that to support that kind of development it would have taken every piece of land in the area." He predicted the Colorado River Valley would have become like "the Ruhr Valley . . . the smell in the air would [have been] that of refineries and sulfur rather than sagebrush and cow pies."[7]

Such a massive transformation of public and private land use patterns demanded an army of lawyers just to process the paperwork and sift through federal and state regulations. Oil shale development required compliance with federal environmental statutes such as the Clean Air Act, Clean Water Act, Endangered Species Act, National Environmental Policy Act, Resource Conservation and Recovery Act,

Exxon also laid asphalt pads for smaller travel-trailers. Young families moved to western Colorado from all over the United States, expecting high wages and years of employment. *Photograph by the author.*

Safe Drinking Water Act, and the Toxic Substances Control Act. Colorado regulations included the Air Quality Control Act, Hazardous Waste Act, Mined Land Reclamation Act, Noise Control Act, Solid Waste Act, and Water Quality Control Act.[8] Exxon officials reiterated their grand scenario with little regard for community or ecological considerations. Their vice-president stated, "Studies have led us to conclude that the United States and in fact the world, are in the early stages of an inevitable energy transition" because of "the uncertainties that surround the supply of imported oil." In spite of major environmental questions and local community impact, Slick added, "We anticipate that second generation plants would be in design and even construction as the first round of plants comes on-stream. We see little to be gained and much to be lost by arbitrarily delaying that process." He continued, "The investment required to attain a production level of 15 MMB/DOE [fifteen million barrels a day oil equivalent] is immense — over $3 trillion 'as spent' dollars," yet he affirmed, "Despite the magnitude of the investments required, we believe they are manageable. The capital markets have demonstrated time and again that given sound investment opportunities, the necessary capital is forthcoming." W. T. Slick acknowledged, "Admittedly, there are many unknowns about the ultimate production levels of shale oil and other synfuels. We believe it is important, however, that as the nation plans for synthetic fuels development, we do so in a way that does not preclude achieving our full potential."[9]

That potential, however, if not limited by environmental, community, and capital considerations, would be limited by water. Ultimately, the industry could not grow beyond the availability of water. "Water from local sources would permit continuous development of a shale oil industry from the late 1990s . . . beyond that level, interbasin water transfers would be required," according to Slick. "These appear to be physically feasible," but he said, "to develop such interbasin transfers for synthetic fuels will require the involvement and active participation of all the affected states as well as the federal government." He continued, "The timing for such transfers is the late 90's, which makes this seem doable, *if we start now.* [Exxon's emphasis] The present challenge is to create action groups to develop plans, not further studies to define constraints." To provide the 3.6 barrels of water it needed for each barrel of processed oil shale, Exxon proposed moving the water from the Oahe Reservoir on the Missouri River in South Dakota in three huge conduits each 9 feet in diameter; the company expected to move a total of 1.1 million acre-feet of water 680 miles from South Dakota to the Piceance Basin. Exxon had chosen Missouri River water for its "interbasin transfer" because unlike the Snake and Yellow rivers, where compacts prohibit out-of-basin transfers without approval of the signatory states, no such compact provisions existed on the Upper Missouri. For electrical power to pump Missouri River water all the way from South Dakota, Exxon intended to divert the million acre-feet through three 1,000-megawatt power plants.[10]

At the Rifle meeting, Slick declared, "I believe many companies involved in synfuels are sensitive to and recognize a responsibility to help mitigate . . . socio-economic impacts. Certainly, Exxon does."[11]

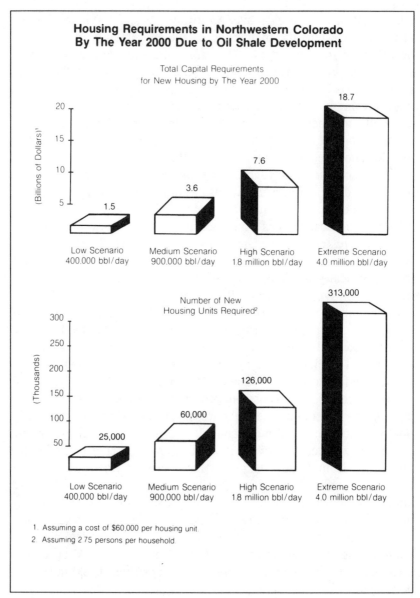

Housing Requirements in Northwestern Colorado By The Year 2000 Due to Oil Shale Development

Total Capital Requirements
for New Housing by The Year 2000

Number of New
Housing Units Required[2]

1. Assuming a cost of $60,000 per housing unit.
2. Assuming 2.75 persons per household.

From Senator Gary Hart's Oil Shale Hearings, Rifle, Colorado.

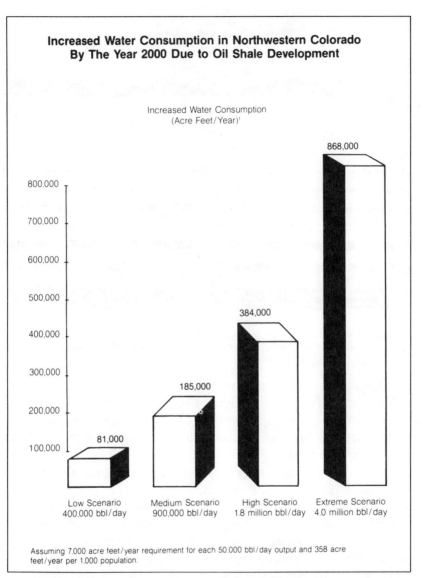

**Increased Water Consumption in Northwestern Colorado
By The Year 2000 Due to Oil Shale Development**

Increased Water Consumption
(Acre Feet/Year)'

| | | | 868,000 |

800,000

700,000

600,000

500,000

400,000   384,000

300,000

200,000   185,000

100,000   81,000

| Low Scenario | Medium Scenario | High Scenario | Extreme Scenario |
| 400,000 bbl/day | 900,000 bbl/day | 1.8 million bbl/day | 4.0 million bbl/day |

Assuming 7,000 acre feet/year requirement for each 50,000 bbl/day output and 358 acre
feet/year per 1,000 population.

Oil shale projections in the late 1970s, with their "high scenarios" for growth, were dwarfed by
Exxon's "extreme scenario." This graph shows increased water consumption in northwestern
Colorado because of industrial development. In its infamous "white paper," Exxon suggested
meeting those new needs by pumping water from the Missouri River basin. *From Senator Gary
Hart's Oil Shale Hearings, Rifle, Colorado.*

Theoretical Open Pit Oil Shale Mine at Maturity,
Horizontal Cutaway View

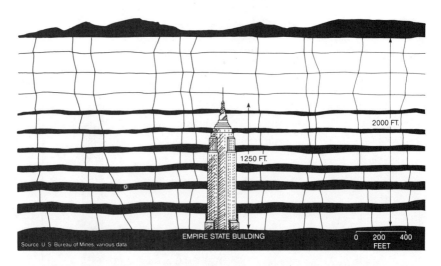

While Occidental Oil Corporation developed an *in situ* underground shale mine, and Union Oil preferred a "room and pillar" mine cut deep into the Book Cliffs, Exxon planned a huge open-pit shale mine. *From* The Synfuels Manual *(Natural Resources Defense Council, 1983).*

Speaking at that Rifle hearing, Senator Gary Hart, who the week before had written a letter to Exxon Corporation Chairman Clifton C. Garvin asking specific questions about Exxon's scenario, said, "It's easy to develop oil shale. The technology is there; the capital is there and the need is there. The question is: What is left behind?"[12] Slick responded by saying, "The potential [for development] is there. The question is: Is there the will to do it?"[13]

Corporate hyperbole reached new heights as Slick finished his prepared Senate hearing testimony with the words, "Development of our full synfuels potential will require the coordinated effort of the private sector and government at the local, state and national levels, and it will . . . require a commitment of a magnitude never achieved in peacetime in the history of our country. Fortunately, if we get on with it, there is still time."[14]

Exxon's "extreme scenario" hit Garfield County with all the force of a financial tidal wave, uprooting everything in its path. For local officials and people working in the service sector, it was like

The size and scope of the Colony Oil Shale Project is vividly seen in this photograph of Exxon's mine bench in which large bulldozers and 85-ton dump trucks with tires more than 6-feet tall seem tiny compared to the immensity of the Book Cliffs. One bulldozer operator earning between $50,000 and $80,000 a year said, "I've got dirt in my blood. These are the biggest toys and this is the biggest sandbox." *Courtesy of the Colorado West Area Council of Governments.*

"walking into a wind tunnel." The delicate social fabric of community and neighborliness that had evolved over generations was stretched to the limit as thousands of unemployed rust belt workers headed west for the land of opportunity and the construction worker's version of the American Dream. Poaching of mule deer increased, as did off-road vehicular traffic. With plenty of disposable income and little desire to buy homes, many boomtown workers who lived permanently in "temporary" housing bought new trucks, cars, snowmobiles, boats, and enough smaller items to put smiles on the faces of even the most dour of local merchants, many of whom soon expanded or sold their businesses.

Pat O'Neill left the *Rifle Tribune* to open O'Leary's Pub in Parachute, which quickly became a haven for construction workers,

deadbeats, local folks, out-of-town journalists, and anyone else need-
ing a cold beer and a hot sandwich. The boomtown euphoria was real;
in one month O'Leary's Pub & Deli sold more Budweiser than any
other bar in Colorado. Everyone made money, and even the unemployed assumed that a good-paying job was just around the corner.
Secretaries, farm help, teachers, and community college instructors
all gave up secure positions for high-paying jobs in the energy industry; others started their own businesses. Exxon began spending $1
million a day in the Colorado River Valley and another million a week
to build the new town of Battlement Mesa. A New Castle bulldozer
operator, who worked on the Colony Project and expected to make
between $55,000 and $80,000 a year, said, "I've got dirt in my blood.
These are the biggest toys and this is the biggest sandbox."[15]

Garfield County Commissioner Larry Velasquez noted, "Ranchers who had held on by the skin of their teeth are now wealthy through
the sale of their land."[16] Parachute's six-gun town marshall succumbed to progress, replaced by a five-man police force for a town
whose population jumped from 300 in 1979 to 1,200 in 1982. As the
population rose and the traffic became bumper-to-bumper, prices
climbed. The only cafe in Parachute had for years served the huge
"Valley Burger," a hefty hamburger with two quarter-pound slabs of
ground beef — for only $.85; by 1981 the price had risen to $3.50.

Mammoth social changes synonomous with the industrialization
and urbanization of the Colorado River Valley included a large influx
of young professionals — doctors, lawyers, teachers, and dentists —
who joined the throng expecting remunerative careers in growing
communities. The urbanization of Garfield County introduced a much
higher degree of professionalism and sophistication in the delivery of
human services, fiscal accounting, police and fire protection, and
municipal government. A "circuit-riding" city manager hired for the
towns of New Castle and Parachute provided valuable professional
assistance, and for the first time, Garfield County communities aggressively pursued state grants and money available from the Oil
Shale Trust Fund. Elise Boulding describes the "order-creating potential of discord" in boomtowns that indeed occurred in Garfield County.[17] As County Administrator Roger Ludwig explained, Garfield
County "changed from being a very typically rural Colorado county

with fairly low levels of expertise" to a professionally managed county with sophisticated planning and zoning procedures "copied by other counties and cities all over the country."[18]

To their credit, Garfield County Commissioners Flaven Cerise, Jim Drinkhouse, and Larry Velasquez did everything in their power to keep the lid on an explosive situation. When Union Oil Company suggested a "man camp," or singles housing, for its construction workers, Cerise and Drinkhouse toured a similar facility in Beulah, North Dakota, to talk with officials there and elicit their opinions. The Union "man camp" was subsequently approved for an area six miles north up Parachute Creek. It helped ease the housing crisis for those construction workers who preferred dormitory-style living and thick, New York cut steaks any night of the week. Modular housing on the 380-acre site provided rooms for 1,000 workers and helped to keep single, male construction workers isolated from the rest of the community. However, such isolation had only a minimal effect as hundreds of unemployed persons came into the Colorado River Valley. Because of the wave of publicity associated with Exxon's purchase of Colony, the unemployed arrived by car, bus, camper, and thumb as they drove or hitchhiked across the United States looking for Parachute. Before he was fired, Parachute Marshall Everett Morrow stated that every time he parked the police car it took him thirty minutes to get away — one man right after another asked where the work was or where they could stay. Exxon had hired Brown & Root as its primary contractor, and when a Brown & Root official parked his truck on a road between Parachute and the Colony job site, cars full of jobseekers converged on him. Men began waiting in line at 6 A.M. to fill out job applications on the hoods of their cars and pickups; their license plates were from nearly every state in the Union. Brown & Root alone processed over 300 applications daily.

William Davis, from the Congressional Office of Technology Assessment, candidly stated, "Boom town problems arise from the sudden influx of large numbers of people" and added, "It doesn't matter whether they are plumbers, pipefitters or out-of-work shoe salesmen." As he concluded, "It may help to know that the welders will come first and then the electricians, but in terms of an overload on the sewer system it doesn't make any difference who is flushing the toilet."[19] Davis's flippant remark aside, one of the most serious problems in Garfield County was the influx of newcomers who lived out of their cars or camped by the Colorado River where there were no toilets. At the request of the state Division of Impact Assistance, a survey of persons camping out in the county was conducted on August 27, 1981, and the results were mailed to Governor Richard Lamm. Seventy-four camps or households were surveyed, though "not all camps in the county were contacted due to remote locations requiring four-wheel drive."[20] Persons camping within city limits were not contacted. The surveyors believed they had reached 30 percent of those actually camping. They found the majority of adults were employed in the Parachute area and commuting 70 miles round trip daily. Human Services Director Ron Johnson stated that almost all those employed were "actively seeking permanent housing" that was "non-existent at this time, regardless of cost." He added that "an alarming number of children were present," particularly "infants and small children. . . . I personally observed no children over 12 years of age."[21] Though they were definitely in the minority, the poor were indeed arriving because of the boom. Roger Ludwig explains, "the people were coming from Detroit, coming from all over the country where the nation was experiencing a terrible recession." He says they were "trying to find work. They came out here with their last dollar, riding in a station wagon with bald tires strapped to the top, and crying dirty kids in the back seat, and they were desperate."[22]

The county commissioners remained firm in their commitment to have deputies peacefully evict squatters, and Sheriff John McNeel complied. In December 1980, he submitted an itemized list to Ray Baldwin, the Garfield County planner, for additional manpower and equipment to cover the Parachute area. The $116,819.80 total included funds for five deputies and three vehicles equipped with mobile radios, light bars, speakers, sirens, shotguns, fire extinguishers, and safety equipment. Union Oil was to pay the costs, but that was only one of many stipulations in their special use permit. Garfield County was being overrun by outsiders, and the county commissioners insisted that industry pay its own way. Lessons learned at Rock Springs, Wyoming, at Beulah, North Dakota, and at Colstrip,

As the boom increased, the Garfield County Sheriff's Office was forced to evict squatters who were illegally camping. This young man is packing up his teepee. The Book Cliffs and their layers of oil shale loom in the background. *Photograph by Pat O'Neill for* The Rifle Tribune.

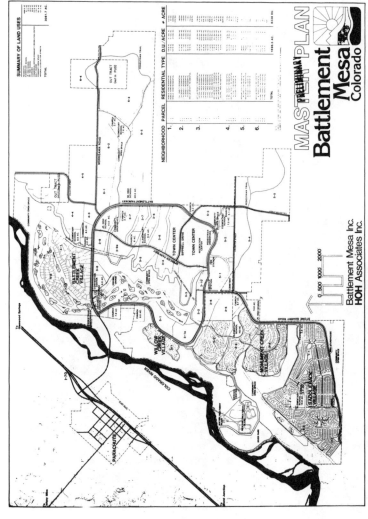

Beginning in the summer of 1980, Exxon spent close to $100 million in eighteen months developing the new town of Battlement Mesa. Fully completed, the town would have doubled the 1975 population of Garfield County. This preliminary master plan shows different types of land use. *Courtesy of Ralph Freedman, town manager, Parachute.*

Montana, would be applied in Garfield County to minimize the impact as much as possible.

Union Oil Company, Exxon, U.S.A., and all other oil companies had to meet strict county requirements on matters pertaining to housing, schools, transportation, socioeconomic monitoring, water and sewer taps, and law enforcement. For example, Union had to guarantee housing for 80 percent of its work force, upgrade County Road 215 for access to the mine, commit $25,000 per year to fund a Parachute police officer, prepay all water and sewer taps, provide worker transportation by vans or buses, produce socioeconomic monitoring reports every three months, and have its permits reviewed every six months. The company also contributed $4.2 million to building the Parachute middle school; $600,000 in Parachute water and sewer tap fees; $251,000 to the Garfield County Sheriff's Department; $36,000 for an Air Methods emergency helicopter; and $25,000 for a Garfield County solid waste study. Because its single-status housing, or man camp, cost $24.8 million, Union Oil Company's total community impact mitigation costs were $62,733,902 or roughly 10 percent of their projected oil shale plant expenses.[23] Exxon also had up-front fees and expenses, but then they were not just building a man camp for single-worker housing, they were building an entire town for 25,000 people.

Although Exxon's public relations office obviously erred in releasing the controversial "white paper," almost all of its other activities in Garfield County were characterized by finesse and careful attention to detail. Some of the company's best executives were called to Colorado to work on the Colony Project, and they performed brilliantly. Whatever the environmentalists may have found to criticize about preparation of Colony's room-and-pillar mine site, work on Battlement Mesa was well done and extremely efficient due to the able direction of Charles Pence, who had started with Humble Oil & Refining in 1956 and had been project manager of Friendswood Development on 30,000 acres near the Johnson Space Center in Texas. Like the Garfield County commissioners, Pence had also visited Gillette, Wyoming, as well as the Alaskan pipeline region. He knew the reputation that big energy companies had for muscling their way into small towns in the rural West, but he wanted to do the best job possible on Colorado's Western Slope.

Pence spent $100 million building the town of Battlement Mesa. Plans called for 7,000 living units (ranging from trailers and trailer space to $200,000 homes), a 100,000-square-foot shopping center, major office buildings, 1,200 acres of park and recreation land, an indoor recreation facility, several schools and churches, and an 18-hole golf course. Pence, president of Battlement Mesa Incorporated, remembers:

I told [my staff] that I felt like we were on the cutting edge of history and that what we did, if we did it well, or if we did it poorly, it was going to be talked about for a long, long time, and it would have an impact either good or bad. We were convinced that we could do it and do it well. The key people I took [from Houston] because of their prior assignments had some know-ledge of Rock Springs, Gillette, and other places which had had problems because of a big influx of people. And we thought because the ingredients were in place we really had a chance to do this thing right. And it would really be a yardstick for other projects. Already the MX [missile system] was being talked about. The remote part of the West was under heavy pressure for the next ten, twenty years. So we actually believed that this whole history of problems with major influxes of construction workers into those thinly populated areas would disappear. It would be obscured by the fact that corporate America could go in and do it well.[24]

Unfortunately, corporate America did not share the personal and professional commitment of Charles Pence and his staff. A handsome man with a firm handshake and a preference for casual western-style clothing, Pence was a superb manager of both human and financial resources. In describing the awesome task of building the town of Battlement Mesa from sagebrush to supermarkets, Pence explains:

You've got to have people willing to work sixteen, seventeen hour days and willing to be really personally inconvenienced. They have to have a maturity level above what you have to have in Houston, because their exposure to the media and to the local people is much greater than if they were off sitting in the Exxon building doing the same thing. They're pretty well insulated [in Houston] and public relations people pick up all the media folk. They [the staff in the Exxon building] are sheltered from all that and they rarely interface with anybody outside the company. But in a remoter area, and very often in Grand Junction, the only Exxon people [locals] knew were the Exxon [employees] that lived next door to them. So that person became The Company.[25]

Though he had lived in much larger communities, Charles Pence had remarkable insight into small town politics. He understood that Exxon needed:

The cooperation of the local government and the local institutions — schools and church, chambers of commerce, whatever. We thought we were moving into a semi-hostile environment. The thing was we had every opportunity there to do it well. We never lost a day to the environmental problem because right up front we told the environmental groups you can come out here anytime and review what we're doing. I told them, "I'll tell you right now we're going to do some things you're not going to like. There's going to be a lot of dust. There's going to be increased traffic. There's going to be an increase in rowdiness in Parachute." I told the Parachute people, two or three hundred of them. Almost the whole town was in the gym one night and I told them everything that was going to happen, and it happened just that way.[26]

Though a career man with Exxon and no stranger to development, Charles Pence also got caught up in the boomtown euphoria. The excitement was real. He recalls:

The euphoria, too. You could see it. It wasn't all just Colony. Union was busy and Occidental was there. Chevron had come in after we did. Oil and gas activity was high. A lot of drilling rigs were running in the area. [There was a] big demand for people and housing, motels and restaurants. Outside money came in. At the peak in Grand Junction we only had 35 or 40 Exxon employees. The 25 or 30 people that [we] moved in had a real impact. Exxon people typically support the United Way very well. Some of our people got involved with hospital fund-raising. So they had kind of a high profile in town. The business community there generally held us in high regard even though we were going to move to Parachute when the plant became operational. We had already laid out a footprint for the office building we were going to build where the whole project would be [housed]. Executives had picked out homesites on the mesa. There was just a whole lot of things going on. It's incredible. The psychology of that. It's unbelievable. It's the only time I've ever had to tell people to take time off and go home. I had to tell 'em that nobody worked on Saturday without permission because some of them would have been there until ten o'clock at night.[27]

Exxon employees were not the only ones working overtime. To meet the human service needs of the county, in December 1981, Reverend Lynn Evans established the Rifle Emergency Committee to assist with housing for those who could no longer camp out because of inclement weather. He also requested that the Salvation Army assess transient camping. Rifle hired a half-time coordinator for a preventive Family Violence Project, and both the Re-2 School District in Rifle and the Garfield County Human Services received grants for innovative newcomer projects to help reduce the alienation and loneliness that had so embittered wives, husbands, and uprooted children in other energy boomtowns.

Joyce Illian directed operation REACHOUT for the county in the communities of Parachute, Battlement Mesa, and Rifle. She dealt with newcomers who had moved up from the South believing that "the company will provide," and she acted as a community catalyst in preventive boomtown care designed to stop problems before they began. Joyce gave twelve volunteers twenty hours of training to assist her in helping newcomers adjust and establish networks of friends and contacts because "normally that sort of thing gets done by informal networks . . . here we need a formalized person."[28] Her primary goals were to reach every newcomer during his or her first week in town and to prepare a forty-page handbook with maps, recreation information, local history facts, school addresses, telephone numbers, and even high-altitude cooking tips.

As the social workers moved into high gear to accommodate boomtown construction workers and their families, other individuals rallied to different causes and sought to preserve as much local history as possible. Elected representatives from eight valley commun-ities formed the Grand River Museum Alliance, using the original name of the Colorado River. The Rifle Historical Society was revitalized by new members, and the Silt Historical Society was established and negotiated a lease from the school district to establish a living history museum on half a block adjacent to the Silt Elementary School. In Rifle, after a decade of neglect, valuable stained glass church win-

John Cozza from Silt typified the local old-timers who went out of their way to help newcomers. Born in 1908 when the Silt bridge was built, he lived to see it torn down and replaced. John was an excellent neighbor who would invite friends to sit on his front porch or come in and have a bowl of "road-killed cat stew." *Photograph by the author.*

dows that commemorated President Theodore Roosevelt's 1905 bear hunting trip were restored.

In Grand Junction, the Two Rivers Citizens Association united local environmentalists for an aggressive letter-writing campaign to call to task developers and oil companies caught up in their massive projections. The Western Colorado Congress and environmental groups sponsored "Oil Shale '81: A Citizen's Perspective." In the Friends of the Earth's Colorado office, Connie Albrecht and her predecessor Kevin Markey "thought Exxon was totally crazy [and] that they'd never build this project" because "they were talking way beyond the scale of anything they could accomplish." After touring the Colony mine site, Albrecht reflected, "There was so much going on and we finally got the scope of it. We said, 'My God, they are doing it.' I mean, we finally became believers at that point."[29]

Socially, the valley changed at all strata. Energy executives, engineers, plant managers, construction superintendents, and their families exerted pressure on local institutions, from schools to churches, as did the hundreds of unemployed seeking shelter or jobs. Newcomers jostled with old-timers for positions in city government, at cafe tables, and for parking spaces. Public meetings, traditionally held in homes or churches and characterized by informal potluck suppers, for the first time were held in new city halls and schools. In 1981, the Burning Mountain Festival at New Castle, an annual event to honor the miners who had died in the Vulcan Mine, was the wildest summer festival the town had ever witnessed. Fire hoses were used to quell partygoers who refused to leave the festival and blocked the main street. In Parachute, voter drives were initiated to quickly register eligible voters and tip the balance of political power to the western end of Garfield County.

Meanwhile, Exxon was preparing for a labor union showdown because its major contractor, Brown & Root, hired only nonunion workers. The corporation requested approval to build a 4,000-car parking lot to be used by Colony employees. The lot was to have two sections, one with 500 spaces for the union workers and the other with 3,500 spaces for nonorganized employees. The paved and fenced lot would have a guard station; union employees would be permitted to picket only in their own section of the parking lot. Exxon also won a 38-year agreement to purchase 7,250 acre-feet of water from Ruedi

Reservoir on the Frying Pan River between Aspen and Glenwood Springs, much to the chagrin of local residents who had fished the reservoir for years and had no idea that it was to be depleted for industrial purposes.

Exxon officials also demanded that two trailer parks be closed — the old KOA campground and the Grandview Trailer Park. Many of the tenants at the Grandview were senior citizens living in antiquated trailers and paying $55 per month rent; in contrast, the new trailer spaces on Battlement Mesa rented for $160 per month, and furnished trailers owned by the company rented for between $600 and $750 per month. The Grandview Trailer Park in Parachute had been owned by Atlantic Richfield, and the elderly tenants there, living on fixed incomes, hoped to move to new trailer spaces on Battlement Mesa. However, they soon learned that their trailers did not meet Exxon's requirements for a "first class trailer park." In addition, the application forms for the Battlement park required answers that the elderly felt were "none of their business," and they were bewildered by the seven-page pamphlet of rules and regulations. As media exposure increased and the eviction date drew closer, Exxon quickly corrected its community gaffe and provided spaces for most of the elderly trailer tenants; only a few of Parachute's senior citizens were actually displaced.

Yet, despite the intense boomtown pressures, at times an almost carnival-like atmosphere prevailed. Just as the oil companies had grandiose expectations, so, too, did local entrepreneurs who saw history unfolding and recognized the opportunity to make a fortune. Pat O'Neill says, "You felt like someone just dealt you one card down and you could go ahead and turn it. It's like somebody gave you a free lottery ticket. All you had to do was scratch underneath and your fortune was probably made."[30]

O'Neill and his partner created O'Leary's Pub in an old Parachute building that had once housed the Grand Valley Lumber and Supply Company. The structure had been essentially vacant for twenty years, yet they had to lease it for $3,800 dollars a month. O'Neill remembers:

It was one of those old buildings, one of those old false-front brick buildings that started at 25 feet high in the front and was 14 feet high in the back and solid brick — two walls of it, and it had been neglected. The guy who had been storing stuff in there was Everett Morrow, the old six-gun marshall. When the roof would leak and the floor would puddle with water, he would just take an old hand drill and drill a hole where the water was and let it rush into the basement. So it was pretty much a mess. It leaked, and the floors were warped, but it was a grand solid old building, and it just had "Pat O'Neill, come make me a bar" written all over it. My favorite tavern in Kansas City is Kelly's Bar, it's the oldest building in Kansas City, and it's laid out almost identical to that, so there's no question I could envision without any problem at all an old mahogany bar down one wall.[31]

O'Neill had carpenters build a sixty-foot hardwood bar, the longest in the county. Behind the polished wood and above the mirror hung a full-sized oil painting of a voluptuous, redheaded, reclining nude modeled after the works of Italian masters. Her fingers gracing an Irish harp, she would have looked equally at home in Virginia City, Cripple Creek, Leadville, or Tombstone. Spitoons were strategically placed on the floor, and guns and knives were routinely requested from unruly or potentially dangerous patrons. As for the hefty lease payment, O'Neill recalls:

You're talking fantasy anyway, from the beginning [but] I knew if anybody could run a tavern anywhere, I could. This was a place ripe for characters and characteristics and I figured an Irish boomtown pub, what the hell! I remember we opened up at 10:30 in the morning on the first day in the fall of '81 [and] about six people trickled in right away. They were nice folks — a superintendent waiting for a job to start and his wife and friends. I thought, "Well, this isn't going to be bad at all." [Then] a couple of cowboy types trickled in and I happened to know a few of them from doing stories on rodeos and stuff and I was all right in their book as long as I didn't charge too much for beer. Pretty soon, about 11 o'clock here come my first two biker couples with chains a draggin' and black leather, and I said, "Oh, man! There goes the neighborhood!" [but] those people were just as harmless as they could possibly be. Then by lunch we were busy and by afternoon we were busy and come evening we were packed. We were just packed. On our poorest day we'd do $1,500 just in beer and booze. And we didn't charge much. We weren't high-priced at all. We were reasonable. In a boomtown you could demand a high price, but we didn't. And we poured a good shot.[32]

As in historical western boomtowns, in Parachute during the oil shale boom there was no time to build churches. Catholic mass was held in the largest building in town — O'Leary's Pub. *Photograph by Nicholas DeVore III / Photographers, Aspen.*

O'Leary's achieved notoriety as a workingman's pub. In a perfect recapitulation of nineteenth-century mining camp life in the Rockies, the saloon even doubled as a sanctuary. Of the nineteen different denominations that competed to build churches on five tracts of Battlement Mesa land, at least one felt an immediate need to serve its parishioners. Father Jim Fox requested permission to use the pub, the largest building in Parachute at the time, for mass on Sunday mornings. O'Neill remembers Father Fox "frequented the joint — being a nice Irish priest — to have a little glass of the wine, don't you know."[33] Being good Catholics, the O'Neills agreed. The nude painting over the bar was discreetly covered when Father Jim Fox said mass, conducted baptisms, and even officiated at weddings.

Bessie Lindauer, the Parachute pioneer who had refused to sell her property and the log cabin her husband had built to oil companies desperately seeking her land and water rights, commented on the old supply store becoming a bar and doing double duty as a church. In saloon-keeper O'Neil's words: "I remember Bessie Lindauer said, 'I shopped here for nails, and I've shopped here for groceries, and I sure

Prominently situated above the middle of O'Leary's 60-foot-long bar, this fetching Titianesque oil painting was a favorite of the local clientele. On Sunday mornings when mass was held in the Parachute pub, she was discreetly covered. *Courtesy of Pat O'Neill.*

never thought I'd come in here to go to church.' She added, 'I don't really approve of it, but if it's necessary and if it gives people a place to go, then that's fine.'"[34]

Among the problems inherent in converting a boomtown pub to a Catholic church was informing all of the pub patrons that the only available drink on Sunday morning was a thimble full of wine for communion. As O'Neill explains:

The very first Sunday we're halfway through the Mass and I didn't lock the side door — I had the front door locked — here come a couple of construction hands all stooped over and groanin', clompin' down the bar to the stools they always went to. They hopped up on them and looked around. They didn't see a bartender and they heard singing behind them. I thought their eyes were gonna fall out of their heads because that's about the time they looked straight up into the mirror and saw all these people in the mirror holding hymnals. They didn't say a word. The first guy just ducked his head, kept looking at the floor, and walked right back out the side door. "God-damn, that was the worst hallucination I ever had." I can hear him now.[35]

Mark Twain wrote that vice flourished during Virginia City's boom; the same could be said for western Garfield County. Two authors wrote that western energy boomtowns were "sprawling and lurid" and would become "melting pots for violence," but that was an overstatement from the perspective of local citizens.[36] In Parachute, prostitution was seen by the old-timers not as a threat to social institutions, but rather as proof that the town was growing and had finally "arrived." Jim Sullivan, *Rifle Tribune* editor, muses:

It was sort of an old vaudeville. You know. Snidely Whiplash. The developer twirling the ends of his waxed mustache and then Little Laura Lee, the farmer's daughter, being fleeced by the real estate developer. Parachute even got its first prostitutes for awhile. There were hookers operating out of Volkswagen buses. Well, hell! That's big time. Parachute came of age! It meant that the boom was real.

I can remember one story. Nick Theos ran [successfully] for the state legislature and he was giving some journalists and Front Range legislators a tour of C-a and C-b tracts. As they were going through [the town of] Meeker, Nick stood up and said, "Look at this. It's just a little quiet country town. Just imagine. In a coupla years there's gonna be whores and drunks on every corner." Nick said it rather innocently, because that's how he felt the boom was going to manifest itself, but the reporters' pens just hit their pads instantaneously.[37]

Newsman Jim Sullivan wrote countless stories about the oil shale boom, but like everyone else in that supercharged atmosphere, he never really knew all that was happening. Sullivan explains:

There was so much going on that I don't think anybody at the time could have sat down and understood it. It's only now that we can sit down and say, "I've got a better idea what happened." At the time we were just guessing as to what was going on. There were so many forces acting upon that community — so many large forces acting upon a very small community — that you couldn't sit down at the time and say, "I know what's going on." You didn't have any idea what the hell was going on. Your time was devoted to reacting to forces. Not only were we being affected by multinational oil companies, but what was going on in the Middle East had more effect on us than any local decisions. Sheik Yamani of Saudi Arabia had more control over Garfield County at one time than our three county commissioners.

The winter of 1982 was mild. In January, work force estimates for the Colony Project were doubled from the 3,000 figure of 1980 to a projected peak force of 6,992 by 1985. Construction continued at breakneck speed on Battlement Mesa. Half a dozen of the largest oil companies in the world — Union, Exxon, U.S.A., Chevron, Superior, Phillips, and Mobil — all worked nonstop to get their oil shale plants "on-line" and operating. Exxon had proclaimed it would be processing between 47,000 and 50,000 bpd by 1985, and since its purchase of Arco's interest, corporate executives had repeatedly made speeches and public appearances around Colorado. In October 1980, Exxon, U.S.A. President Randall Meyer flew to Grand Junction for a private dinner party with local officials and businessmen. By April 1981 he was addressing a crowd of young engineers at the Colorado School of Mines and proclaiming, "at the peak rate of development, the industry would require some 8,400 engineering personnel . . . and would employ directly some 870,000 people." He exclaimed, "we must have the foresight, the will and the commitment . . . to achieve the national goal."[39] The Colorado School of Mines published Meyer's Earth Day speech and stated that the Exxon, U.S.A president "has long been regarded as one of the giants of American industry" and that "Mr. Meyer's comments and predictions are based upon extensive study by his firm."[40]

As shale development accelerated, oil companies were gratified by the low number of accidents and few fatalities. One bulldozer operator had died building a service road at the Colony mine site, and Occidental Oil had a fatality while building its huge mine shaft, but Occidental had an accident frequency rate of under 1.0 the first year and 2.3 the next year, while the mining industry as a whole averaged 21.0 accidents for the same number of per-thousand man hours. The emerging oil shale industry was a very safe place to work.

As hundreds of laborers earned a median wage of $16 per hour, well-placed community and local government officials found lucrative jobs with oil companies, for the industry actively sought to purchase their local expertise and goodwill. A Western Slope television newswoman became an industry public relations representative, and a former state legislative aide became a legislative affairs administrator for an oil company. Bob Demoz, director of the Colorado West Area Council of Governments, was hired by Multi-Minerals Corporation. But the prime catch was Garfield County planner and native Ray Baldwin, who made $30,000 a year working for the county and turned down an industry offer at twice his salary plus a $15,000 cash bonus. He received twenty-one different offers from oil companies and was eventually hired by Tosco.[41]

In October 1980, Harvard scholar Henry Lee authored "Oil Shale Development: A Perspective on Certain Regional Economic Issues" as a report for the Energy and Environmental Policy Center of the John F. Kennedy School of Government at Harvard University. Although Lee stated, "Presently, no oil shale project in the United States has produced more than 800 barrels per day," he explained that "[i]f all of these projects come on line by 1990, the total production will be in the vicinity of 250,000 barrels per day or slightly more than one-half of the President's goal."[42] On March 23, 1981, Senator Gary Hart delivered an oil shale address in Denver titled "Colorado's Energy Challenge," and that month the Colorado Energy Research Institute at the Colorado School of Mines published *Colorado Oil Shale Development Scenarios 1981–2000* for the Governor's Blue Ribbon Panel. Statistics and bar graphs clearly illustrated the projected impacts of growth and development on the Western Slope.

Everything looked promising for the summer of 1982. Business was booming throughout the Colorado River Valley as oil shale development infused millions of dollars into the local economy. By the last week in April, the three-story Regional Energy Center in Rifle was almost finished. It would be the tallest commercial building in a town whose population of 5,000 was destined to swell to 30,000. Plumbers and electricians had only to hook up the rooftop air conditioners, and carpet-layers needed only to finish laying the carpet in the plush upstairs offices.

As summer approached, social service workers in the county feared they were going to be overrun, but their fears never materialized. For on the morning of Wednesday, April 28, Exxon's board of directors in New York City voted to close the Colony Project. A day later, Exxon, U.S.A. President Randall Meyer requested a meeting with Morton M. Winston, president of Tosco, for the next day in Los Angeles. Exxon and Tosco were partners in the Colony Project. (Tosco at the time had its own problems because Denver real estate developer Ken Good was trying to take over the company in a proxy battle. Good had options to purchase thousands of acres near Rifle, Colorado, for his La Mesa subdivision.) Then, on Friday, April 30, because of a contract agreement to buy out Tosco's 40 percent share of Colony in the event of a shutdown, Randall Meyer and Robert P. Larkin, Exxon, U.S.A.'s synthetic fuels manager, met with Morton Winston and John Lyon, Tosco's executive vice-president for shale oil. It was there that they heard the totally unexpected news that Colony would be closing. After the meeting, Tosco officials went for a walk to discuss strategy, and within hours, lawyers were drafting the requisite paperwork to allow Tosco to exercise its option and sell its share of Colony for $380 million.[43]

On Sunday, May 2, Tosco's board of directors met at 9:30 A.M. and voted to exercise their option to sell. A representative flew to Houston with the proper legal documents. Charles Pence was telephoned and told to go to his Grand Junction office and wait for a phone call from Frank Barrow, who also called Garfield County Commissioner Flaven Cerise. The oldest of the three county commissioners, Cerise asked Barrow, "Frank, we've been very close, but you never called me on Sunday afternoon before. What are you fixing to do — shut the project down?"[44] No one else — not even the governor — knew until late in the afternoon.

Elsewhere in the Colorado River Valley, on this first balmy Sunday of spring, a contractor was hosting an outdoor party with barbecued beef and pork, kegs of beer, and a live band for the 400 partygoers. Parachute construction workers at the party were anticipating overtime pay and large bonus checks that summer, as well as an opportunity to get into the mountains after the snow melted off the high peaks of the Flat Tops, the Cline Tops, and Battlement Mountain.

At 5 P.M. on Sunday, May 2, 1982, news of the shutdown came over radio and television.

5

From Boom to Bust:
The Tiger Empties the Tank

The West has never had enough to come back on. It is the one section of the country in which bankruptcy, both actuarial and absolute, has been the determining condition from the start. . . . Looted, betrayed, sold out, the Westerner is a man whose history has been just a series of large-scale jokes.

> Bernard DeVoto
> "The Plundered Province"
> *Forays and Rebuttals*

When Exxon announced on Sunday, May 2, 1982, that it was closing the giant $5 billion Colony Project, 2,100 people became unemployed overnight, and 7,500 support workers began to worry about their future.

Overnight, employees of Brown & Root, T.I.C., Daniels Construction, and Gilbert-Western knew they would be laid off.

Overnight, hundreds of businessmen who had rapidly expanded their businesses began to question the size of their inventories and the number of their employees.

Overnight, construction on Battlement Mesa ceased, and the historic nineteenth-century pattern of "boomtown-to-ghost-town" seemed likely to be repeated.

And overnight, planning for growth stopped. There had been countless plans for a boom, but not a single plan existed for a bust of such epic proportions.

In the absence of coherent facts, rumors quickly circulated. Within twenty-four hours, three main opinions had emerged on why Exxon had closed the Colony Project. None of the rumors was correct, but then no one wanted to face the truth. No one wanted to believe that the oil shale bubble had really burst.

No one could conceive that any company, even the largest corporation in the world, could simply turn its back on a $920-million investment.[1] Because the first shale boom from 1915 to 1925 had failed, Garfield County citizens had been skeptical of this recent boom, but most had finally become convinced and invested accordingly. The thousands of newcomers, the hundreds of new houses and streets, the out-of-state license plates on expensive pickup trucks, even the soft southern accents of the bearded construction workers had all verified that the towns of western Colorado were irrevocably changing from rural, agricultural communities to industrialized small towns. On Battlement Mesa alone there were twenty-six general contractors, each of whom had ten subcontractors working under him.

Then, overnight, because of a decision reached in a Manhattan boardroom half a continent away, all activity stopped at the Colony mine site and on Battlement Mesa. In one swift move, nineteen managers on Exxon's board of directors had radically altered the lives of thousands for whom Black Sunday would forever remain a benchmark day in their lives, their fortunes, and their futures. The parachute had failed to open. *Fortune* magazine commented that Exxon's departure from oil shale had all "the abruptness of a teenage driver making a screeching U-turn."[2] Saloon owner Pat O'Neill, locked into a $3,800-a-month lease for his Parachute pub, caustically commented on the speed of "the corporate guillotine."[3]

When the largest construction project in the world was shelved, so many journalists arrived in Parachute that a newly built motel had to open a week early. The story of the Colony shutdown was carried by every television network and featured as front-page news in the *New York Times*, the *Wall Street Journal*, the *Washington Post*, and

Courtesy of The Free Weekly Newspaper.

virtually every newspaper in Colorado. By the next week, stories appeared in *Time, Newsweek,* and *U.S. News & World Report.*[4]

The force of that single event, the shutdown of the Colony Project, sent shock waves through the Western Slope's economy. And in retrospect, the oil shale bust can be seen as the turning point for the entire petroleum industry. The economies of the oil-patch states of Texas, Louisiana, and Oklahoma still boomed, but within three years the drilling industry there would be experiencing layoffs unparalleled since the Great Depression. Black Sunday — May 2, 1982 — would soon have repercussions in the U.S. state capitals of Austin, Baton Rouge, and Oklahoma City, as well as the foreign capitals of Tripoli, Riyadh, and Mexico City. The roller-coaster ride of energy price escalation and double-digit inflation had ended. The coaster had careered to the top in western Colorado, then plummeted. Citizens in Garfield and Mesa counties were the first to feel the devastating effects that, within a few short years, would rock international money markets and lending institutions around the world.

For everyone living on the Western Slope, absolute certainty about their communities' growth, their own employment potential, their friendships with neighbors, and their proximity to family members all changed in the space of one weekend. Soon local women

As a spoof, *The Rifle Tribune* published a "Ghost Town Tribune" on May 1, 1983. This posed photograph of tumbleweeds in Rifle appeared on the front page. An interior illustration featured happy, cheering people proclaiming, "You can't put a good town down." A year later many of those residents had left, and for financial reasons the newspaper ceased publication in 1985. *Photographs by Don Thompson for* The Rifle Tribune.

would become "weekday widows," as their husbands drove further and further out of the valley in search of work. Rising expectations of rural people, who had previously been satisfied with a farm-based income, were crushed. Farms and ranches that had been sold at high prices reverted back to their former owners, but titles were mired in legal entanglements and encumbered with much higher taxes.

Because it was a shared, group experience, in many ways the social and psychological effects of the bust replicated those of a natural disaster, with all its concomitant social and economic consequences. Like victims of a natural disaster, residents felt overwhelmed by grief and tragedy. Those who made it through that first, uncertain winter referred to themselves as "survivors"; they even held a gala street party on May 1, 1983, to prove to the world, and to themselves, that they were still there. As a spoof, the *Rifle Tribune* published the "Ghost Town Tribune," with a front-page photograph of the main business street, Railroad Avenue, deserted and covered with tumbleweeds. The masthead read, "Serving the Survivors" and the issue featured stories titled "Noted Psychic Says Rifle Haunted, But That Ghosts Are Friendly" and "Local Tumbleweeds Called 'Ideal' for Western Movies." Both stories had been written by a reporter named "I. M. Left." Inside the front page, the real newspaper appeared with a bold headline that declared, "It's Been a Year, and We're Still Here!" That page of the special edition carried a photograph with the same view of Railroad Avenue, but the tumbleweeds were gone and the street was full of laughing, cheering people. In front of the crowd was a sign that read, "You can't put a good town down!"

There have been three historic bonfires in Rifle's history. The first bonfire in 1912 celebrated the completion of the ill-fated Havemeyer Ditch that washed out a month later. Then, in 1925, the town had a street dance and bonfire to celebrate the first oil shale boom, although it was already coming to an end. Finally, on May 1, 1983, the Black Sunday "survivors" had a third historic bonfire — but they called it a "roast" and threw shale from the Colony Project into the flames, sending thick, black clouds of smoke wafting above the street. The crowd drank beer, congratulated themselves on their resilience, and vilified Exxon. Both the local and national press covered the 1983 anniversary of the bust, as well as the "survivors' picnic" held in Parachute during the first week of May 1984. But by the third year, many of the survivors, depressed, disillusioned, and bankrupt, had been forced to leave. Despite boosterism and bravado, Black Sunday continued to take its toll.[5]

The power of the bust affected everyone — from Danny the Bum who slept in the back of O'Leary's Pub and swept out the bar in the morning, to Frank P. Barrow, project director for Colony and a thirty-year Exxon veteran, who had been ready to commission an architect to draw plans for his retirement home on Battlement Mesa. Like Charles Pence, Battlement Mesa's president, Barrow had already picked out his lot, featuring a stunning view of the Colorado River to the north and the Battlement Peaks to the south. In April 1982, Pat

The Parachute-Battlement Mesa merchants in appreciation of your support invite you to the...

ANNUAL SURVIVORS DAY PICNIC

★ Hamburgers ★ Hot Dogs ★ Chips
★ Pepsi ★ Basketball
★ Volleyball ★ Horseshoes

WHEN: Sunday, May 6, 1:00 pm to ?
WHERE: Cottonwood Park
WHY: Because we deserve it!

Bring your family, lawn chairs, a salad, side dish or dessert for an afternoon of fun and festivities.

A SPECIAL THANKS TO OUR CUSTOMERS FROM THE THESE BUSINESSES:

Battlement Beef and Beverage
Brass Pig
Cache Creek Inn
Chamber of Commerce
Children Corner Playschool
Country Bazaar
City Market
Dons' Liquors
Donut Company
Doxol Propane
1st National Bank of Battlement Mesa

Foxy Guys and Gals
Gilcomart
Guzzler Ltd.
J.M.S. Inc.
Letson's Service
Main Event
Stuart & Dan'l Mershon
McFritz's
Dr. Nemer
Ninety-Six Ranch
Old Bank Saloon

Old West Pizza
Parachute Auto Parts
Parachute Center Real Estate
Parachute Chiropractic Clinic
Parachute Insurance Agency
Parachute Plaza Motel
Parachute Service Center
R&S Sales & Welding
Rainbow Video
Reed Texaco
Rifle Realty

Bob Risley
S&H Laundromat
Saddleback Maintenance
Smitty's
Stod's
Taco Johns
Thunder River Furs
Rober E. Traul Jr. D.D.S.
Union Oil
Valley Store
Valley Petroleum

May 1, 1983, inaugurated the "Annual Survivor's Day Picnic." The event lasted a few years but is no longer occurring because too many people have moved away. *Courtesy of* The Rifle Tribune.

Dalrymple, the president of Aspen Savings and Loan, had said, "If one were to be anywhere during the recession, western Colorado would be the ideal place. I think the Western Slope economy is possibly the strongest in the nation." But just two years later, unemployment levels there had reached 9.5 percent, and by the end of 1985, 14.2 percent of all Grand Junction residences were vacant.

People may never recover emotionally and financially from the devastating consequences of the bust. Confidence in their own abilities has been badly shaken. Younger men have watched their dreams dissolve, and older men who expected a secure financial future cannot even afford to retire. For businessmen, it may take years to regain lost credit. In one instance, two California developers filed a $58 million lawsuit against Exxon and lost; Exxon countersued, but a jury awarded the multinational corporation zero dollars and zero cents.

Exxon had promised state and county officials an "orderly shutdown" to accompany its "mothballing" of the $5 billion project, but what actually happened was far from orderly. All rental trucks and trailers within a ninety-mile radius were leased within four days of May 2, 1982, and within a week after Black Sunday, an estimated 1,000 people had left Parachute and Garfield County. The exodus had begun. Mesa County had a population of 94,000 people in 1980, but by 1985, only 83,000 remained. Some $85 million in annual payroll evaporated from the economy of Colorado's Western Slope. The tiger had emptied the tank, and thousands of lives were knocked over like so many dominoes. Only now, seven years later, are the full ramifications of the bust being understood.

In her book *On Death and Dying*, psychiatrist Elisabeth Kubler-Ross describes the stages of grief family members must go through when a relative dies.[6] In western Colorado, where communities acted collectively, one family's financial distress only mirrored the losses of others. And like families in bereavement, Western Slope residents went through stages very similar to those outlined by Kubler-Ross. First came denial, then rage and anger. The third stage was an attempt at bargaining, and then came the final stage of depression and, at last, acceptance. Robert Nuffer, a counselor and director of the Sopris Mental Health Center in Glenwood Springs, Colorado, explained:

What we saw was the very typical grief reactions that you see with a loss. The first was a sense of shock and denial. This can't be happening. This isn't real. I don't believe it. Wake me up. And then the next stage that people often move into is kind of an anger, angry at Exxon, angry at the government. A lot of anger focused at Exxon over the fact that they pulled the rug out from under us after giving us the promise, after saying that oil shale really has arrived because the biggest corporation in the world is investing in it. And then came bargaining. That's the third stage. Trying to somehow work a deal so that this won't turn out to be as bad as it turns out to be. And people move back and forth between all these stages. Then it's into a depression, a loss, a sense of hopelessness, an overwhelming sadness, a tendency towards despair before people finally get [the conflict] resolved. This process can take time. Depending on the magnitude of the loss anywhere from several months to several years.[7]

Courtesy of the Copley News Service.

The heaviest impact of the bust has not been on the multinational corporations like Exxon, Mobil, Chevron, and Occidental Oil who abandoned their projects, transferred their middle management workers, absorbed their losses and moved on. Nor has the impact fallen most heavily on the rust belt workers who came West and belatedly returned to their eastern roots. The greatest impact has been on the local communities in the Colorado River Valley, but this impact has been largely ignored. In his article in *Science*, for example, John S. Gilmore defined the stages of boomtown growth, but he neglected the bust phase.[8] It has taken a few years for all those millions of dollars circulating in the local economy to filter out. Black Sunday is the memorable event — a benchmark in western Colorado — but the bust itself continues long after.

As much social change occurred with the bust as had occurred with the boom, yet the social science investigators are now gone. Their interests waned as their research dollars did. Just when they could have been of service to the energy-impacted communities they had studied during the boom years, those same researchers failed to return.[9] Reverend Lynn Evans of the Rifle United Methodist-Presbyterian Church explains that, during the boom:

We began to lose the community caring, commitment, and concern for each other. When everybody became concerned about getting rich themselves, then we lost that deeper concern for everybody in the whole community. Then [after the bust] I think it got worse. Then they were hard up. They really began looking out for number one. They were overextended. They were deeper in debt — myself included. I bought into the boom and went into debt, too. Bought a house, a lot more house than I needed to buy. I'm overextended, and almost everybody in Rifle is overextended and that makes you even more grabby, greedy, and looking out for number one. So it got worse. The new set of poorer values that got started in the boom became worse in the bust.[10]

To understand the momentous significance of Black Sunday, it is critical to concentrate on the events of the first week after Exxon's announcement. Like the confusion and disbelief that comes with the awareness that a dam has broken and a swollen river has moved the highway and carried off your house, there was a sense of utter disbelief and numbness among the people who survived the oil shale bust.

Rhonda Atchetee worked for Charles Pence in Exxon's Grand Junction office. She vividly remembers Black Sunday and describes the first week of the bust and the conflicting feelings staff members experienced, as well as the difficulties they had in explaining to their friends and neighbors that, even as Exxon employees, they had not been forewarned:

We got home that evening at about six o'clock and the telephone was ringing. When I answered it was Charlie Pence and he told me that a decision had been made to shut down the project. He read [me] the press release. He said, "I've been trying to get hold of you all day. I didn't want you to see this on the news." He did it for all of us. It wasn't just me. It was everybody in the company. [He called his staff] because he felt that commitment. To be honest, I cried for a week. It was just hard to function, it was real hard.

Right after I hung up the telephone from talking to Charlie Pence, I turned to [my husband] and told him what Charlie had told me, and right then the news was coming on and we saw it on television. Then our next door neighbor and his wife came over — they just rang the doorbell and they said, "We've been trying to get in touch with you all day. Have you heard?" I said, "We just did." His wife was crying, I was crying. We all just sat on the steps and we talked. It was like we were at a funeral.[11]

Everyone interviewed clearly recalled what he or she was doing when the news broke. Rhonda Atchetee is no exception:

We were outside the house, a cool clear night, and then all the neighbors from across the street came over so there were twelve of us out on our front porch just talking about it. And everybody was very, very quiet asking very thoughtful, calculated questions. They weren't attacking me or trying to pump me for information, they were very sympathetic and very concerned. But they really just wanted to know what I knew — which was nothing. And I felt like I had to make them believe that I did *not* know anything about it. I was not tricking anybody. I think they believed it. These people were our friends. They believed me. It wasn't as easy out on the streets.[12]

The work week would become interminably long. Careers, mortgages, plans, investments — all were suspended. Many younger Exxon employees had their first serious doubts about the corporation they believed in. Rhonda explains:

We went into the office on Monday morning and Charlie had a staff meeting at eight o'clock. He wore a suit that day. I'll never forget it because he never wore a suit. He was always in his jeans and checkered shirt, his western look. I said, "What's the occasion?" And he said, "Well, you heard the old adage, dress up and it makes you feel better," but I [felt] like he was dressed for a funeral. There was just a lot of sad faces and teary eyes and the shock of walking into your office and looking for all the projects you had started on Friday and knowing which ones were going in the trash and which ones you needed to start all over with.

Everyone just sort of walked around like "What's going to happen to me?" And at that point there were absolutely no assurances. Everybody was in shock. We had all worked so hard to build the trust of the people there and then it was just like the rug was jerked out from under us. And there was an intense anger on my part towards the company. My feeling was these guys are making decisions in New York up in the board room and they don't realize what they've done to these people. I just wanted them all to come down to Grand Junction and to Battlement Mesa and just see what was happening. From a management perspective I don't know if it would have been any better to phase it down or pull the plug like they did. But it was so traumatic the way they did it.[13]

The trauma of the bust was in direct proportion to Exxon's grandiose expectations. Because everyone had believed in oil shale and Exxon, the bust created deep feelings of anxiety and doubt, coupled with realistic fears of financial failure. Stability had become instant instability, and for many workers a good job on Friday was a pink slip on Monday. Rhonda Atchetee had planned to implement construction goals at Battlement Mesa, but instead she presided over the sad exodus of hundreds of workers. She explains:

My job that week was to go up to the mobile home park and set up an accounting office there and make refunds of security deposits to the people who were moving out. I was to make final rent settlements for the people who were leaving Battlement Mesa. Just seeing those people for two weeks was very difficult. A lot of people came in saying, "Hey, I don't have any place to go. I don't know where I'm going. I don't know if I'll have a job. We came out here and we knew we were going to make big money and we were going to go back to Tennessee [or] Detroit and build our dream home."

There were a lot of sad stories, and most of it was just fear that they didn't have a job, and a lot of them had no place to go, but they knew they were getting out of there. There was no reason to stay. The job wasn't there and they knew there wouldn't be any [work]. They just wanted out. It was a painful, painful time. I'll never forget it.[14]

Rumors of violence occurring in Parachute, Colorado, were unfounded but nevertheless widely circulated in Texas. Friends and relatives telephoned, fearing for Rhonda's safety:

By [the end of the first week] we were getting a lot of response from home, from Texas. The pictures hit the newspapers of some guy who just had a fit and kicked out a fence at Battlement Mesa. [The picture] made the front page of the [Houston] Chronicle. People [in Texas] thought they were tearing the town apart. We were trying to communicate back home to tell

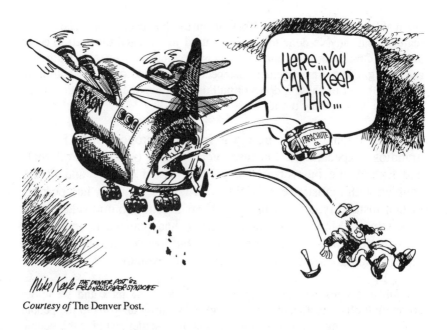

Courtesy of The Denver Post.

them what the real story was. It was just like someone had died. I was getting
sympathy calls from my friends in Houston because they knew how much I
loved that project. It was a funeral, that's what it was.[15]

Rhonda Atchetee's friends and relatives actually had little reason to be concerned, but the extent of the rumors is another social-
psychological indicator of how critical an event Black Sunday was to
the Western Slope. As early as Monday, May 3, 1982, rumors circulated that trailers were being burned and fences destroyed. Members
of the sheriff's department received hundreds of outrageous reports
about looting and pillaging in the new community of Battlement
Mesa. Supposedly, the National Guard had been called in, and Governor Lamm was said to be flying by helicopter to Battlement Mesa to
talk roving bands of oil shale workers out of wholesale rioting.
    What actually happened that day is a very different story. After a
seventeen-mile drive up a winding dirt road along Parachute Creek,
workers who had not yet heard the news arrived for the morning shift
at 5 A.M. and listened as the Brown & Root supervisor told them the
job was over; they could pick up their checks in two days. Severance

pay amounted to mileage to and from the job site and two hours extra pay. Because of the sheer size of the project, these workers had expected to be in the area for several years, and many had moved their families for the first time. They had been promised a career, not just a job, and they expected to stay in one place long enough to see their children graduate from high school. But because of the early May shutdown, dozens of children did not even finish the school year.

In Parachute and Battlement Mesa that Monday morning, gangs of out-of-work construction crews converged on the two liquor stores as soon as they opened. Fists pounded on the glass doors at O'Leary's Pub, and the owner opened early, for the crowd was in a foul mood. By 11 A.M., both bars were full, and when authorities shut down the Guzzler Liquor Store on Battlement Mesa and beer was taken off the shelves at the grocery store, rumors flew that armed construction workers had commandeered a tractor-trailer rig and were headed to Grand Junction to bring back bourbon. As one observer noted, by midday "the tension was so thick the only thing that could penetrate it was a well aimed fist."[16]

Journalists arrived expecting violence. When the print and television reporters descended on the bars and asked, "What's your reaction?" angry construction workers became even more irritated. Pat O'Neill remembers that "at times the bellowing and cursing were almost deafening."[17] The Parachute police chief, Steve Rhoads, was told by the sheriff to close down the bars that evening, but he refused, saying, "Those guys are angry and they're going to drink. I'd rather keep them here than have them on the road endangering innocent people."[18] The telephone kept ringing off the wall at both O'Leary's and the liquor store, with reporters calling in from around the nation to confirm "the hostile reaction" of laid-off workers, but there really was no hostile reaction — only intense frustration and diffused anger. By late afternoon, the "rioters" were thoroughly drunk and had either passed out or were milling around elsewhere.

Social worker Joyce Illian spent the day in Parachute listening to the rumors. She recalls:

The part that amazed me is that about dinner time, I went back down to O'Leary's and a lot of the county commissioners and the director of Social Services and the director of the Mental Health Clinic were all in the bar sitting over in the corner, looking, watching, and saying, "Joyce, tell us what they're saying."

So that was kind of interesting going back and forth. It was like so many of those folks never really touched base with the reality of the construction people there. It was like they were somewhere up above dealing with the honchos and couldn't really carry on conversations with a lot of the workers. And the bar cleared out so early it was an amazement to me. By seven o'clock there were three people left in the bar and one of them was Ralph [Freedman], the city manager, and he had never been in O'Leary's before. It's real vivid for me. There was only a handful of people in there and there was a crack of thunder that was real loud. Someone said, "See, even God's gonna get exiled," and it poured down rain.[19]

Charles Pence also remembers that afternoon:

I was in Grand Junction at the time. The first rumor I heard about two o'clock was that they had shut down all the liquor stores and bars in Parachute because they were fearful there was going to be a horrible uprising. Then along about 3:30 or 4:00 somebody else got a rumor that there were trailer truckloads of whiskey being loaded in Grand Junction — being taken over [to Parachute] and all kinds of stuff. So I finally decided I would get in my car and see what was going on. We had a fellow who was our chief of security for Colony, named John Hunt, who lived up on Battlement Mesa in a house that's on the point and overlooks the river, and so I went up and found him. There were guys around drinking beer, and lots of people here and there. We were up there walking around. In fact, I drank a couple of beers. Some of those guys weren't all that friendly, but they were impressed that old John Hunt and I were up there. Some of them were really hot at Exxon, but they didn't get personal about it. When it started to rain, I left. I think it was handled just right — God even helped because of that cold rain. I'll tell you it was cold. The drops were as big as quarters and cold. And that happened about dusk, drove everybody in. It rained for about an hour and a half or two hours — not in a torrential downpour, but just steady with big drops.[20]

Reporter John Colson of the *Rifle Tribune* wrote that during the day the streets were relatively deserted except for small knots of people who had gathered on the corners, yelling and swearing. Jittery deputies "backed by intense weaponry and sporting protective protective 'body armor'" waited for what they assumed would be a "big party at the Brown and Root camp" or construction site, but there was no violence, only an ominous silence. Colson explained, "all day long the weather had matched the mood — alternating between sullen threats of storm and sudden outbursts that quickly petered out — so the sky continued to reflect what went on below." The tension dissipated with the first large drops of rain.[21]

Perhaps there would have been a violent outbreak if not for the rain. A fence was kicked in, and a photograph of the incident appeared in the *Houston Chronicle*. The photo had alarmed Rhonda Atchetee's friends, but it is possible that it was faked; the young worker giving a karate kick to a wooden fence could have been inspired by an eager photojournalist looking for action. (Charles Pence claims that a cameraman on the scene at Battlement Mesa who witnessed an angry construction worker heave a six-pack of beer bottles across a street requested the laborer to pick it up and do it again while the cameras rolled.)[22] But other than a few broken fence slats and some knocked-over trash cans, there was no destruction. Violence simply did not exist. The force and magnitude of the closure resembled a natural disaster, not an angry worker-management confrontation. People do not react violently after a tornado; they did not act violently in Parachute. On the night of Black Sunday, Pat O'Neill remembers, "Numbness was the most common reaction, as across town a silent sort of shock was setting in."[23]

John Colson wrote a column for the *Rifle Tribune* titled "Sorrow and Rage With the Bust That Was Not Supposed to Happen." He stated, "In the bars and around the towns, the media vultures stood with hooded eyes as they inwardly lamented the calm enforced by the storm." He continued, "Attracted by the smell of doom and disaster, they had gathered from afar, circling as they watched and waited for some frenzied outburst or choking death rattle." But there was no violence for the media to report, and Colson categorized the reporters' feelings. "Disappointed," Colson wrote, "they dispersed into the night to see what tomorrow might bring."[24]

As if on cue, the day ended with a brilliant rainbow. The Parachute town council held a special meeting that night in a brand new, 5,800-square-foot town hall. Marvin Wamboldt, the Garfield County building inspector, commented on the shutdown, "We've seen this before and we'll see it again,"[25] but that was small comfort for the hundreds of workers who would wake up the next morning hung over and out of a job.

On Tuesday, May 4, men lined up at 7:30 A.M. to receive their final paychecks from Brown & Root. As *Denver Post* writers observed, "By the hundreds, the displaced workers of the Colony Oil Shale Project closed their bank accounts, drank beer, shed a few tears, and prepared to move out to pursue another American dream."[26] Though many had earned $14.85 an hour, they were just settling in and had new debts from purchases of campers, cars, pickups, and trailers. Their only choice was to find work elsewhere.

Joseph P. Prinster, president of City Market grocery stores, had planned to open a 55,000-square-foot "superstore" on Battlement Mesa on September 1. He was quoted in the *Rocky Mountain News* as stating, "Everybody is kind of shell-shocked at the moment. Everything is in a holding pattern right now."[27] From full speed ahead, Garfield County had now ground to a halt, and in the wake of Exxon's decision, people waited and reassessed their positions. The *Grand Junction Daily Sentinel* published an editorial titled "Exxon Cuts and Runs" and compared the infamous "white paper" to Exxon's promise to shut down the multimillion-dollar development "in an orderly manner." The editor wrote, "Pardon us for retaining a similar measure of skepticism about Exxon's assurances of due regard for all the people affected by the Colony project's closing."[28]

Governor Richard Lamm accurately described the bust as "a disaster for Garfield County," and added, "It's a blow for the state and also a blow for the country, which needs alternate energy resources." He observed, "This is part of the boom-and-bust cycle the West has been experiencing throughout its history."[29] Charles Pence was also interviewed by the *Denver Post*. He stated, "We had a plan for everything but this, and now we don't know what we're going to do. This thing, the announcement by Exxon, U.S.A., that it was shutting down its Colony Project, caught us by surprise."[30] As the U-hauls moved out and the newcomers left town, Pat O'Neill wrote that "carpetbaggers buzzed around like flies on an outhouse."[31] Some bought televisions and stereos for ten cents on the dollar, others bought furniture, appliances, and automobiles. Quick-thinking stencil artists even sold shirts, caps, and bumper stickers advertising the "Bust of '82."

By Wednesday, May 5, new graffiti began showing up in the bars, with inscriptions such as "Exxon: The Sign of the Double Cross" and "Welcome to Colorado's Newest Ghost Town, Compliments of Exxon." People referred to the "screw job" that had occurred, and a new batch of very popular T-shirts proclaimed "Exxon Sucks Rocks." Another version of the T-shirt had the same motto, but the word "Rocks" was covered by a large X. On Wednesday, a young couple arrived at O'Leary's Pub in a battered station wagon; they had driven 1,800 miles in hopes of finding a job with Brown & Root. The bewildered father explained that they had $25 left and babies to feed.

Charles Pence stated in an interview, "With my 26 years in this, if someone had told me to prepare a Dunkirk scenario, I probably would have smelled a rat and done things differently," but added, "I was never given any indication that we were in any mode except go. There are forces at work here I am not aware of."[32] By Wednesday, La Sal Pipeline Company, an Exxon affiliate, canceled plans for a $100 million pipeline that was to have carried synthetic crude from Colony to a refinery in Casper, Wyoming. Exxon also backed out of a $22 million power-transmission line that it had been negotiating with Public Service Company of Colorado, and a $2.3 million Mountain Bell telephone switching facility to handle Battlement Mesa calls had been put on hold. Yet, just three days after Black Sunday, Victor Schroeder, president of the U.S. Synthetic Fuels Corporation, told a Denver audience that the Colony shutdown was a "big glitch," but that synfuels development was still a certainty. Ironically, on that same day, May 5, the state's Cumulative Impact Task Force, programming growth scenarios into an elaborate computer model to predict development patterns, had finally come on-line with conclusive projections. Had all three major oil shale projects been in place, the computer would have projected a total employment in Garfield County of 18,000 by the end of 1982 and 29,000 by 1990. Now, three days after the shutdown, the same computer predicted a loss of at least 6,000 jobs in Garfield County alone![33]

The following day, tales were being told of the real reason the project had been shut down. Rumors flourished that Exxon had been disgusted with cost overruns by Brown & Root, and corporate managers had closed the project so they could fire its general contractor; once the Brown & Rooters were gone, the project would start up again. A new batch of bumper stickers appeared stating, "Jesus came to Parachute but Exxon laid him off," and beer-drinking talk included such witticisms as, "If Dolly Parton lived in Parachute she'd be flat-busted." That night, 300 people attended a meeting in DeBeque to hear Chevron talk about its proposed $6 billion Clear Creek Shale Oil Project, still in preliminary stages. DeBeque Mayor Wood Smith was not convinced. "It ain't going to happen," he said.[34] By Friday, May 7, 1,000 people were gone, and a headline in the *Washington Post* read, "World's Largest Oil Company Leaves a Streak of Rage and Fear."[35]

The exodus continued over the weekend. In the Sunday, May 9, issue of the *Grand Junction Daily Sentinel*, a realtor for the Rocky Mountain Land Exchange explained, "We've just gotten a little taste of Detroit," and Rick Becvarik, working for a Rifle concrete firm, stated, "Everything looked so good a week ago. Now it's all gone."[36] A letter to the editor in the same issue expressed the views of one pioneer family:

Thanks Exxon! If you succeeded in anything it was that you DID spend lots of money in the Parachute area. You DID open up a huge amount of oil shale cliffs at the head of Parachute Creek and expose thousands of acres of Battlement Mesa land. Never mind that we asked that the process be orderly and gradual. But you said you were No. 1. You had the expertise, the incentive, the hundreds of millions of dollars! Never mind that we said, "Yes, but we've seen it all before."

We were born on Parachute Creek. Our dad, now 77 and living here still, was born on Parachute Creek. And, he said, they always pulled out and they left a hollow place. So we questioned the thousands of acres of ground laid bare so that a city of thousands could be built. Our questions were, "Why so much all at once? Why thousands? Why not hundreds? Why not a step at a time? Why?"

But you could handle it. You had estimates. A contractor. Experts who would supervise the spending of your hundreds of millions of dollars. But even hundreds of millions of dollars do not last. Hundreds of millions only leave a larger hole. — *Charline (Benson) Jones* [37]

Pat O'Neill wrote about the speed of the "corporate guillotine" after Exxon decided to abandon the Colony Oil Shale Project, throwing 2,100 people out of work overnight. Because of "Black Sunday," May 2, 1982, O'Neill lost O'Leary's Pub and went bankrupt, but he still kept his jaunty smile. *Courtesy Pat O'Neill*.

Other states began to be affected. On the same day that Charline Jones's letter was published, an order for fifty-six modular homes from a Nebraska construction company was canceled. But on May 9, as pioneer families in Parachute lambasted Exxon's fickle financial commitment and Nebraska workers were thrown out of jobs, the lead article in the business section of the *Sunday New York Times* was titled "The Singular Power of a Giant Called Exxon." John D. Rockefeller's corporation was celebrating its hundredth birthday.

In the second week after the bust, the Rifle chamber of commerce demanded a response from Exxon officials. By now, dozens of houses were up for sale, immediately deflating the housing market, and contracts for everything from nails and screws to multimillion-dollar housing developments were voided. Yet mayors and county officials breathed a sigh of relief and explained that everything had been happening much too fast; perhaps the Colony shutdown would offer time to catch up and retrench. Another angry letter-writer, beekeeper Blane Colton, stated in the *Rifle Telegram*, "I, for one, am truly pleased to know that Exxon is going home to Houston. I will be even more pleased if they stay there." He continued, "Now, hold on a moment: it's not that I have no empathy for the wrecked businesses and lives left in Exxon's wake. On the contrary, I know all too well how it feels to be squashed by a corporate giant" because "my life and business was turned to shambles by Exxon and others two years ago. I used to make my living from the alfalfa and topsoil that they scraped into the gulleys to make way for the trailers." As Colton added, "Exxon may not be gone forever, but the topsoil is."[38]

Other county residents, at least early in the bust, had strong feelings of ambivalence best expressed in this gem of local folklore which was one of the proverbs told in Garfield County bars. Exxon's departure, the story went, was "a lot like your mother-in-law driving over a cliff in your new Cadillac. You have mixed feelings about it." From construction workers to city planners, most people enjoyed a respite from the intense development pressures and they appreciated a return to the slower pace that had attracted them to the Colorado River Valley in the first place. But who could tell what direction, if any, the local economy would take?

Two weeks after Black Sunday, the bust had begun to enter Phase I — the period of shock and denial that lasted for approximately nine months. Even though construction work slowed down considerably, many projects that had been started earlier were completed, including dozens of apartments on Battlement Mesa — but these were only finished on the outside for appearance sake. Throughout the summer, transients continued to arrive looking for work that they thought still existed. The problem of transient labor in the energy boomtowns would exist for years, and the wanderers would become burdens to both social services and to community hospitals. But in the late summer of 1982, the on-going problem with transients was just beginning. The main feature of this early bust phase was community denial. Jim Sullivan, editor of the *Rifle Tribune*, remembers:

When Exxon announced its shutdown the reality of the world energy market hit home with thundering force. It was incredible. It was like going to the altar and finding out your wife-to-be had been sleeping with the minister. Nobody wanted to believe it. This is how the community as an organic entity reacted. It was like having a child snatched away from you or having one run over by a car at the age of eight or ten. You just don't believe it. It can't happen. It's not real. People sat there and believed, "Well, Colony may be gone, but oil shale's still here so I'm going to open my flower shop." That's the perception versus the reality. Things were going on that so clearly foretold what was going to happen, but nobody wanted to accept it. I mean if you were a banker and you had millions of dollars in loans and all of a sudden the belly fell out of the real estate industry you'd have a tendency to say, "This can't be happening." And if you say that long enough then it isn't happening.[39]

Denial also played an important role in business plans because residents simply would not accept the fact that their fortunes had changed overnight. As Jim Sullivan explains:

I had a real estate saleswoman come up to me [and say] "You know this community has to survive. We have to sort of find the silver lining in the cloud and write about the positive things going on in the community." The long and short of it is that she wanted me and that newspaper I worked for to no longer write anything about the bust, and this was two weeks after the fact. Let's ignore it and it'll go away [was her attitude].[40]

The Sentinel's editorials

SUPERCHICKEN
HAS FLOWN THE
COOP THIS TIME!

COLONY

EXXON

LOCAL
GOVT.

HAMILTON

Colony lesson

After years of supporting oil shale, the *Grand Junction Daily Sentinel* felt bitter disappointment with Exxon and the shale shutdown. This political cartoon ran on the editorial page the week of Black Sunday. *Courtesy of the* Grand Junction Daily Sentinel.

Denial continued despite a huge three-day auction of surplus equipment from the Colony Shale Oil Project in late October 1982. Over 1,200 bidders netted Exxon $5 million for the sale items. (The Parks-Davis auctioneer said that "every last thing" was sold and the only larger auction they had managed was at the Alaskan pipeline project in 1977.) For some local businessmen, denial may have been their only means of coping. Gaylord Henry's family, for example, had been in the dry goods and clothing business in Rifle for generations. They had a well-stocked store downtown on Railroad Avenue and had decided to expand into a new shopping center. The week of May 12, the family opened this additional store with $350,000 worth of merchandise displayed in an 11,000-square-foot facility. Their store featured designer clothing and intended to cater to Rifle and Parachute's new class of executives and their wives. Similarly, other businesses also opened after the bust. Caught up in the momentum of financing and construction plans, new businesses started whether or not they made economic sense. The inertia of boomtown growth particularly crippled Grand Junction, where the 500,000-square-foot Mesa Mall opened and immediately began to lose tenants who had signed expensive leases. Inspite of that, the mall threatened the commercial viability of downtown merchants. In another example, the Grand Junction airport terminal facility was expanded by 450 percent after Black Sunday, only to have airlines reduce and cancel flights. A new Grand Junction Hilton built after the bust consistently had the lowest rates of any Hilton in the state; by spring 1986, it had gone into receivership.[41]

The shrewd out-of-state investors who had come in to make a killing in the real estate market cut their losses and ran. Within six months, they were out of the housing market or had defaulted on their land purchase options. The Western Slope had been a realtor's dream; now, after the bust, office after office closed, and salespeople were laid off. Some developers had clauses in their contracts stating that, in case of default, initial payments would be credited toward whichever acres those developers chose to retain. For example, if a house and twenty acres had been purchased for $200,000, or $10,000 an acre, and the developer had paid $20,000 down, he could choose whichever two acres he wanted to keep — usually the land with the house on it or those acres with the best irrigation rights.

The Boulton family has ranched continuously on Divide Creek in Garfield County since before the turn of the century. With this recent oil shale bust, Alice Boulton notes:

Many local papers shared the feelings of the *Grand Junction Daily Sentinel*. In this political cartoon, Exxon is running away having left Garfield County with a bag of excrement. *Courtesy of* The Free Weekly Newspaper.

Many of those ranchers sold the land with an agreement that the down payment paid for a certain amount of land. That down payment was all they ever got. When the other payment was due the buyer said, "Nothing doing. I own your house and choice land around it. You can have the rest of it." Those men who took the down payment and put it on another piece of land were left with a larger debt than ever and some lost everything.[42]

The first phase of the oil shale bust was characterized by a gradual downward spiral in the economy and the beginnings of a major social reorganization. Money continued to float for a while in local communities, and the rumor mill sustained ranchers, bartenders, bakers, and even bankers who were convinced that things would get better in 1983. Unfortunately, they did not. More houses showed up on the market. More people left. And more oil companies abandoned their expensive oil shale projects. Almost all the young, single construction workers from out-of-state were gone as soon as the work dried up. Men who had moved their families across the country stayed a bit longer and continued to deplete their savings until they, too, were forced to leave.

Middle management superintendents had their homes bought by the company they worked for, and away they went. But leaving the Western Slope was never easy. The spectacular landscape, the friendly people, and the immediate access to mountains and streams with unsurpassed fishing and hunting caused many families to put off the inevitable as long as they could. But even within Exxon's highest echelons, such a serious corporate shakedown had its ripple effects. During the first six months after the bust, many managers transferred or took early retirement. The bust also shattered the careers of Frank Barrow and Charles Pence, leaving them as corporate casualties. Both men had been loyal to Exxon, had dutifully climbed the corporate ladder, and had expected to retire with honor in the model community they had built. The depth of their commitment to the project was reflected in the depth of their loss. Frank P. Barrow, project director for Colony, had worked for Exxon for thirty-one years. Under his direction hundreds of millions of dollars had been spent. He states:

There is no pretty way to shut down a construction project, absolutely none. Once you decide that you aren't going ahead, then you better cut it clean. Once the decision is made that you aren't going to build it, then it's wasteful to continue. Tough, mean-assed tough, but that's the way life is. Nothing else makes any sense. You aren't serving the shareholders by throwing more money away, so it's just time to cut it clean. And construction companies understand that, and most construction workers understand that.[43]

Perhaps construction workers did understand, but it came as a slap in the face and a punch in the pocketbook nevertheless. The largest construction project in the world in the early 1980s had slammed to a halt. As Frank Barrow remembers, "Now there were some risk-takers out there, some entrepreneurs, one motel builder, and some other folks like that and they cried bloody murder. That's just part of business."[44]

But being "just part of business" did not count for much when dozens of local businessmen found themselves forced into bankruptcy. The corporate moguls like Barrow had golden parachutes and

Construction workers on break in Parachute. *Nicholas DeVore III / Photographers, Aspen.*

a safe place to land. The head of the Colony Project took early retirement, and though he was financially secure, like so many others he was bitterly disappointed. Barrow explains:

I retired on October 1, 1982. Thirty-one years [with the company], that's why I could take early retirement. Had there been another project, then I could have gotten up the firehorse adrenalin, if you will, and gone and gotten it. But the company's expansion plans at that point in time were such that I couldn't get a clear message of when I was likely to see anything resembling that kind of action again. I was looking forward to staying there for the rest of my life. Eventually we would have shut the Denver office down entirely and all of us would have gone over there. But you know, here I am, 54 years old, with a motto of saying — I'm doing the thing I had the most fun with in my professional career. I'm running a $5 billion project. I'm starting a team from scratch — I mean from absolute scratch, and I've got a project that'll take me till I'm 59 or 60 years old to get it finished and start it up. As soon as I get to that point , I'll throw in the sponge. That'll be a great cap on a professional career. [The Colony Project] was to be the crown jewel. And that Sunday it was gone. So that was quite a blow.[45]

Charles Pence also felt the Black Sunday blow. He worked rigorously on mothballing the Colony Project and phasing it down. He helped all his employees transfer or relocate, but he failed to make provisions for himself, and it cost him dearly. He reflects upon the dedication of his staff:

The depth of commitment that existed, not just at the top of this — not just myself and the manager, or the guy that was the superintendent for the contractor, but the depth of commitment ran from top to bottom — I mean it went all the way through. That's why we got so much done as fast and as well as it was done. It was one of those things where you thought, well, you know, this is not a drill. This is for real. In our case what we did we were going to be living with. It wasn't like we were going to build it and leave it. We were going to be out there driving by it every day and I used to tell the staff, "Look guys, remember, we're going to be our own toughest critic because we're going to know every single mistake that's made here and we're going to drive by it every day and that's what you're going to see. You're not going to see the flags on the flagpoles and stuff, you're going to see the mistakes you made. So bear down. Let's minimize those things."

Just as Frank Barrow expected to build a house and return to Battlement Mesa, so, too, did Charles Pence. Exxon officials assumed that the project would go to completion, and they wanted to become part of an exciting new community. Pence explains:

I had a place to build a house. I can see it right now, looking toward the Book Cliffs. The back part of it would have [had an] unobstructed [view] back toward the Twin Buttes at Battlement Mesa. Great location. Development had gotten to where it was ready to build on. Utilities and everything. In fact, had they not pulled the plug, we would have built the next year. I guess 15 or 20 people had picked out lots.[47]

Because of its isolation, the Western Slope has always had close-knit communities, but the Exxon employees were welcomed with open arms in Grand Junction. Family ties were strengthened and corporate employees felt very close to one another in their dedication to oil shale development. Charles Pence describes the family-like closeness among his employees that was shattered by the bust.

I'd never had anything shut down that way. I think the reason it had the impact it did and probably one that's lasting [is because] I had never been in a place where the company employees and their families were as close as we were there. You knew everybody. You knew their children. You knew whether they were getting good grades [or] bad grades, you knew almost all of them. And you're working at this fever pitch and then all of a sudden you go phllumpp. It was really hard on some people. It was like a funeral almost. I thought it was kind of brutal, but after thinking about it, it's probably the only way you could do it. I mean, why cut the dog's tail off an inch at a time — just go ahead and whack it. I really did work hard at getting the other people placed and getting the phase-down carefully communicated in the proper sequence to the town and the county and the state and to Exxon, U.S.A. and to Exxon Corporation in New York and all those things. And suddenly I realized that everybody was taken care of except me.[48]

Dedicated to his staff, dedicated to building an entirely new community in the American West, Charles Pence was indeed the selfless vice-president who easily led people because he inspired intense loyalty. After the bust, he repaid their loyalty and eased his staff's transition to new jobs in new locations. But he was too busy to think about himself, and the time for cutting deals with the corporate bureaucracy at Exxon had come and gone. Pence explains that twenty-six years of service meant little:

The final deal was they wanted me to stay out there as a caretaker type and I was not psychologically equipped to do that. I've got no patience for sitting on a dead horse. So I said, "Well, gee, guys, if that's all you've got, I think I'm gonna go my way." And I did. And I think that surprised some people in Exxon and other places. I'd been with them about 26 years, but the thing is I'd always had timing on my side. I'd always been at the right place at the right time — and all of a sudden after 26 years of being that way — you can't expect it all your life. And I ended up being at the wrong place at the wrong time. It's not the corporation's fault and it's not my fault, it's just circumstances. It's one of those things that happens. The only thing that disappointed me, I felt like with all those guarantees I'd been given, somebody might have worked a little harder to find a place that was acceptable to me, but they can't spend a lot of time on one person. It's like a battle wagon that just keeps on plowing. If you fall overboard they throw a life raft off, or a ring off and say "Well, I hope you can find it in the water."[49]

Charles Pence went back to Houston. For the corporate executives, the forced relocation was traumatic, but for the locals, the trauma was only beginning. Pence stayed long enough to see the disastrous consequences. He remembers:

The ripple effect of all that cash flow went out of the motels. Cash flow went out of the restaurants. Office space went vacant. Houses were for sale everywhere when we left. Out of forty houses there had to be at least ten for sale. And nobody to buy them.[50]

The housing market continued to plummet, exacerbated by the actions of the oil companies who seriously damaged the market in two significant ways. First, they were obligated to buy back houses from executives like Pence and sold more than a hundred houses belonging to management for far less than their assessed value. Thus, neighborhood property values were further lowered. Second, within twelve months, both Exxon and Union drastically lowered the rents on apartment buildings they had built on Battlement Mesa or in Parachute or Rifle.

The first phase of the bust lasted from Black Sunday to Christmas, or approximately nine months. In August 1982, Virginia Senator John Warner (R) tried to get the Department of Defense to take over the oil shale lands and develop them for national security purposes, but his bill never made it to the Senate floor for a vote. The second phase of the bust lasted for eighteen months, from Christmas 1982 to spring 1984, and proved to be the most debilitating. Garfield County investors learned what it was like to have a corporate neighbor who had decided to disinvest. Two-bedroom furnished apartments on Battlement Mesa (complete with pool, tennis court, fireplace, cable television, $300 worth of coupons for food and furniture purchases, all paid utilities, and the seventh month rent-free) now leased for $295 per month. Under no circumstances could private investors in the valley compete with such rental rates. Yet by May 1984, the housing market was so poor that Exxon had only 35 percent occupancy. Most of the community and social trauma occurred during this second phase when denial of the shale bust ceased to be a psychological alternative. On Kubler-Ross's continuum for grieving, this was the phase for rage, bargaining (with creditors), and acute depression.

Exxon exacerbated the decline in the local housing market by selling executives' homes below market value and renting Battlement Mesa apartments at rates so low that no one could compete with it.

Institutions that had arisen with the boom collapsed. Social services were greatly reduced. Church membership declined dramatically as people moved away, leaving congregations that had expanded into new facilities with large debts spread out over a much smaller segment of membership. Religious men and women who were experiencing personal financial stress found it increasingly difficult to meet their tithing obligations.

Eighteen months after Black Sunday many local businesses had failed including over 200 in Rifle alone. Bars that had been receiving five busloads of miners after every shift closed their doors for lack of customers. During the boom in Rifle, the local auction sales ring for cattle buyers had been converted into a country-and-western discotheque called the Cattle Company; it, too, folded. Just as growth and development brought in a new slate of political candidates, so did the bust wipe the slate clean. New county commissioners were elected, and they took a hard line financially to keep the county afloat by making massive layoffs and drastic reductions in department size and function. The layoffs were controversial, and whether or not they were truly needed from an economic standpoint, they exacerbated local fears and anxieties caused by the bust. Unlike the previous county commissioners, who had grown in their skills and expertise while handling the boom, the new slate of commissioners overreacted and intensified the sense of crisis. Ordinances that had been passed during the boom were repealed. A Garfield County ordinance that had established laws against stray dogs and other pets was abolished, along with the position of county humane officers; stray dogs found running loose in a farmer's pasture could once again be shot.

As the boom imploded and the bust intensified, personal tolls on families increased, yet there were few places to turn for help and support. As a direct result of eroding incomes, attitudes began to change. People became isolated and alienated and stopped visiting friends and neighbors because they did not want to discuss financial troubles. The sense of living in the Colorado River Valley, in a psychological and physical space determined by the river and the mountains, began to change. Residents began to think of themselves as living in their own small communities of New Castle, Silt, or

Parachute rather than in the valley as a whole. Reverend Lynn Evans in Rifle noted:

Suddenly you start trying to plug economic holes. There really are people who go hungry in a bust town. There really are kids who don't have enough to eat and don't have medical care, and there are young pregnant women who do not get prenatal care. People with that kind of need often come to churches, not to worship services necessarily, but come to clergy for help and suddenly most of your days and time and efforts go to trying to plug those holes — holes that are in people's lives. Family relationships turned ugly and violent after the bust. Then we had a lot more abuse. When the bust came, suddenly [people] were a lot less well to do. He would take his frustrations out on her face with his fists, or she would take to the bottle and/or start smacking the kids around.[51]

Communities and families that had once thought of themselves as part of "the valley," socially and emotionally, now fought for limited resources. A particularly divisive contest occurred over recreation district legislation that had been passed during the boom. Deciding where in the valley the recreation facility would be built became a major issue. Meanwhile, county officials could not adequately conceptualize the shift from boom to bust, so mental health services were cut back just as the need for counseling increased. Schisms developed between the newcomers and the old-time families. Those families had networks of friends and relations to turn to, and as the cash economy began to wane, they once again bartered for goods and services. But the newcomers had to seek professional counseling for financial and marital problems. One source of family fallout among both newcomers and long-time residents was the need for role redefinitions for fathers who had lost their jobs and were forced to babysit if their wives were still employed. These housekeeping and child-raising chores often violated paternal self-concepts, and men became uncomfortable in their forced domestic roles and homebound isolation.

In many cases, even the home — typically a family's greatest personal investment — was lost. Construction workers and businessmen in the valley had enjoyed a large cash flow during the boom, and they spent accordingly at a time when housing prices were high and double-digit mortgages were common. Now, families were faced with imminent financial disaster. Their initial response was denial. Then came the second stage, panic, and finally the third stage, acceptance of the inevitability of losing their homes. Like business leaders, family heads went through conceptual phases of disbelief, panic, realization of loss, depression, and collapse of self-esteem, before making the decision to go bankrupt and/or to leave the Western Slope. After awhile, many people simply quit making their mortgage payments, knowing that it would take six months to a year for the bank to evict them. In some cases, there was a two- or three-year time lag on foreclosures. When finances became exhausted, there were 250 foreclosures in western Garfield County alone. People said, "We lost our house" or " We let it go back to the bank," and neighbors understood. In some cases, individuals had to save money even to declare bankruptcy — at least to pay the lawyer and the filing fees in district court.[52]

Editor Jim Sullivan faced bankruptcy himself. He explains:

There are stages. You've lost your job, but you'll get another one because you've never been without work before. But you've got your $700 a month mortgage. Well, you can't make it this month. But you've got savings so you can make it. I can still afford it [you say to yourself, because] I can get another job. So you go and you find out that there aren't any other jobs. So you tell yourself again, well, I've been without work before, but I've always found another job. So you go and you keep looking and you keep looking, and all of a sudden you don't have any money to make mortgage payments. You're maybe a white collar worker, not a blue collar worker, and you don't have any income. Where do you go? You don't go to social services. People like you don't go to social services, but what are you going to do? There was denial, but then you needed to blame somebody. So they blamed Exxon, or those goddam politicians, or those goddam Arabs. Nobody could inflict that much harm on you and not be a villain.[53]

The work ethic that had sustained the first pioneer families and their descendants meant little in the face of community financial collapse. Sonja Seivers Friztlan was the great-granddaughter of German families who had worked in the Aspen mining camps and over the years moved down the valley to ranch. During the bust, despite years of hard work and fiscal prudence, Sonja lost her business and her house. Yet, she resolutely refused to file bankruptcy, as did many other local people. Newcomers typically filed bankruptcy and left, but most old-time families perceived their obligations differently. As Sonja Fritzlan states:

We still have indebtedness from when we left the [boarding stables and] barn. And I finally decided . . . I sat down and wrote people letters. I said, "Dear Sir, I haven't forgotten you. I still don't want you to think that we're fly-by-night people and we intend to shirk our obligation to pay you this bill at this time, but at the [present] time we are financially strapped. I promise that when I get it, you will." No, I'd never [file bankruptcy] because there's people that we owe money to who are people just like us, and they're hard-working, decent people. I think that would be sinful. I do. I really believe that. They're nice people, and you just wouldn't want to get next to them like that.[54]

After an energy boom dies in the Rockies, there are few places to turn for employment in the West. Even those people with solid roots in the area find difficulty making ends meet, and for most newcomers, wholescale dislocation occurs. Thus, a collapsing economy forces people to leave. Jim Sullivan, who left the *Rifle Tribune* for the *Grand Junction Daily Sentinel*, has seen the effects of the bust throughout the valley. He observes:

The long-range impact is as much psychological as it is anything else. People are sort of battered. Attitudes aren't good. You know you're in a bad situation when people are looking forward to the bottom. They're not talking about things turning up; they want to hit bottom. If someone goes belly-up that affects you, because he probably owes you money. You did some business with him or your neighbor did business with him. So you can piss and moan, but you've got to sit down and understand because it's affected you. And it's going to hurt you. While you may be embittered by it, you may be next. Everything was very interlocked. You couldn't help but feel an empathy if not a sympathy for someone else's financial trouble because it may portend your future.[55]

Though there is trauma, a bust also brings out human compassion. People with little are willing to share, even if all they can offer are the stories that sustain them. Couples who have lost their security can provide solace to husbands and wives who are losing theirs. Jim Sullivan tells a poignant tale:

I was talking with a lady whose husband is a carpenter and hasn't worked steady in a couple of years, and she is just mortified by the fact that they are probably going to have to walk out on their mortgage and their home will go into foreclosure. She was still working, but her income wasn't enough. She was having trouble accepting that, but it was inevitable. It was just a matter of time and they'd have to pack up their bags and move. But another woman sitting at the same table sort of leaned over and said, "Well, honey, it's no big deal. We did the same thing. Me and my husband. You'll survive. You'll survive because you have to survive. If I can help you in any way, I will." It's always easier being the second and the third person filing for bankruptcy. The first person has a tough time of it.[56]

Family dislocations after the bust affected almost all of the young, professional people who had come into the valley and revitalized it. They had different views and educated backgrounds, and they were committed to the scenic and recreational values that they had found in western Colorado. But their positions were eliminated. The Northwest Area Council of Governments in Rifle, for example, went from a paid staff of fifteen professionals to one lobbyist and a secretary. The city managers for New Castle, Silt, Rifle, Glenwood Springs, Grand Junction, and Parachute were replaced or their salaries were reduced. This departure of growth management officials so essential to the boom altered the county's municipal expertise and totally destroyed any collective managerial memory that would have been useful in mitigating the effects of future booms. The town planners had been important decision-makers during the boom, but they were forced to move on to other municipalities or county governments where they became cogs in a bureaucratic wheel.

With bankruptcies come divorces, but it is impossible to accurately link divorce rates to the bust because marital problems that may have arisen in Garfield or Mesa county led people to file for divorce in another county or even another state after the exodus. Equally pernicious is the long-range effect of the boom and bust on local youth who became accustomed to high wages and have since left the area and severed their family ties. Old-timers had finally welcomed the boom because it meant full employment for their children and grandchildren, some of whom had returned from lucrative jobs elsewhere; now, their descendants have left the area again in order to earn a living. The pattern of out-migration has always existed, but before the boom, people who chose to stay in the valley could always find work. That is no longer easy to do.

Just as there were corporate casualties among Exxon's staff, the ripple effects of the deepening depression profoundly affected the business community in Grand Junction. The chamber of commerce had to borrow $200,000. Motels and restaurants closed, as did small factories and branch offices set up by Denver businesses on the Western Slope. In Mesa County, the situation became more dismal each year. In 1980 there were 98 foreclosures; in 1981, 107; in 1982, 157; in 1983, 465; and in 1984, 1,042. An article in the *Atlantic Monthly* of April 1985, proclaimed, "Within four years the mortgages on one out of every twenty houses in the county were foreclosed — financial ruin on a scale not seen in most midwestern steel towns."[57]

Along with the devastating financial consequences came a profound social impact. Jane Quimby and her family were among those whose lives were changed by this impact. Jane and her husband had lived in Grand Junction since 1964. They raised six children, and she achieved prominence as a member of the Grand Junction city council, the Energy Impact Advisory Committee of the State Department of Local Affairs, and the Colorado Municipal League, where she was vice-president. She was also elected mayor of Grand Junction. In April 1981, she and her husband and ten other local dignitaries met with Randall Meyer, president of Exxon, U.S.A., at a private dinner party in Grand Junction. In a published interview, Mayor Quimby recalled asking herself, "What am I doing having dinner with the president of the largest company in the world?" The evening was "not a business meeting," she noted, but "a get-acquainted time," and she found Meyer "dignified but warm" and "genuinely wanting to know more about our community."[58] Her husband, Robert "Bob" Quimby, also enjoyed the intimate dinner with Exxon, U.S.A. President Meyer. Robert Quimby was president of the First National Bank of Grand Junction, which, in 1981, was rapidly expanding and would soon begin construction on a new downtown building. In a matter of months, however, he would be faced with the economic disaster of the bust. His First National Bank would be in serious financial jeopardy despite massive infusions of dollars loaned by Denver financial institutions. The entire economy of Grand Junction and the Western Slope would erode like a sand castle before a wave. On April 28, 1982, the Exxon board of directors voted to shut down the Colony Project, and exactly two years later, Robert Quimby committed suicide.

Two years after the bust, much of the economic shakedown had already occurred, and depression and malaise at last gave way to the first purposeful attempts to regain community stability and begin economic recovery. As the Western Slope entered Phase III, bitter attitudes of anger and depression finally acceded to acceptance, adjustment, and accommodation. Yet the bust was far from over. In fact, the statistics seemed to indicate an increasing financial toll, together with one stark and unexpected fact — there was no returning to even a pre-boom economy. On May 9, 1984, the *Rifle Tribune* announced that the bottom had been reached, and the paper printed population and sales tax figures that indicated that the local economy had leveled off. But on January 9, 1985, the paper itself became a victim of the bust and ceased publication. The headline that day read,"Adios, Amigos," and Pat O'Neill wrote one last column for all his friends in the "Sagebrush School of Journalism." At that time, however, O'Neill himself was living in Kansas City; his pub had gone bankrupt, and he and his family had joined other Western Slope exiles beginning anew somewhere else.

Government officials and city council members told citizens to be patient and wait for the return of the pre-boom economy, but other factors have entered into the picture in recent years. Businesses that had successfully operated for generations have folded. The value of ranchers' agricultural products has declined, coal has become less valuable, and the oil and gas industry has continued to spiral downward. People in the Colorado River Valley now ruefully realize that, after stretching and expanding to accommodate boomtown growth, communities and businesses do not soon rebound and take their former shape. Fervent desires for economic equilibrium remain unfulfilled, and personal boomtown losses eclipse any boomtown gains. Statistics tell the grim story. Office buildings sat empty, and of 41,000 homes in Mesa County, over 3,000 were up for sale. In September 1984, a survey of Grand Junction families found that 10 percent, or about 7,400 people, would be leaving. Mayor Mike Pacheco stated in the *Daily Sentinel*, "I had an idea a significant number of families, because of economic reasons, had to leave, but I had no idea it was that high. That represents the last 15 years of [population] growth in Mesa County."[59] In 1985, foreclosures reached 1,600, and lawyers who had come for real estate developments found themselves spending 85 percent of their time on bankruptcies.[60]

In Rifle, a drugstore in business for thirty years closed its doors in October 1985; across the street, half a business block was vacant. As mental health counselor Robert Nuffer stated three years after the bust, "I think that many of the communities are moving through that final stage of depression into some kind of acceptance and resolution and trying to look at getting on with life," but he added, "There are still businesses closing in the Rifle area, and every time a business closes people that have shopped there or other retail businessmen feel a sense — a renewed sense — of loss and fear. Are they going to be next?" [61]

The fourth and final phase of the bust is adjustment, and there have been a number of important changes in this period. A Garfield County Economic Development Steering Committee was formed, and in December 1985, it released "The Garfield County Economic Development Report" to spur economic diversification of the county, although noting that since 1981 the county had lost 6,472 jobs and 3,745 residents. By 1988, economic development funds had been spent on several projects, including raising oysters in tanks near Silt, but few permanent jobs had been secured.

But in Mesa County, several major industries and businesses that had existed for more than ten years failed, including an agricultural seed company, an electrical component firm, and a 22-year-old independent grocery store. The area Brown & Root office tried to sell ten 85-ton dump trucks with tires more than 6-feet tall and buckets capable of holding 189 cubic feet of material; the gigantic trucks, which cost $350,000 each in 1981, had been idle since the bust. An

Instead of helping to cure blight and decay and renovating the historical town of Parachute, Exxon built its brand-new community south of the Colorado River. Some corporations, however, built closer to Parachute, as seen in this photograph of new apartments with Mt. Callahan in the background. *Photograph by the author.*

article published in the *Daily Sentinel* on May 4, 1986, to commemorate Black Sunday lamented, "A whole new tier is beginning to fall. People who have pulled every trick to stay out of bankruptcy are now finding that it still hasn't been enough."[62]

As for the great experiment in oil shale housing, Exxon successfully filled its Battlement Mesa townhouses and apartments with senior citizens after a major media campaign was launched in the spring of 1985, touting the mesa as "The Liveable Mountain." But significant issues of emergency health care for those senior citizens remain unresolved, for it is a long ambulance ride to either the Rifle or Grand Junction hospitals. Meanwhile in Parachute, old buildings that were never renovated during the boom remain abandoned and boarded up as mute evidence to Exxon's insistence on creating its "city upon a hill" rather than rejuvenating the existing eighty-year-old community. It may be decades before vacant lots in Parachute are ever utilized. Former Parachute town administrator Ralph Freedman states, "We could have infilled 5,000 people in Parachute. Instead, [on Battlement Mesa] you now have 3,000 acres of sprawl — trailers on one end, recreation facilities and housing on the other."63

The new municipal facilities also have their drawbacks. In Rifle, the water plant would run more efficiently with a population of 12,000 people, for without a sufficient volume of water usage, sewer wastes remain in the new pipes and are not adequately flushed. The new water plant in Parachute, built to accommodate four times as many residents as the town now has, is extremely expensive to operate, costing thousands of dollars monthly in electric bills. And the miles of new roads and streets require regular maintenance, yet city and county maintenance funds have been severely curtailed.64

Just as everyone hoped that the county would stabilize to a pre-boom economy, they assumed that once the newcomers had left, the region would return to the same earlier mixture of old-timers, ranchers, farmers, and small businessmen. But out-dated publicity on the oil shale industry continued to attract a transient population of hard-core unemployed — latecomers who brought totally different values and norms to what was once a stable agricultural community. This influx of latecomers has changed the social fabric of these Western Slope towns. Filling up the area's apartment buildings and small rental houses were welfare recipients from Denver and other areas of Colorado, attracted by the lowest rental rates in the state. These latecomers posed additional problems for the county because they needed family and individual counseling and public health services at a time when staff had been reduced. (By the end of 1985, for example, the Garfield County manager, the director of social services, three social service caseworkers, and seventeen people in related positions had been fired.) Because of the poor educational backgrounds of new students, Rifle High School began to offer three levels of English to accommodate varying student abilities. A new influx of latecomers changed the social fabric of Colorado River Valley towns.

In another development, a new legal decision has resolved an important oil shale issue. Following the 1980 Supreme Court decision, on May 1, 1985, Chief Judge Sherman G. Finesilver of the Denver District Court ruled that the Department of the Interior had been negligent and had acted irresponsibly in failing to release land patents on oil shale claims filed over half a century ago. Release of those claims as patented lands cleared up years of litigation and established a unique hegemony of hydrocarbon wealth for a few Colorado families who had tenaciously maintained their faith in "the rock that burns." Descendants of those oil shale entrepreneurs, the Savages and the Ertls, have at last been vindicated and they may pass on to their heirs a fortune in petroleum reserves.

For area farmers and ranchers, the prospects are less optimistic. The sale of thousands of acres of agricultural lands and water rights during the boom has resulted in a serious, ongoing problem with weed control on uncultivated farmland. Weeds proliferating on abandoned subdivisions now scatter seeds throughout Garfield County and lower the value of crops. In Mesa County, however, the precipitous drop in real estate prices caused farmers to replant peaches in platted subdivisions that were never developed; some of the peach orchards even have curbs and gutters. Fruit-growing, which began in the Colorado River Valley at the turn of the century, has made a comeback near Grand Junction, and in an area between Silt and Rifle, a new salesyard has been built for livestock buyers and sellers, replacing the old sales ring that saw limited use during the boom as a country-and-western bar. The remaining oil company officials and resident ranchers even have a new restaurant — The Bullshipper's Cafe.

As for the oil companies, after spending millions of dollars in Garfield County, they have yet to produce a single barrel of commercially viable shale oil. Union Oil of California, now called Unocal, continues to experiment with its retort facility up Parachute Creek. Union president Fred Hartley had a deep commitment to oil shale and personally called the offices of the *Grand Junction Daily Sentinel* on Black Sunday to inform the paper that Union had no intention of giving up its 10,000 barrel-per-day facility; however, Hartley is no longer president of Union Oil. A May 14, 1986, front-page story in the *Wall Street Journal* titled "Coming up Dry, Unocal Struggles on with Attempt to Get Crude Oil from Shale" points to the company's continuing frustrations. The "rubber rock" that jammed retorts during the

One of the major benefits of the oil shale boom was the upgrading of sewer and water lines in the impacted oil shale communities. This photograph shows new water lines in Rifle, Colorado. *Photograph by Randall Teeuwen.*

first boom in the 1920s still confounds engineers. And now that Fred Hartley has retired, Union's oil shale plant may be in jeopardy for it cannot pay its own way without federal price supports.[65]

The back-slapping, smooth-talking developers with real estate contracts in their back pockets have all gone elsewhere. Those rare individuals like Charles Pence who were truly committed to the Colony Project and building Battlement Mesa as an exemplary community have departed. The current corporate management displays less finesse. After nearly seventy years of dominating the hopes and dreams of the Western Slope, the oil companies and their representatives are still not satisfied with their land holdings, their water rights, and their taxes. These companies have begrudgingly met state requirements for land reclamation and are building lakes and dams to protect their water rights for the next shale boom, yet they are also arguing about the tax assessment on their shale lands. Nearly all the 180,746 shale-rich acres in Garfield County are privately owned, but, in 1985, the oil companies were dissatisfied with the agricultural assessment of their oil shale properties. They paid a tax of only $.09

cents per acre on those lands in 1984, or a total of $17,624, but in February 1985, they proposed HB 1204 in the Colorado legislature to limit their assessment to $5,397 for the same acreage. The bill's sponsor angrily withdrew the legislation once he understood its full implications.[66]

As a final capstone to the tumultuous oil shale boom of the 1980s and a symbolic conclusion to this hundred-year community history of the Colorado River Valley, Congress abolished the Synthetic Fuels Corporation on December 19, 1985. After an initial $8 billion allocation and unending media hoopla, the corporation died an ignoble death. As one observer commented, the SFC "slithered out of existence with long time critics kicking it and making political hay on the way out."[67] Energy self-sufficiency and "the moral equivalent of war," like so many other grandiose concepts imposed upon the West by Congress, ended only in disaster and economic chaos. In the final analysis, the largest corporation in the world did not choose to commit the financial resources to develop oil shale; neither did the United States government. Yet, the greatest concentration of oil reserves in the free world is still to be found in the Piceance Creek Basin, in a remote corner of western Colorado first traversed by Fathers Dominguez and Escalante in 1776 and surveyed by the great explorers John Wesley Powell and F. V. Hayden a century later.

The first oil shale boom was spawned by dire predictions of a gasoline shortage during World War I. The discovery of the Texas and Oklahoma oil fields in the 1920s discouraged shale development until the late 1970s, when an international cartel of oil-producing nations leveraged the price of oil drastically upwards and caused worldwide inflation. Now the boom has passed, and communities in the Colorado River Valley have been forced to live with dislocated economies. People have been psychologically bruised by the rapid change in their fortunes. But on the environmental side of the ledger, eagles are returning to their nesting areas. There are fewer incidents of poaching deer and elk, and little danger exists to the threatened species of Uintah Basin hookless cactus at the mouth of Roan Creek.

In Bernard DeVoto's famous essay, "The Plundered Province," he chronicled "an unending stream of gold and silver and copper," — western mineral wealth "which was one of the basic forces in the national expansion." He explains, "It has not made the West wealthy. It has, to be brief, made the East wealthy." DeVoto could easily have been describing oil shale when he wrote, "Congress helped out by passing . . . a series of imbecile laws which, even if no other forces had been working to that end, would have insured the West's bankruptcy."[68] Though the recent oil shale boom poured millions of dollars into the Western Slope of Colorado, on the human side of the equation, the net result was only economic instability and personal chaos.

6

The White Paper, Black Sunday, and Corporate Responsibility in the West

What are the losses and who bears them? . . . We need an answer to the question "just who pays?" . . . The older merchants stay and pay; the younger ones, and those with no stake in the community will move; but the value of their property will in both cases largely be gone. . . . Those pay who are, by traditional American standards, most moral. In short, "good citizens" who assumed family and community responsibility are the greatest losers. Nomads suffer least.

> W. F. Cottrell
> "Death by Dieselization,"
> *American Sociological Review*

The cyclical nature of boom and bust in mining communities of the Rocky Mountain West continues from one century to the next. The national and international forces that spurred the massive mining booms that built Virginia City, Leadville, Tombstone, and Cripple Creek continue to affect the present. Local communities have little say over the use or misuse of adjacent natural resources developed by multinational corporations that are headquartered half a continent away. In the last quarter of the nineteenth century, booms in remote areas of the rural West were stimulated by the search for and extraction of precious metals. Now that national wealth is no longer tied to a gold or silver standard, the price per barrel of oil has become an international fiscal denominator.

The recent boom in the last quarter of the twentieth century was an energy boom, not a precious metals boom, yet the catastrophic pattern of expansion and contraction of rural boomtown communities has been repeated. Excess always has its aftermath, and disparity between plans and outcomes in western development continues. Despite the impressive gains of new schools, city halls, libraries, streets, and other municipal improvements, social and psychological losses have damaged small, agriculturally based ranching communities that overnight became boomtowns because they were located near vast energy resources of uranium, coal, oil, or oil shale.

This study has focused on community history in the towns of New Castle, Silt, Rifle, Parachute, and Grand Junction during the boom and after the bust. Rarely in the last decade have any other small towns in the United States been buffeted by such dramatic social change and subjected to such intense developmental pressures. Boomtowns, microcosms reflecting larger changes in American society, are characterized by rapid urbanization. But unlike diversified urban areas that may deteriorate slowly, boomtowns suffer swift community collapse due to their dependence upon a single resource. Outside capital has always been essential to western development — whether it was to inaugurate the fur trade, complete the transcontinental railroad, irrigate the Central Valley of California, or plat a frontier town — yet that capital has fled when the resources became depleted or prices dropped.

Recent western booms offer the opportunity to raise necessary ethical issues, to study the past as prologue, and to analyze a historical continuum of boomtown development, urbanization, dramatic social change, and equally dramatic decline. Young, single men who swung hammers and drills in the bowels of the Sierra Nevada in California or frequented saloons in Goldfield, Nevada, and Helena, Montana, in the nineteenth century had a great deal in common with oil shale construction workers in Parachute, Colorado, in 1981. They, too, would have bellied up to the bar at O'Leary's and cast longing glances at the Titian-style nude above the sixty-foot-long hardwood bar; if they were Catholics, they might even have returned to the pub on Sunday morning for Father Fox's mass.

Because of the myriad social forces at work in boomtowns, adult residents typically experience boomtown euphoria, a stimulating blend of greed, opportunity, esprit de corps, and joie de vivre. Boomtown euphoria is a genuine phenomenon, worthy of serious scholarship, that affects most adults in a boom community, be they nineteenth-century mine promoters peddling worthless stock or twentieth-century real estate brokers eagerly anticipating large commissions. Everyone "wants in" on the rosy, redeemable future, and the past becomes the present as the Old West and the New West merge in an amalgam of pickup trucks and gun racks, jeans and boots and cowboy hats, and prime agricultural lands subdivided into countless ranchettes. The folklore of success and the greed of personal ambition fuel boomtown growth with a furious intensity.

The exploitation of mineral resources and concurrent boomtown development on Colorado's Western Slope is at once typical of other western boomtowns and unique because of the proximity of the White River National Forest, the Flat Tops National Wilderness Area, the Colorado National Monument, and the miles of open meadows, dense aspen groves, and large stands of Engelmann spruce. Above all, there is the closeness of the West's great red river, the Colorado, which drains a quarter of a million square miles and flows through some of the most spectacular and varied landscape in the United States. The fact that the region's vast oil shale resources on Parachute Creek are adjacent to the Colorado River makes environmental issues concerning water purity of prime importance to millions of Americans in the West.

The first oil shale boom produced no boomtowns, and its major effects were the subtle shifts in property ownership and water rights from the public domain and small ranchers to Union Oil of California, Standard Oil of New Jersey, Getty Oil, and other firms that had no intention of building shale processing plants. Instead, they quietly consolidated their resource positions and bought out those earnest but naive entrepreneurs who thought they could start an industry with common stock capitalized at a penny a share and retorts that resembled outdoor barbecues. Having achieved virtual hegemony over the shale lands, the corporations then diverted their finances to pumping west Texas crude.

The first oil shale boom went bust because the price of oil plummeted; the second boom followed the same pattern, but with additional national attention focused on shale resources because of the widely held belief that high oil prices were here to stay. The boom was considerably larger and so, of course, was the ensuing bust.

Boomtown changes in the valley were a direct result of a national oil crisis, heightened by a president's insistence that energy self-sufficiency become "the moral equivalent of war" and the creation by Congress of the Synthetic Fuels Corporation. This recent oil shale boom remains unique in the annals of western history and is of special import for the future because the shale still lies unutilized while the United States continues to import vast quantities of foreign oil.

In the late 1970s and early 1980s, an international energy crisis orchestrated by OPEC brought about the second major crude oil shortage in the history of the United States and confronted Colorado River Valley towns with unprecedented community expansion. Industry demanded that shale resources be developed on a scale that threatened water supplies in the entire Colorado River Basin, as well as clean air over the Flat Tops National Wilderness Area and even metropolitan Denver. The erroneous belief persisted that because "national security" issues were at stake and energy self-sufficiency had reached the level of a federal crusade, a technological fix would ultimately be forthcoming in the true spirit of American pragmatism and competitive corporate culture. However, that technological breakthrough did not occur, and the boom busted because the price of oil began to fall. The energy economists had erred and the technological fix was never achieved. Even Exxon succumbed to the volatile international energy market.

Gains from the rapid urbanization of Colorado River Valley towns include lasting infrastructural improvements, but positive social changes have vanished as rapidly as they occurred. The "crucible effect" of young professionals learning their skills rapidly under near crisis conditions and infusing their communities with fresh ideas and perspectives has had little permanent effect because most of the professionals in the valley — the newspapermen, nurses, physicians, social workers, city planners, teachers, and town administrators — have left because their jobs have been eliminated or their salaries cut. They took with them their enthusiasm and collective experience. During the boom, urban pressures confronted rural values and resulted in community disorganization that sociologist Elise Boulding describes as the "order creating potential of discord," yet the oil shale bust created an entirely new set of social problems requiring more complex solutions.[1]

Black Sunday, May 2, 1982, becomes a benchmark day in the history of western booms and busts and validates the cyclical theory of resource exploitation and a boomtown continuum from the nineteenth century to the present. As Patricia Limerick notes, "Historians of the future . . . will find the 1980s to be a key period in Western American history."[2] But historians and social theorists have yet to match contemporary bust scholarship with the volume of scholarship published on the energy boom. To John Gilmore's model of boomtown stages should be added bust stages. To the social science categories of old-timers and newcomers must be added the new category of latecomers, the hardcore unemployed who relocate in failed boomtowns for the cheap rent, but then require extensive social services just as those services are being cut back. The quiet agricultural communities of hard-working farmers, ranchers, and small businessmen only slowly regain the social mix that had previously resulted in generational stability. Mistrust, selfishness, and other poor values brought about by boom pressures become ingrained due to personal financial crises caused by the bust. People feel isolated and cut off, and they are unwilling to talk with friends, neighbors, and relatives who might ask embarrassing questions about income and expenses. Community caring changes for the worse. Rural values and simple neighborliness have been discarded, yet there are no substitutes, for the urbanization process was never completed. No longer rural, not yet urbanized, boomtown communities gone bust, must, like the residents who remain, seek a new identity. For inevitably, the cycle will recur. There will be another boom. The strategic importance of 500 billion barrels of oil within a 100-mile radius in the middle of our western states cannot be underestimated.

Short-term planning for development of a major national resource only results in catastrophe for communities adjacent to that
resource. Oil shale may indeed become essential for national security,
yet the present corporate policy of Exxon, U.S.A., owner of the
Colony Project and Battlement Mesa, is to advertise its new town as a
retirement center. What will happen when another energy crisis results in a housing shortage for oil shale workers? Will serious social
and environmental concerns brought on by another boom be taken
into account, or will state and local governments bend over backwards to accommodate oil companies promising large payrolls? The
potential impacts for local citizens could be far greater in the future
than they were in the past.

It is essential to assess the past in order to confront an inevitable
future. In the late 1940s, sociologist W. F. Cottrell studied community
response to rapid economic and technological change. For his research, he chose a small, one-industry town in the West that was
totally dependent upon railroading — a town in which men had built
their houses of brick and concrete because they were certain that the
railroad would always be there and that trains would always stop for
water and coal. Cottrell's study focused on community change and
"death by dieselization," because his community, which he called
"Caliente," was being phased out as a maintenance stop on the railroad. Smoke-belching, water-guzzling, coal-consuming steam locomotives were being replaced by more efficient diesel locomotives,
and in Caliente, the busy roundhouse would soon be used only for
storing locomotives and standby equipment. The company knew what
its losses would be: 39 private dwellings, a modern clubhouse with
116 single rooms, and a hotel with dining room and lunch counter.
Cottrell, however, was interested in losses that would never appear in
an accountant's corporate ledger; he was interested in the residents of
Caliente, the impact of their shattered security, and the intangible
losses to their community. Cottrell wrote, "The story is an old one and
often repeated in the economic history of America. It represents the
'loss' side of a profit and loss system of adjusting to technological
change," but he added, "Perhaps for sociological purposes we need an
answer to the question "just who pays?"[3] Many of the significant
issues raised in his research are equally germane forty years later in

the Colorado River Valley and the small towns of New Castle, Silt, Rifle, and Parachute, and the mid-sized town of Grand Junction, where wholesale community disruption has occurred because of the energy boom and bust.

The Colony shutdown was not just an isolated incident of an industrial project gone sour, but the largest, most expensive, and fastest mining boom and bust in the history of the West. For those reasons, it should also be the focal point for a major debate on corporate responsibility, laissez faire economics, the disparity between plans and outcomes, and the philosophy that "letting the marketplace work" serves all interests.

These are critical issues in American life and society that extend to the heart of both an individual's and a corporation's right to property, as well as a community's right to its own salvation. Uncomfortable precedents abound with similar booms and busts throughout the United States, but in the West, as with striking desert and mountain landscapes, the issues are always in dramatic relief because the economic downturns are so severe. Unlike diversified areas of the United States, where jobs are plentiful and workers usually find alternative employment after a manufacturing plant shuts down, in the rural West there are virtually no alternatives. Agriculture, mining, and federal employment have been the economic mainstays in the intermountain West, and though tourism is on the increase, displaced workers can only be absorbed slowly.

The history of the settlement of the Colorado River Valley began with a pioneering heritage as ranchers and farmers grubbed out the sagebrush for hayfields, raised and branded cattle and horses, built houses of stone, and dug by hand miles of irrigation ditches to provide precious water for the semiarid soil. But today, the agricultural heritage of Garfield County has been compromised, both by low prices for farm products and by oil company purchases of land and water rights. Quiet, rural communities that had been content with congenial lifestyles and a strong sense of neighborliness and solidarity quickly became energy boomtowns. Just as quickly, those boomtowns went bust, and values that had sustained residents for years were threatened and in some cases destroyed. Now that the boom has passed, communities seek solace in old ways and traditions, yet too much changed as the area's economic equilibrium was shattered. Communities have been traumatized and have faced a distinct loss of identity and self-definition.

Exxon Chairman Clifton Garvin, Jr., has said, "Successful business does best in communities that are alive, healthy and secure. And that means that business has to look beyond its basic economic function." He continues, "To stay in business, we have to make a profit. To succeed in business, we have to share some of that profit, beyond the dividends and taxes we pay, for the public good."[4] Those are well-chosen words and appear to reflect a sound corporate policy of community caring and concern, but they were never followed through in Colorado.

Mrs. Thomas Brimhall sent a letter to the editor of *Exxon, U.S.A.* magazine. Her letter specifically addresses communities that are far from "alive, healthy and secure." The letter, published in the February 26, 1986, *Rifle Telegram* read:

Dear Editor:

The recent issue of your magazine, *Exxon U.S.A.*, carries some heart-warming articles about the studies made of your company['s] environmental impact on Alaskan and Colorado wildlife. It is commendable that such a large company cares enough about God's creatures that it will spend so many precious months and hundreds of thousands of dollars to protect the animals and birds from even the slightest adverse effect of the Alaskan pipeline or the Colorado industrial development of oil shale.

What a pity you did not have the same concern for the human beings in Colorado in 1982 when your company began the oil shale project and required immediate housing and support services for hundreds of people brought into Rifle or Parachute and Grand Junction. The local businessmen and entrepreneurs rose to the need to provide those services. They built apartment houses, stores, restaurants, service stations, churches, homes — expanding to meet the requirements of your employees and their families. Then, without so much as a week's notice or a single dollar spent on any kind of an "impact study," you locked your door on May 2, 1982, and not only put 2,000 of your own employees out of work, but drove hundreds of other citizens into foreclosures and bankruptcy. There has been an ever-increasing record high of tax sales and "business troubles" in this valley —

shock waves from your uncaring attitude towards the people who gave you and your employees the support you required.

In the Grand Junction area alone, three long-time well-established restaurants closed in one recent month, a local bank has gone broke due to real estate loans that purchasers could not repay, a savings and loan association is desperately seeking financial aid to save its life, a hotel of a chain renowned throughout the world has voluntarily gone into receivership in the past week, four major grocery stores have abandoned their premises, weeds are growing high around countless empty houses with vandalized windows and fences because the owners have no money and no work and have either moved in with relatives that are little better off or left the area completely to seek some kind of livelihood somewhere in some other city or state. . . .

In response to your "business reply card" enclosed with your magazine: Please remove my name from the *Exxon, U.S.A.* mailing list. An empty lot remains at the address to which your magazine was sent. The Brimhall Motel Apartments did not survive your retreat from this valley, either.

Yours truly,
Mrs. Thomas J. Brimhall

Mrs. Brimhall is certainly correct in her assessment of economic woes in the Colorado River Valley, but conservative economists would argue that such are the risks of all venture capitalists, whether they are building a small motel or annexing eighty acres of choice residential land. But investors like the Brimhalls bought property based on assurances from the largest corporation in the world that oil shale would indeed be developed and that the federal government believed synthetic fuel production essential to national security. To paraphrase W. F. Cottrell, not only should the question "Who pays?" be asked, but also, "Who is at fault?" Though financial setbacks and reverses are common, rarely does Adam Smith's invisible hand of the marketplace so closely resemble a clenched fist with brass knuckles. The pounding received by residents in the Colorado River Valley requires a thorough review, not just a cursory dismissal in the name of laissez faire economics.

Mrs. Brimhall is incorrect, however, about Exxon not filing an "impact statement." Indeed, one of the reasons Exxon bought the Colony Project from Atlantic Richfield is that Arco had successfully completed all the necessary permits — the project was ready to begin.

Part of the problem, then, as Mrs. Brimhall tries to point out, lies with the environmental impact process itself and its total inability to deal with human, as opposed to environmental, issues. Major changes are needed in environmental impact statement criteria. During the late 1970s, for example, as economists erroneously predicted a continuing rise in the price of oil, social scientists, using sophisticated econometric computer modeling with projective, evaluative, and directive assessments, created inaccurate "state of the art" impact assessments that had no provisions for community change and no consideration of nonempirical phenomena. Individual human behavior, much less the aggregate behavior of energy-impacted communities, is far too complex to be reduced to a simple computer assessment. Environmental impact statements fail to address the significant social impacts of energy booms because few attempts have been made to understand local culture.[5] Nor is there a requirement to look at the possibility of rapid shutdowns and their subsequent impacts. In the future, the crucial issue of industrial shutdowns needs to be integrated into every environmental impact statement.

The problems of socioeconomic safeguards for boom-and-bust cycles in the West are compounded by the western myth of rugged individualism that originated in the region's pioneer roots. To live on the land is not necessarily to own it, as Garfield County ranchers ruefully learned when they sold their property in good faith in the 1970s and, under default rules, received only portions of it back. To the complex question of how one breaks a boom-and-bust cycle when the mainstays of the economy are mining and agriculture must be added the unadulterated truth that some westerners love a boom regardless of its consequences. Infusions of capital and investment during a boom provide the only means for some people to get ahead. As Roger and Diana Oliens write in their history of the Texas oil fields:

For despite hectic and occasionally rugged conditions of life, to the boomers, drifters, workers, and their families, oil booms offered economic opportunities that outweighed the attendant hardships of boom life. It was the chance to get ahead, rather than the "social chaos" so shocking to non-participant commentators on oil booms, that meant the most to those who took part in petroleum development. Difficulties were temporary: economic advancement, whether for communities or individuals, was real.[6]

However, the Oliens fail to point out that the people who really benefit from a boom are the nomads who leave when the bust occurs. Because there is always that sense of boomtown euphoria and open-ended opportunity, private yearnings of ambition accompany every boom. Surprisingly, even individuals who have gone bankrupt admit that they would do it all again, for the boom was a high point in their lives. Pat O'Neill, writer for the *Rifle Tribune* and co-owner of Parachute's O'Leary's Pub before it went bankrupt, explains:

Bankruptcy was like a little tiny escape hole at the very, very end of the tunnel. If you couldn't get out you had an emergency exit. And that was it. Everything you touched was turning to financial ruin. It was out beyond your control because the economy was on a downward spiral and you can't stop water from going down the drain. There was nothing you could do to stop it going down. You'd drive down the street and say, well, who's next? I betcha he's going. He can't make it. That poor bastard, what's he doing here? He's crazy if he thinks he's going to last. That person's got his house for sale. Been in here with the 32nd classified ad and dropping the price again. And they're still not going to sell it.[7]

O'Neill was interviewed just a few months before he moved from Garfield County back to Kansas City, Missouri. As a reporter, editor, and businessman with a thriving saloon, he had seen it all. Yet, despite his financial reverses, he had truly enjoyed himself and felt like a major participant in an exciting event. He even compared Parachute, Colorado, in the 1970s and early 1980s to Mark Twain's raucous Virginia City. O'Neill explains:

I think that in spite of it all, even with that damn cancer I've got in my pocket book, I wouldn't have traded it. I was glad I was there because I saw something that most people never get to experience. If it wasn't a vital, exciting, wild, experience worth having, they wouldn't have written volumes on the booms of the 1880s. Mark Twain wouldn't have written *Roughing It*. There's color and glamour and a kind of sensuous brush with prosperity, and [there's] familiarity, intimate familiarity with loss, personal and financial. [I enjoyed] watching people at their most delightful and at their strangest and at their saddest and at their happiest. I'd read Twain for years, and I'd read the boom camp stories just because I love the color of that era, and here I happened to find myself in [a boom camp]. As a writer I wouldn't have wanted to be anywhere else in the world. People, damn it, they don't change. What I saw in front of me was Virginia City personified a hundred years later. Instead of horses, they rode Harleys. Instead of Stetsons they wore welding caps and instead of — no, we had the dust streets for God's sake, and we had people living much like they lived before. Single guys [who were] on the make for money or on the run from something [were] being as free spirited as you'll ever see anywhere.[8]

Yet O'Neill admits that after the bust, despite the romance, "You don't like to leave the game the loser, and I really had a stigma in my heart. You're going out of town with your tail between your legs, because somebody owed me money and I owed somebody else money."[9] O'Neill and his family came and left like so many others during the boom and after the bust. They tried to stay, but without the security of owning property or a close network of kinfolk, they were forced to return to their roots.

For those families who have always lived in the Colorado River Valley, leaving is not so simple. This is home, as it has been for generations. Many of those families still want development — they believe in it and see booms as an opportunity for the community to thrive. Attorney John Savage, whose grandfather helped stake some of the first oil shale claims up Parachute Creek, sees energy booms as integral to development and progress. He notes:

In sociological/cultural terms, I believe that a neighborhood, a town, a country, or a species must be either progressing or regressing. It is impossible to maintain the status quo for very long. If you are not going forward, you will fall behind. In Colorado you have the east slope [Denver residents] fighting to save the environment and out here we're still trying to survive it. The only hope is mineral extraction. [If] you can't make money raising corn in Iowa, you surely can't do it here.[10]

Indeed, the positive infrastructural gains in the Colorado River Valley are impressive. Thirty years of municipal and educational improvements were made in the space of three years. Certainly there are maintenance requirements with new streets and water systems, but other communities with potholed streets and aging sewer lines would welcome such problems. The valley now has an excellent stock of new housing that is very affordable to people with steady jobs. In fact, so much new infrastructure was built that 20,000 people could move in overnight and be accommodated. Garfield County Re-2 School District in Rifle has a new administration building, two new elementary schools, a new high school, and a new vocational building. In Parachute, there are two new schools, a new city hall, a water plant, and paved streets. For the first time, Silt, Rifle, and Parachute also have community libraries. County offices have been decentralized, and services are now offered in Rifle that required a twenty-minute drive to Glenwood Springs in the pre-boom days. All these are the physical manifestations of progress that John Savage credits to the recent oil shale boom, yet they came about not because of corporate largesse, but because hard-headed county commissioners insisted that oil companies pay front-end money to help mitigate their impact.

Those county commissioners were correct in making the corporations pay their own way. Both Garfield and Rio Blanco counties set significant legislative and zoning precedents that will alter mining and energy permits for future western industrial development — but it has not been enough. The commissioners are not patting themselves on their backs, for the bust has been too severe, the economic downturn too sharp. They were not re-elected, and their friends and neighbors lost assets acquired over decades. The oil companies rightfully paid impact assistance monies through oil shale trust funds and bond guarantees, to insure that the county and small towns would not be at financial risk. But they should have paid "backing-out" money, as well, to mitigate the chaos they created when their glorious projections became empty promises. This is the answer to Cottrell's question, "Just who pays?" Certainly the communities have paid in disrupted lives, multiple foreclosures, mental illness, marital discord, and personal bankruptcies.

At the Exxon stockholders meeting in New York City on May 13, 1982, Chairman Clifton Garvin explained that the Exxon board of directors was "taking a hard and comprehensive look at all major projects" and that the decision to dramatically close the Colony Project had been reached "reluctantly because we were conscious of the human problems that could arise as plans were disrupted." Garvin continued, "We were reluctant, too, because we continue to believe that alternative fuels, such as shale oil, will someday play a significant role in meeting energy requirements."[11] It is essential to ana-lyze a corporate mentality that would issue a statement as provocative as Exxon's "white paper" in the summer of 1980 and then totally reverse itself in May of 1982 with an announcement closing the Colony Project and cutting the number of employees from 2,800 to 30. Such corporate schizophrenia is unprecedented. Corporations are fallible, yet "the singular power of a giant called Exxon" must be kept in check.[12] No nineteen managers on any board of directors should have the power to cause so much economic disaster and dislocation in the rural West where alternative employment opportunities are nonexistent.

The size of the bust is directly proportional to the size of the boom, and the size of the boom can ultimately be traced to the "white paper," which was a deliberate, premeditated attempt to shock the nation into utilizing its synthetic fuels potential and to secure a national consensus for Exxon's grandiose scenario. In the "white paper," Exxon suggested that its Colony Project would produce 50,000 barrels per day by 1985, rising to 600,000 bpd by 1990 and culminating in 1.5 million bpd in 2010. Simultaneously, population in the Colorado River Valley was to grow from less than 100,000 to 1.75 million.[13]

Exxon's "white paper" projections smack of corporate hubris and need to be examined not only because the Western Slope was sacrificed, but also because Exxon, U.S.A. itself has suffered and needs to study its own mistakes. "Citing the drastic drop in oil prices and a pessimistic outlook for the oil industry," in mid-April 1986, Exxon announced the forced retirement of 40,000 employees despite a 37 percent rise in first-quarter profits. Because of the Colony debacle, Exxon's second-quarter profits plunged 51.5 percent in July 1982.[14]

In an interview on May 14, 1984, two years after Black Sunday, Bill Ekstrand, manager of both Battlement Mesa, Inc., and the shelved Colony Project, stated, "It would be nice for the public and the political leaders to stop saying that Exxon was the cause." He continued, "I'm not trying to say we didn't cause any disruption. No doubt about it . . . We were the biggest, the highest profile, the loudest . . . We probably overpromised. We probably over spent," but he added, "It's just a shame that so much energy is spent looking backward."[15]

To the contrary, far too little energy has been spent looking backward. Historians and social scientists have been unwilling to thoroughly examine this recent boom and bust, but business professors see in the Colony Project a classic case study of business strategy and policy. In a senior level undergraduate business textbook, Garry Smith, Danny Arnold, and Bobby Brizzell explain that "no company in the United States has ever grown as big and wealthy as Exxon Corporation, a giant among giants in the most prosperous of industries." They note that "Exxon's size magnified the scale of its losses," though even the most free-spending of multinational managers must question why "less than two years . . . after investing about $1 billion at Colony, Exxon appeared to have abandoned the biggest and most promising synthetics fuels project in the United States."[16]

The issues of investment, disinvestment, and corporate ethics are significant. But so, too, are the dozens of houses that sat vacant in Rifle and Grand Junction, the 1,600 foreclosures in 1985 alone, the high local unemployment rates, and the depression, loss of self-esteem, spouse abuse, child abuse and bust-related suicide. A letter to the editor of the *Grand Junction Daily Sentinel* began, "Bye! Since Hallmark doesn't make a farewell card which encompasses a quarter of a community moving at one time, I thought it best to say goodbye this way."[17]

Two assumptions underpinned the corporate bravado of the "white paper." The first came from a complex set of uniquely American values and contradictions that are at the heart of our international and economic success as a nation and at the root of our country's combined environmental and ecological problems. That assumption comes under the heading of a "technological fix," or the notion that corporate research and development, given enough time and money, can engineer a solution to anything. The second underlying assumption is much easier to assess. It was tied to the mob psychology of the oil industry that prompted Exxon to jump into oil shale development

Cartoon by Charlie. *Reprinted by permission of Tribune Media Services.*

when, in fact, no company had then or has now a commercially viable shale retorting process. Global needs for capital investment and technical expertise, together with the complex vertical integration of multinational oil companies, limit innovation in the competitive worlds of energy exploration and development. Consequently, a mob psychology prevails, and Exxon found itself in the embarrassing position of being the only major corporate player without an oil shale project. So the synthetic fuels division of Exxon chose to make up for lost time with a vengeance. Exxon soon joined Mobil, Chevron, Tosco, Multi-Minerals, and Occidental Oil in a frenzied rush to develop shale, while Union Oil doggedly continued to tinker with its 10,000-barrel-per-day oil shale plant. The "white paper" can be seen as Exxon's contribution to oil industry group behavior and the belief that synthetic fuel development, and oil shale in particular, would save the nation. In fact, Exxon boldly appeared so committed to oil shale that it scorned loans and price guarantees from the multibillion-dollar Synthetic Fuels Corporation, insisting it had the financial resources to go it alone.

By purchasing the Colony Project, Exxon immediately became the new kid on the block in the Piceance Creek Basin, and its executives were determined to demonstrate their corporate machismo by bringing a 50,000-bpd plant on-line by 1985. Their ambitious plans, of course, never materialized, and today Exxon is doing nothing in oil shale development except some land reclamation and earthen dam building to keep their permits current. Rather than scale down the project to a more realistic goal of 5,000 or 10,000 barrels per day, they have "mothballed" it indefinitely.

Exxon's other assumption — that a giant technological fix would be forthcoming — also undermined the Colony Project. In addition, a "big is better" philosophy failed to account for Americans conserving energy and driving smaller cars out of financial necessity. That factor helped cause the economic projections for $40-a-barrel oil to go awry as did the introduction of North Sea oil, cheating on quotas by OPEC producers (specifically OPEC nations in Africa), and increased production in non-OPEC areas. Economists became entranced with parabolic curves showing ever-increasing energy consumption, but the solution was not in finding more energy; it was in using less. Like turtles who withdraw into their shells, bureaucracies and corporations often turn defensive rather than reassess unsuccessful decisions. Bureaucratic failure is generally not made public and, therefore, rarely exhumed and studied.

From a fiscal perspective, there is little question that Exxon made the right decision in closing the Colony Project. The precipitous decline in the price of oil, the gold standard for all energy fuels, was correctly predicted by the board of directors who closed the project.[18] Subsequent events, including hard times in "the oil patch," have proved the financial wisdom of Exxon's shutdown decision, but just as corporations have obligations to their share-holders, they have obligations to the communities in which they do business, especially after promising such exorbitant financial commitments. Publicly, Exxon announced they were closing Colony because of cost overruns, but that is only a half-truth. Both Colony and Battlement Mesa were extremely efficient operations, and within the goals set by the corporation any additional expenses could have been absorbed. Instead, Exxon's board of directors forgot all about the nation's twenty-first-century energy needs that they had been preparing for and decided to jettison the project rather than rationally continue on a smaller scale. They abandoned their planned technological fix, and they abandoned oil shale. Subsequently, so has every other oil company except Union, and Union may soon be next. Yet at one time Exxon Corporation Chairman Clifton Garvin had stated, "Shale oil . . . is part of the bridge between fossil fuels and renewable fuels — a bridge that could last up to 195 years."[19] The rhetoric, the crusaders' zeal for "national security," and the millions of dollars spent have all been conveniently forgotten, except by people in the Colorado River Valley.

Former U.S. Senator Gary Hart's oil shale files contain an elaborate 1982 brochure simply titled "COLONY" in embossed gold letters. The first page is an old black-and-white photo of miners with a color photo inset of Parachute Creek and the shale cliffs. The text begins, "An age-old epic of man's relationship to the land — of human endurance and survival — of human success and triumph. This latest advance is just beginning." If those lines seem grandiose, the following prose, extracted from the same brochure, is equally purple:

Shale Oil — An Idea Thats [sic] Time Has Come

The world has changed dramatically in recent years. Oil shale development is no longer a dream — it has become a political, economic, and strategic necessity for America and its people.

The Pioneering Spirit Lives On At Colony

With a pioneering spirit — a sense of adventure that has become a tradition in the American West — Exxon Corporation and Tosco Corporation have joined forces in the multi-billion dollar Colony Oil Shale Project. Like the Indians, explorers, settlers, and miners who came before, the people of Colony have been drawn to the land and its resources. Like their predecessors, they are willing to work hard and to face risks, but they are determined not to repeat the mistakes of the past.

They are dedicated to preserving the environment and avoiding the boom town/ghost town syndrome. They are building a new community — Battlement Mesa — with deep concern for sound community planning. The Colony Oil Shale Project is looking long into the future to provide jobs, planned growth, prosperity and energy for decades to come.

The story of oil shale began some 55 million years ago. The Colony Project and Battlement Mesa are the next chapters in the age-old epic of man's relationship to the land, of human endurance and triumph. And this next episode is just beginning.[20]

Unfortunately, the "next episode" never began. Corporate hubris is perhaps too poetic a term, but no other suffices to describe Exxon's posture. The company's "white paper" and glossy promotional brochures like the one just quoted utterly transformed communities in the Colorado River Valley. No local officials were asked in advance to comment on the release of the "white paper," and they certainly were not asked in advance to offer opinions and suggestions on the bust. But the power of the boom was directly related to corporate hyperbole, which encouraged rampant speculation. Ralph Freedman, former Parachute town administrator, remembers the impact of the "white paper" when it was presented locally:

Exxon held a gigantic public meeting in Grand Junction in 1980 where they basically laid out their scenario for oil shale development. There must have been 800 local and civic leaders and business people from the Grand Valley that were there and [Exxon] talked about 8 million barrels per day of oil shale, the need for 50 cities of 50,000 people each to handle all this construction and the new people that would be coming. They talked about bringing

water from South Dakota because there wasn't enough water in the Colorado River for oil shale. When you have a meeting like that and Exxon,
which is the largest oil company in the world, says they're going to do it, all
of a sudden everyone across the country started to watch Parachute and was
interested in how it developed. And of course that triggered a lot of speculation. Prices went from almost nothing to people on Main Street asking $25 a
square foot for undeveloped land. [It] seemed like everybody who was
anybody was sitting at that meeting, called to Grand Junction by the king-
pins of the oil industry to listen to their whole spiel about how oil shale was
going to make this area just go crazy. After that, the speculation started and
that's when people were calling up trying to find out about land, trying to
find out whether there was any industrial property for sale, trying to find out
about zoning, trying to find out what needs the community had or what was
there. It got to the point that you were paying as much in Parachute,
Colorado, as you might in Denver for downtown space.[21]

   Freedman observed the effects of the "white paper" on Parachute while he was working to bring a sleepy little nineteenth-century
farm town into the twentieth century. John Gilmore knew all about
boomtowns from his experience as a newspaper editor and publisher
in southwest Colorado during the uranium boom of the 1950s and as
a senior research fellow for the Denver Research Institute at the
University of Denver in the 1970s. He comments on Battlement Mesa
and the impact of the "white paper":

[Battlement Mesa] was planned for far more people than Exxon would
employ. It was a grand gesture to show that Exxon was serious when it had
published, in one of the greater minor faux pas of corporate history, a White
Paper predicting a tremendous future for synthetic fuels in general and oil
shale in particular. [The paper] focused in Northwest Colorado without
[Exxon] taking the trouble to tell the governor of the state or either of the
two senators or anybody else that they were publishing this thing. [The
"white paper" had] all the prestige of the industry which Exxon's annual
energy industry papers enjoy. And you had some very angry, very senior
politicians in Colorado after that paper was published. Now, I think that was
a minor factor, but it did make Exxon people realize that since they had
pointed to oil shale as being a huge thing, when it came time to start up the
Colony Project, somebody made a decision by God they were going to do it
right. Battlement Mesa, until it was shut down, was being done on an almost

cost-is-no-object basis. The only constraint, I think, was pretty good management by the people who were running it.[22]

Gary Schmitz is a newspaper reporter who covered the oil shale story from the Garfield County courthouse and the mine benches on plateaus above Parachute Creek to the floor of Congress, where he reported the decision to abolish the Synthetic Fuels Corporation. Schmitz worked for the *Glenwood Post* in Glenwood Springs, and the *Grand Junction Daily Sentinel*; currently, he is an energy specialist with the *Denver Post* in its Washington, D.C., bureau. He reflects:

I think the White Paper was another instance in which the stakes were raised considerably. [Exxon] admitted that it was their intent to raise the level of the debate rather than talking about 10,000 barrels a day here and another 10,000 barrels a day on the next mesa over. When they started adding all this up, what the nation needed and how much oil shale's out there, the resource was tremendous. You started reading things about how there's as much oil shale as there is oil in the Middle East and it got your attention. So whatever their ultimate aim was [the "white paper"] is probably still open to debate. I'm not sure we can ever answer [what the intent was], but we can look back and determine what the effect was. [Entrepreneurs] ran around to California and New York and got investment money to build new condominiums and subdivisions.[23]

In contrast to the speculators who stampeded the Colorado River Valley, environmentalists rallied round their own flag. Schmitz explains:

Those types were saying, "Hey, this is real. Look what they're talking about. They're going to trash the Colorado Plateau, and for what good reason? It doesn't make sense. We've got to do something about it." So each of the respective factions used it to their advantage. Assume for a minute that [Exxon] believed it. If they did, I'm not sure that it was such a bad thing. It may have been a responsible thing to do. I don't think it worked out that way. I think the ["white paper"] for the most part blew up in their faces. [24]

The "white paper" certainly made Exxon stand out above all the other oil companies who were trying to make their projects work on a smaller scale. Yet Exxon itself may not even have had a clear picture of what it was promoting. The controversy that immediately surrounded the release of the paper baffled industry representatives who were so insulated within their own corporate mindset that it was difficult for them to comprehend why anyone should be upset with their shale development scenario or Exxon's plans for inter-basin water transfers to bring Missouri River water from South Dakota to Colorado. Understanding the Exxon decision-making process is difficult because relevant records are "proprietary" and this author has been denied access to them.[25] "The Company," as it is known by the people who work for it, seems unwilling to review publicly a very expensive but very poor management decision.

Today, Exxon's synthetics fuels division is considerably smaller, but in the late 1970s it must have been a force to be reckoned with. Gary Schmitz offers these insights:

Corporations at some level have personalities. Early on, I think, [the county commissioners] saw Fred Hartley [president] of Union and some of these other guys as Horatio Algers. County commissioners saw these guys as industrial champions here to save us. The argument [existed] that we were here to help the nation, that the world needs this resource and it's our duty to provide it. There was always a misconception that there was a monolith of thought among big oil as to how this would play out. They didn't know. The division among Exxon must have been horrendous. Exxon, because it was such a huge corporation, had all the same bureaucratic problems as does any public institution of similar size. It had trouble communicating with itself. Decisions were made on one level that may not have been well researched with those at another level. Things were driven by broad policy rather than hands-on, minute-by-minute observation.

A lot of things were floating around that no one understood the importance of until months, years later. There were a lot of milestones that we can only now determine that at the time didn't seem like anything. After [the "white paper"] hit the newspapers, after it became the standard talk, not just of the landed gentry of Garfield County, the ranchers and everybody else — by the time it filtered down to the bar crowd, and they were talking about it, it was only then that Exxon decided, "Well, we've got to set the record straight. This is what we're talking about." Then they adopted this [stance concerning the "white paper"], "No, we're not promoting it. We're just saying this is what could be happening." When they came to Washington saying "get the government out of our way," of course they were promoting [the "white paper"]. When they went to Garfield County and spoke to the Sierra Club they were saying, "This is our cautious appraisal and we need to take steps to ensure that this doesn't happen." So they were talking out of both sides of their mouth.[26]

The "white paper" also had tremendous clout inside the corporation. Gary Schmitz explains:

At different times they would use [the "white paper"] to even sell the project within their own organization. A corporation, especially as large as Exxon, is not any monolith of thought. [Departments] are competing for resources. The offshore people would have loved to have had the $5 billion that was at one point allocated to the oil shale project. So those people have to justify their own existence. They're building their own empires. There's constant war in oil companies between economists, engineers, and lawyers. The petroleum engineers who used to run oil companies just loathe the attorneys who they think have gummed the whole process up because you should be able to go out there and just build something. What's all this damn paperwork![27]

To the public, Exxon seemed to know what it was doing, but internally, as Schmitz relates:

They were competing within themselves. The pro-synfuels forces used that paper within the organization to rally their cause. We all assumed that this is a corporation, the largest in the world, that knew what it was doing. That it had some kind of well-charted, well-planned course. That they had figures which indicated that it still made sense to spend a million dollars a week even though other companies had pulled out and the prices were softening and going the wrong direction instead of the $60-a-barrel or whatever the hell they needed to justify a project of that magnitude. But in fact, the board was juggling this project against a variety of others. The board was buffeted by the same kinds of uncertainty in the international oil market as everybody else was. Their economists have had just as bad or worse a track record at predicting the price of oil as any economists in private or public endeavor. [But] everyone assumed they knew what they were doing. They were still spending a million dollars a week, and finally they compared it with all the other things they had done, and low and behold they said, "No, this doesn't make any sense." Rather than any kind of cautioned approach to slowly shutting off the valve — the money valve — in any kind of measured doses and increments, they halted everything in one fell swoop and hence, Black Sunday.

In historical terms, the bust simply replicated previous boom-and-bust cycles in the West. However, for the residents who lived through it, the bust represented a turning point in their careers and fortunes; it was a cataclysmic event that would shatter their lives. As an energy specialist for the *Denver Post*, Gary Schmitz draws these conclusions:

People weren't injured. Nobody was killed. Nobody drowned. It's more of a psychological blow. And the bust wouldn't have been as severe if the boom hadn't preceded it. It was new. It was exciting. Things were expanding and growing. Kind of tumultuous, kind of chaotic, but hey, it was fun, too. A lot of beer was flowing, a lot of money, a lot of backroom poker games. But if you hadn't had that rapid growth, if things had been stable before it, the bust wouldn't have been as tremendous as it was. Just as there was no charted course as to how a corporation should respond to a boom, there certainly was no charted course [as to] how a corporation should respond in the face of a bust. There is no policy statement that some Exxon middle manager can pull out of his job description and say, "Now, here I have to do this, this, and this." It just doesn't exist, nor did it exist on the state level or the government level, either. People were playing things day by day. People on the high level [at Exxon] didn't know Garfield County from Saudi Arabia. It was just another spot on the map. It was just another hole they dumped money down. So Exxon becomes the whipping boy, and maybe rightly so. I don't feel sorry for them, but at the same time there were just forces at work far in excess of Exxon, if you can imagine.[29]

Unfortunately, just as there were no national laws regarding plant closings, there were no local laws tied to mining permits that would have required Exxon to mitigate the bust they had created. Exxon had no shutdown plan for Colony, nor was a plan required. Colorado land reclamation laws, however, were clearly in place and Exxon estimated it would spend $30 million revegetating the shale cliffs it had sought to mine. But why is the landscape better protected than the people who live there? Reclamation should exist for communities of people as well as for ecosystems of mule deer and red-tailed hawks. The Colorado River Valley reeled from the combined economic chaos of drastic falloffs in all the energy industries — oil shale, gas, coal, oil, and uranium.

Garfield County did a fine job in dealing with the impacts of the boom. In fact, few local governments in rural America have ever dealt so effectively with such massive industrial development. The bust became a disaster because no shutdown laws were in place. In the future, all permits for mining development should have shutdown clauses. Garfield County did not have such a legal stipulation in its mining permits, yet Exxon had bust provisions in its own legal contracts, and Tosco had a shutdown clause that forced Exxon to buy out Tosco's 40 percent interest in the Colony Project at a multimillion-dollar profit. Industry failed to provide for a shutdown in dealing with the county, but made certain that it could minimize its own financial liability if a shutdown occurred. Charles Pence, the consummate community builder of Battlement Mesa, explained a tiny clause he inserted in all his agreements with contractors and subcontractors. He says:

In our contracts with our contractors we had a paragraph that [stated] in the event the project was shut down certain things would happen and the contract would be canceled. A certain formula came into play for compensating the contractor. As a result, I didn't have a single claim from a contractor or a single lawsuit in the time I was there. In the contract, we had language that was standard that dealt with closing in the event we shut down the project before the contract was terminated. I never for a minute thought that would be invoked, but it turned out that it saved us a lot of agony. I put it there because I've got a lot of scar tissue from things that happened in the past, and I felt, well, it'll be a lot simpler if both of us know what is going in [to the agreement]. The wording was a little different in each one, but basically it said "in the event of termination or marked decrease of activity of the Colony Oil Shale Project [that] will impact the need for goods and services and/or product over the term of the contract, then the contractor will be paid for work completed" plus some percentage that would allow [contractors] to demobilize.[30]

So Exxon had shutdown agreements when the county did not.

Exxon protected itself, but the giant corporation made no provisions to protect communities in the Colorado River Valley. Consequently, these communities had to shoulder enormous economic

Page 24-A The Aspen Times May 6, 1982
SAL A. MANDER

Sal A. Mander cartoon. *Courtesy of* The Aspen Times.

burdens. For example, small towns had to absorb the costs of medical services the citizens could not pay for themselves. Boom-and-bust clients created a $400,000 deficit for Clagett Memorial Hospital in Rifle, and the hospital in Meeker experienced similar difficulties.

The chaos that Garfield County was forced into with the shutdown announcement on Black Sunday was compounded by the fact that it took twenty-four days before corporate plans for an "orderly shutdown" fully emerged.[31] Exxon representatives had no contingency plans for a bust; the company believed its own rhetoric and at no management level within the huge corporation had anyone prepared delay or abandonment plans for the Colony Project. At one point, Battlement Mesa employees even considered bulldozing unfinished buildings.

Faced with massive social disruption in the Colorado River Valley, Reverend Lynn Evans and other concerned community members had a novel solution:

We went to them as an organization called Lift Up. At that time [Exxon owned] a lot of real estate in Rifle. They bought their executives' — or their white collar folks' — houses when they left town. So Exxon owned an awful lot of property in Rifle. I'd hate to guess how many houses, a couple of hundred, though. We wanted a couple of those houses for people to stay in. We had teenagers being thrown out because of stress in the family. We had women being abused and run out. We had people being foreclosed on and being literally moved into the street. We had a lot of that stuff going on, especially at first, and we wanted — the deal we offered Exxon was that if they gave us the keys to a couple of their houses we would take care of them. We'd put it in writing that we'd hand the houses back to them at the end of three years, or whatever, in as good a shape as we got them. We'd paint them up. If a window [got] broken we'd replace it. We'd keep the plumbing. We'd take care of all that if [they] just gave us the real estate on a long-term lease, about a year or so. But they didn't go for that. Their response to us was, "We don't owe you anything. You were greedy. We didn't promise you that the merry-go-round would never stop. If you jumped on and got hurt that's your fault. Why should we pay for that?"[32]

Operation Lift Up and the Pastoral Center continued their work nonetheless. To its credit, Exxon finally gave the center $5,000 and has continued to support other worthwhile projects, including the Flight for Life helicopter at St. Mary's Hospital in Grand Junction, that had been initiated as an emergency medical service for oil shale workers. But the damage has been done. Whatever credibility sincere employees like Charles Pence had earned was destroyed in the aftermath of Black Sunday. During the beginning of the boom, Exxon, U.S.A. president Randall Meyer was quoted in the *Rocky Mountain News* as saying, "We want to make sure that our coming does not cause undue dislocation in a community," Meyer declared. "And, once we are there, we are prepared to carry our share of the load. We want to be welcome in an area over a long period of time and to be able to operate in other areas where our reputation may precede us, so we conduct ourselves accordingly."[33] Reverend Lynn Evans has a few words about Exxon's reputation after Black Sunday:

I still get mad at Exxon. Somebody asked me one time, Lynn, how long you gonna stay in that little church — because I've had chances to move on to supposedly bigger and better kinds of things, [but] I want to be here when Exxon wants to come back. I'll stay a thousand years if I have to. When those turkeys come back and want in again, oh, am I gonna make them pay. I still have that kind of bitterness and anger at being worked over by the big corporations. The real old-timers, they just kinda laugh and slough it off. It's happened to them so many times before that they can handle it. I won't tell them [the oil companies] they can't come. They will anyway. I can't stop them. Yeah, I'll cry louder. I've got more history. I don't have any illusions about the president of Exxon ever hearing that even, but some of those

In 1983, Ken Smith loaded one of the last shipments of oil produced at Anvil Points and the Paraho site. Now, the New Paraho seeks to make oil shale competitive, not for oil production but for the manufacture of oil shale asphalt. *Photograph by Randall Teeuwen.*

middle management folks will have to deal with me. And they'll wish I wasn't here, because I will remember.[34]

An opportunity exists to dispel the lingering bitterness that remains in the Colorado River Valley. Unlike the Midwest, where entrenched corporations hold communities hostage by threatening to relocate if wage and tax concessions are not met, in the resource-rich areas of the West, mineral extraction must occur where the resources are found. Consequently, local and state officials have leverage via zoning regulations and land use permits required of all industrial developers. Combining bust mitigation plans and procedures with land use permits should become standard. For all those corporate promises given and promises broken, goodwill earned and goodwill lost, the most important aspect of any bust mitigation plan or delay-and-abandonment clause should be economic diversification. Carefully written zoning regulations and revised environmental impact statement criteria are essential to prevent international corporations from riding roughshod over small communities. Local governments are serving notice that they have important obligations to their constituents that they intend to meet.

With the ending of the hundred-year history of oil shale development in the Colorado River Valley comes the beginning of a deeper awareness of the rights of rural communities to their own salvation and security. For resource development in the West, the issue is clear. Radical swings in international markets cannot be anticipated. Corporate responsibility must be spelled out to the letter; it cannot be assumed. Grandiose promises and projections mean nothing in the face of declining prices. Talk is cheap when oil gets cheaper.

Seven years after Black Sunday, experts are predicting long gasoline lines by the mid-1990s. The vast Tell Ertl oil shale holdings have been sold to Shell Oil Company for $37 million, and critics and congressmen complain about the settlement of half-century-old oil shale claims. Exxon has finished the golf course, clubhouse, and swimming pool at Battlement Mesa and built 200 new townhouse units. The U.S. Geological Survey has even published a new, comprehensive professional paper titled "Oil Shale, Water Resources, and Valuable Minerals of the Piceance Basin, Colorado."[35]

Yet the larger issues of capital versus community will continue to plague the West and the nation as the economy shifts, the population ages, traditional industries fail, and major corporate employers vacate the premises. "Boomtown blues" are not limited to the West, but it is there that the historical cycle is most pronounced. It is there that the cycle must end. Consistent with the recent upswing in conservative ideology is the belief that local, not federal, control is the more appropriate form of government. New legal ground has been broken with rural counties stipulating requirements and provisions for multinational corporations doing business in those counties. The next step is to insure that both boom and bust provisions become standard in the local government regulations of any resource community not blessed with economic diversity.

Bernard DeVoto was correct in calling the West a "plundered province." The recent oil shale boom in the Colorado River Valley was blatantly manipulated from the start without adequate consideration for the people whose lives would be most affected. The bitter irony of a major oil shale project called Colony and the ephemeral commitment of a fickle Congress to "the moral equivalent of war" must not be forgotten. Despite impressive gains in the intermountain West after World War II, only the oasis cities of Denver, Phoenix, Tucson, Albuquerque, and Salt Lake City are economically diverse enough to withstand drastic economic shifts. And contrary to much recent scholarship in western history, there has been little change for small communities. The rural oil shale boom and bust is the classic case in point.[36]

As *Boomtown Blues* goes to press in the autumn of 1989, Exxon remains the big kid on the block, and Battlement Mesa has become a haven for 1,800 upscale retirees. Right after the bust, Exxon did almost anything to get renters into Battlement Mesa apartments, and its initial strategy welcomed retirees on limited budgets. Now those people have been pushed out. The eighteen-hole championship golf course is complete and, today, only well-to-do retirees can afford Exxon's "city on a hill." Animosity within the small town of Parachute continues, for, though locals can work on Battlement Mesa, few area retirees can afford to live there. Though Exxon provided some low-rent apartments for the elderly, corporate hubris continues. What Exxon would do with their housing in the event of major oil shale development remains unknown.[37]

Housing prices have stabilized and even improved since 1985, but Armand Hammer's Occidental Oil Corporation has abandoned its much-heralded "in situ" shale plant, throwing more people out of work. The oil corporations are still squabbling about their local taxes and suing Garfield County because they feel their taxes are too high. Union's oil shale plant sputters along with ever-increasing threats of closing down altogether, casting doubts on the job security of their 500 local employees. (Union shut down once before, in the 1950s.)[38] A national plant closings bill finally passed Congress; it may help to prevent boom-and-bust swings in the future, or the legislation may affect only existing industrial plants, not those being built as Exxon's Colony Project was in 1982.

In retrospect, Black Sunday on the Western Slope was the falling domino that sent the "oil patch" states of Oklahoma, Texas, and Louisiana into an economic tailspin. The oil shale bust also helped create the "new poor" in the oil patch — white oil workers out of jobs and on the move. Because of low oil prices, the Texas real estate market is in shambles and Texas savings and loans totter on the brink of insolvency.[39]

As always, the price of oil continues to be a major factor. From its 1981 high of $41 a barrel to its 1986 low of $11, oil production continues to shrink in the United States, putting us in an even more precarious position than before OPEC began its embargo. We have lost valuable refining capabilities and the count of oil rigs actively searching for new sources of crude is perilously low. Texas, for example, had as many as 1,300 working rigs operating in 1981, but only 281 rigs operated in 1988.[40] A recent report from the U.S. Energy Department claims that oil will stay below $20 per barrel through 1994. Other experts say there may be a serious oil shortage in the future.[41] Ominously, our dependence on foreign oil will increase to 55 percent of our daily usage by the year 2000. (During the energy crisis in 1973, our dependence on foreign oil was only 36 percent.)[42] Yet oil shale may no longer be the energy answer. As reporter Jon Klusmire states in a recent issue of High Country News, "In addition to being intertwined with the topsy-turvy world oil market, oil shale is also locked in a race with improved energy efficiency and development of alternative liquid fuels based on alcohol, biomass and natural gas." [43]

Environmentalists and irate congressmen howl about the "great oil shale giveaway" of 1986, when 252,000 acres changed hands for $2.50 an acre in the final settlement of decades-old oil shale claims by the Reagan administration. Actually, the federal government did not really give away land at $2.50 an acre; instead it simply processed old mining claims that had been held up for years. Yet the dispute rages, and once again the public feels betrayed by oil shale entreprenuers.

The old Paraho Oil Company research facility has become the New Paraho, with plans to turn oil shale into asphalt. Perhaps the very qualities of the "rubber rock" that have confounded petroleum engineers for years may at last be put to beneficial use filling America's potholes. Test strips of oil shale asphalt have been laid on state highways.

This 1989 photograph shows the New Paraho Research & Development Center seven miles west of Rifle. Test strips of oil shale asphalt have been laid in Colorado, Utah, and Wyoming. If the tests prove successful, a new industry will develop. *Courtesy of New Paraho.*

After surviving through the Great Depression, the First National Bank of Rifle folded because of the oil shale collapse and the failure of real estate loans that accounted for 54 percent of the bank's assets. The building is now a restaurant. Here, local citizens line up to receive the balance of their bank accounts from the Federal Deposit Insurance Company the week of August 27, 1986. *Photograph by the author.*

Exxon's 8,800 acres of shale lands for the Colony Project remain idle, except for environmental monitoring needed to maintain the permits. As synthetic fuels coordinator B. D. Wims explains, the project is on hold until "the time frame is correct." Exxon maintains the Colony Project and continues to do some research into mine shale technology so that it has "an option to participate when the time is right."[44] As for oil geologists, their employment picture has not brightened. With the continued low price for crude oil, local folklore in Colorado these days includes this joke: "How do you find an oil geologist in a Denver restaurant?" Answer: "Just say, 'Hey waiter!'"[45]

Geologists may be out of work, but resort construction in the Colorado Rockies is booming. New gas wells are being sunk in the valley, and the economic stimulus from international ski resorts like Vail, Beaver Creek, and Aspen has worked wonders at decreasing unemployment and filling up available housing in New Castle, Silt, and Rifle. There are plenty of jobs for workers if they are willing to commute one and a half to two hours each way, but there is no economic diversification. The local economy is healthier than it has been at any point since May of 1982. Seven years after Black Sunday, the energy bust is finally over but only at great personal and financial cost; the economy of Colorado and the Western Slope is still painfully vulnerable to international market conditions. In 1986, Colorado bankruptcies rose by 55.8 percent. Throughout the energy states, from Alaska to New Mexico, a new bumper sticker is appearing on ten-year-old Cadillac and Lincoln luxury cars. The sticker states in no uncertain terms "Lord, let there be another oil boom and let me not piss this one away."

Meanwhile, the Reverend Lynn Evans has left the Colorado River Valley. He accepted a church east of the Rockies where he can build a new life for himself. Former Garfield County Commissioner Eugene L. "Jim" Drinkhouse, once one of the most powerful men on the Western Slope, has not been so lucky. On August 1, 1988, he was sentenced to one year of unsupervised probation and fined $4,110 for forging his wife's signature to obtain a bank loan.[46] Bankruptcy, marital problems, and divorce have plagued many valley residents, and Drinkhouse is no exception.

Rifle, Colorado, has long called itself the "oil shale capital of the world." The First National Bank there weathered the Depression in the 1930s, and bank administrators bet heavily on oil shale in the late 1970s. They lost, and the bank folded. Today, the bank is a restaurant, and the oil shale survivors who have remained in the community dine in quiet comfort in rooms where they once squirmed under the scrutiny of loan officers intent on double-digit interest rates and imminent foreclosures. The restaurant is a popular place, and residents return to laugh about their bad debts and think about the past. In quieter moments, they even speculate about oil shale and the future.

Endnotes

Notes to Introduction

1. The estimate of the recoverable oil amount is based on veins more than 5 feet thick with a richness between 25 and 60 gallons per ton. See Donald C. Duncan and Vernon E. Swanson, *Organic Rich Shale of the U.S. and World Land Areas*, U.S. Geological Survey Circular 523 (Washington, D.C.: U.S. Government Printing Office, 1966). Other estimates vary from a high of 800 billion barrels, if shales that yield 10 to 25 gallons per ton are included, to the extremely conservative 52 billion barrel figure from the "Research News" column titled "Oil Shale: A Huge Resource of Low-Grade Fuel," in *Science,* vol. 184, no. 4143 (21 June 1974): 1271.

2. S. David Freeman, *Energy: The New Era* (New York: Vintage Books, 1974), p. 77. This text, like so many others, predicted a totally new alignment of international power and money based on the actions of OPEC and other cartels. A book on the same theme is Peter R. Odell's, *Oil and World Power* (Middlesex, England: Penguin Books, 1979).

3. Charles F. Cortese and B. Jones,"The Sociological Analysis of Boomtowns," *Western Sociological Review,* vol. 8 (1977): 76–90.

4. This description of Gillette, Wyoming, comes from the controversial paper "Social Consequences of Boomtown Growth in Wyoming," presented by El Dean V. Kohrs at the Regional Meeting of the American Association for the Advancement of Science at Laramie, Wyoming, in 1974. Numerous social scientists have objected to Kohrs's stereotyping of construction workers. Also see Montana Energy Advisory Council, *Energy Information Booklet: Supplement* (Helena, MT.: Office of the Lt. Governor, 1975).

5. Wallace Stegner, *The Sound of Mountain Water* (New York: Dutton, 1980), p. 20.

6. William R. Freudenburg, "Boomtown's Youth: The Differential Impacts of Rapid Community Growth on Adolescents and Adults," *American Sociological Review,* vol. 49, no. 5 (October 1984): 703.

7. See Kenneth P. Wilkinson, James G. Thompson, Robert R. Reynolds, Jr., and Lawrence M. Ostresh, "Local Social Disruption and Western Energy Development," *Pacific Sociological Review,* vol. 25, no. 3 (July 1982): 275–296, with commentary titled "Balance and Bias in Boomtown Research," pp. 323–338, by William R. Freudenburg.

8. John S. Gilmore,"Boom Towns May Hinder Energy Resource Development," *Science,* vol. 191, no. 551–2 (13 February 1976): 535–540.

9. These statements are paraphrased from the numerous speeches, reports, and publications that predicted an imminent energy shortage that would necessitate synthetic fuels development, despite the fact that technologies for oil shale and

coal gasificiation were unproved. The best collection of such predictions is found in Terrell J. Minger and Sherry D. Oaks, eds., *Growth Alternatives for the Rocky Mountain West: Papers from the Vail Symposium V* (Boulder, Colo.: Westview Press, 1976).

10. John Wesley Powell, *Report on the Lands of the Arid Region of the United States* (Washington, D.C.: U.S. Government Printing Office, 1878).

11. Exxon's oil shale "white paper," officially titled "The Role of Synthetic Fuels in the United States Energy Future," was first presented to Club 20 at Grand Junction, Colorado, on 25 August 1980. Exxon refused to give me a copy of the "white paper" and has ceased making it available because the paper severely damaged Exxon's credibility and weakened the strength of its other "white papers" that had been considered major policy statements by banks, brokerage houses, etc. My copy came from the files of the *Rifle Tribune*.

12. Edward Abbey, cited in Terrell J. Minger, ed., *Vail Symposium/Six — The Future of Human Settlements in the Rocky Mountain West* (Vail, Colo.: The Printery, 1978), p. 227.

13. The Robert Wamsley interview is from *Rifle, Colorado: Boomtown of the Seventies,* a videotape produced by Candi Harper for Grassroots Television, Aspen, Colorado, 1975.

14. The best comparison to a natural disaster is found in Kai T. Erikson, *Everything in Its Path: Destruction of Community in the Buffalo Creek Flood* (New York: Simon & Schuster, 1976).

15. Bernard DeVoto, "The West: A Plundered Province,"*Harper's Magazine*, no. 169 (August 1934): 335–364.

16. Patricia Nelson Limerick, *The Legacy of Conquest* (New York: W. W. Norton, 1987) and William G. Robbins, "The 'Plundered Province' Thesis and the Recent Historiography of the American West," *Pacific Historical Review*, 60 (1986): 577–597.

17. Gene M. Gressley, "The West: Past, Present, and Future," *Western Historical Quarterly*, 71–1 (January 1986): 5–24.

Notes to Chapter 1

1. Walter Gallacher, *The White River National Forest 1891–1981,* rev. ed. (Glenwood Springs, Colo.: White River National Forest Regional Office, 1983), p. 46. Citizens of Rio Blanco County, who now profit from tourism and hunting on the Flat Tops Wilderness, initially opposed establishment of the White River Forest Reserve (as it was first termed). The *Meeker Herald* of 10 October 1891 urged, "Citizens of Rio Blanco County rise in your might and protest against this damnable outrage. Will you allow the county to be robbed of vast taxable property? We think not. Then be up and doing!"

2. Frank Waters, *The Colorado* (Chicago: Swallow Press [1946], 1984), p. 361.

3. Information on Dominguez and Escalante's crossing into the Colorado River Valley is from Jerome C. Smiley, *History of Colorado,* (Chicago: Lewis Publishing Co., 1913), 1:20. See Joseph Cerquone, *In Behalf of the Light: The Dominguez and Escalante Expedition of 1776* (Denver: Paragon Press, 1976). For a recent translation of their journals, see Angelico Chavez, trans., and Ted J. Warner, ed., *The Dominguez-Escalante Journal: Their Expedition Through Colorado, Utah, Arizona, and New Mexico in 1776* (Provo, Utah: Brigham Young University Press, 1976). Some historians dispute the fact that the friars crossed at Streit's Flat. Other writers argue that they came up the North Fork of the Gunnison River and over Muddy Creek through Balm of Gilead Park to camp near Collbran, then they rode over Battlement Mesa to cross the Colorado River above DeBeque before going north up Roan Creek. Coming down Divide Creek and crossing at Streit's Flat seems a more logical route. Dominguez and Escalante's historic journey was duplicated during the nation's bicentennial.

4. John Wesley Powell, *The Exploration of the Colorado River and Its Canyons* (New York: Dover [1895], 1961), pp. 117–119. Wallace Stegner, in *Beyond the Hundredth Meridian* (Lincoln: University of Nebraska Press, [1953], 1982), analyzes some interesting errors in Powell's book in which he combined expeditions that were actually undertaken several years apart.

5. Powell, *Report on the Lands of the Arid Region of the United States* (Washington, D.C.: U.S. Government Printing Office, 1878). For a recent reprint of this important work, see Wallace Stegner, ed., *Report on the Lands of the Arid Region of the United States with a More Detailed Account of the Lands of Utah* by John Wesley Powell (Cambridge, MA: The Belknap Press of Harvard University Press, 1962).

6. William H. Goetzmann, *Exploration and Empire: The Explorer and the Scientist in the Winning of the American West* (New York: Random House, 1966), p. 498.

7. F. V. Hayden, *Tenth Annual Report of the United States Geological and Geographical Survey of the Territories Embracing Colorado and Parts of Adjacent Territories Being a Report of Progress of the Exploration for the Year 1876* (Washington, D.C.: U.S. Government Printing Office, 1878), pp. xvi.

8. Jonathan Lash and Laura King, eds., *The Synfuels Manual* (New York: Natural Resources Defense Counsel, 1983), p. 12.

9. Hayden, *Tenth Annual Report,* pp. 170, 173.

10. Ibid., p. 172.

11. Ibid., p. xviii.

12. Ibid., p. 333.

13. Alice Wright, "Room for All of Us," *Westworld* (Sunday magazine of the *Grand Junction Daily Sentinel*), 14 August 1977, p. 6. The article is an interview with Daisy Hurlburt Green, daughter of the founder of Parachute, Colorado.

14. Hayden, "Report of George B. Chittenden, C .E., Topographer of the White River Division, 1876," pp. 351–352.

15. Ibid., p. xviii.

16. Lena M. Urquhart, *Cold Snows of Carbonate* (Denver: Golden Bell Press, 1967), p. 7. Also see Andrew Gulliford, *Garfield County, Colorado: The First Hundred Years 1883–1983* (Glenwood Springs, Colo: Grand River Museum Alliance, 1983), and David F. Halaas and Gerald C. Morton, "Boom and Bust," *Colorado Heritage News*, no. 1 & 2, (1983), pp. 9–24.

17. Wallace Stegner, *The Big Rock Candy Mountain* (Lincoln: University of Nebraska Press [1938]), 1983), p. 30.

18. Sarah Jane Boulton, "Sketch of Divide Creek and Dry Hollow from Early Days." (Mansucript from the collection of the author, 1954, rev. 1956), p. 3. The first settlers on Divide Creek not only walked into the area from Leadville, but they walked back for supplies. One settler returned to purchase a batch of bread dough, one box of 45.70 shells, salt, and flour. He brought the items back on a sled.

19. Erlene Durrant Murray, *Lest We Forget: A Short History of Early Grand Valley, Colorado, Originally Called Parachute, Colorado*, 3d ed. (Grand Junction, Colo.: Quahada Corporation, 1981), pp. 1–2.

20. Information on families of settlers and their countries of origin is from *Progressive Men of Western Colorado* (Chicago: A & W Bowen Co., 1905). Also see Len Shoemaker, *Roaring Fork Chronicle*, 3d ed. (Silverton, Colo.: Sundance Publications, [1958], 1979).

21. Private homestead filings on the public domain ceased with the passage of the Taylor Grazing Act in 1934. In her memoirs, *Dry Hollow Ranch Memories* (Silt, Colo.: privately printed, 1965), Margaret Irene Trusty Boulton writes, "In the early 1930s, we all decided to file on homesteads to provide for ample grazing in the future. To prove up on these we had to fence them, build cabins and establish homes."

22. John Grigor, "Rounding Up the Strays." (Poetry manuscript in the Western History Collection of the Rifle Public Library, Rifle, Colorado, 1921). Cowboy poetry, like cowboy songs, is its own folk genre. See David Brose, "Cowboy Poets Maintain Long Tradition," *Colorado Heritage News* (January 1986) and Carol A. Edison, ed., *Cowboy Poetry from Utah: An Anthology* (Salt Lake City: Utah Folklife Center, 1985).

23. Andrew Gulliford, *America's Country Schools* (Washington, D.C.: Preservation Press, 1984), p. 242.

24. Theodore Roosevelt, "A Colorado Bear Hunt," *Chronicles of Colorado*, ed. Frederick R. Rinehart (Boulder, Colo.: Roberts Rinehart, 1984), pp. 149–150. Excerpted from Roosevelt's *Outdoor Pastimes of an American Hunter* (New York: Charles Scribners & Sons, 1908).

25. Ibid., p. 153.

26. Ibid., pp. 134, 137.

27. Elmo R. Richardson, *The Politics of Conservation: Crusades and Controversies 1897–1913* (Berkeley: University of California Press, 1962), p. 9. Also see Michael McCarthy, *Hour of Trial, The Conservation Movement in Colorado and the West, 1891–1917* (Norman: University of Oklahoma Press, 1977).

28. Pinchot arrived in Glenwood Springs one month before the law would take effect. He read a personal letter from President Roosevelt that began, "In dealing with this problem I should like to have you remember that recent investigations have demonstrated the destructive character of the Free Range System." Fred Light, from Snowmass, Colorado, purposely let his cattle trespass on Forest Service lands in June 1907. The entire western cattle industry watched the development of the Fred Light test case as it went before the United States Supreme Court in 1911. In the intervening years, there were numerous violations. For a detailed analysis of the local effects of the case see Jim Cayton, "The Fred Light Test Case." (Manuscript, in the possession of the White River National Forest, Rifle Office, Rifle, Colorado, n.d.).

29. Proof that blacks worked in Garfield County coal mines is obtained from photographs in the collection of the Frontier Museum and Historical Society, Glenwood Springs, Colorado. Black miners were photographed at the South Canyon mines, ca. 1906. See Gulliford, *Garfield County, Colorado*, p. 14.

30. Information on the Boston and Colorado Coal Company is from promotional literature in the collection of the Frontier Museum and Historical Society, Glenwood Springs, Colorado. The best publication on the Garfield County coal industry is Anna Johnson and Kathleen Yajko, *The Elusive Dream: A Relentless Quest for Coal in Western Colorado* (Glenwood Springs, Colo.: Gran Farnum Printing, 1983).

31. *First Biennial Report of the Bureau of Labor Statistics of the State of Colorado, 1886–1888* (Denver: Collier & Cleaveland Lithography Co., 1888), p. 117.

32. Dave Fishell, "The Vulcan Mine Disasters: Tragedy at New Castle," *Grand Junction Daily Sentinel*, 18 February 1979, p. 6. The front page of the *New Castle News*, 18 December 1913, which announced the 1913 disaster, is permanently displayed behind the front desk in the Garfield County Public Library. For additional information, see Libby Doak, "The New Castle Mine Disaster." (Manuscript in the Garfield County Public Library, New Castle, Colorado, n.d.).

33. Mary Wade and Gladys Prendergast, "History of New Castle." (Manuscript in the Garfield County Public Library, New Castle, Colorado, 1966), p. 8. For specific names of businesses, see Judy Haptonstall, "A History of New Castle." (Manuscript in the Garfield County Public Library, New Castle, Colorado, 1977), p. 5.

34. *New Castle News*, 11 January 1896. The best general reference that places the New Castle miners' disputes into larger perspective is George S. McGovern and Leonard F. Guttridge, *The Great Coalfield War* (Boston: Houghton Mifflin, 1972). For a recent appraisal of coal baron John C. Osgood, see Sylvia Ruland, *The Lion of Redstone* (Boulder, Colo.: Johnson Books, 1981). Also see Eric Margolis, "Colorado's Coal People: Images from Turn-of-the-Century Coal Communities," *Colorado Heritage*, no. 4 (1984), pp. 10–24, and "Western Coal Mining As a Way of Life: An Oral History of the Colorado Coal Miners to 1914,"*Journal of the West*, vol. 24, no. 3 (July 1985).

35. *New Castle News*, 18 February 1896.

36. Ibid.

37. Ruth Louise Duffy, Silt, Colorado. Interviewed by author on 13 June 1977. She and her family were living in New Castle at the time of the second Vulcan explosion. She vividly remembers seeing the body of a mining victim on her family's dining room table when she was nearly ten. Text of this interview is in the Western History Department of the Denver Public Library.

38. Wade and Prendergast, "History of New Castle," p. 4. There were enough Italian miners to establish a New Castle chapter of The Sons of Christopher Columbus.

39. McGovern and Guttridge, *The Great Coalfield War*, p. 162. After making his crass offer of $75 per family toward funeral expenses, the new owner died one month later from poisonous gases inhaled at the entrance to the Vulcan. In a unique turn of events, Josephine Roche, a social reformer with a master's degree in social work from Columbia University, assumed control of the giant Rocky Mountain Fuel Company in March 1929. As David Fridtjof Halaas writes in "Josephine Roche, 1886–1976: Social Reformer, Mine Operator," *Colorado Heritage News*, (March 1985), p. 4, "Rival coal mine operators received the news with shock and dismay. She was, after all, a progressive who supported labor, a radical who held dangerous beliefs, a social reformer, and a woman meddling in a man's world."

40. Hayden, *Tenth Annual Report* (Chittenden report on the White River District), p. 352.

41. From the Antlers Orchard and Development Company papers courtesy of Lovena Michelsen, 4951 233 Road, Rifle, Colorado. Her parents were German-Russian immigrants who came to the valley to work in beet fields. In 1899, Bulletin No. 1 of the Colorado Sugar Manufacturing Company advertised "500 farmers wanted in the Grand Valley to raise sugar beets for The Colorado Sugar Manufacturing Co." in its Grand Junction factory.

42. Stegner, *Beyond the Hundredth Meridian*, p. 308.

43. Murray, *Lest We Forget*, pp. 80–83. Reading Club of Rifle, Colorado, comp., *Rifle Shots: The Story of Rifle, Colorado* (Rifle, Colo.: Reading Club of Rifle, Colorado, 1973), pp. 138–141.

44. Murray, *Lest We Forget*, p. 49.

Notes to Chapter 2

1. Data on the agricultural base of Garfield County between 1950 and 1960 is from John S. Gilmore and Mary K. Duff, *Policy Analysis for Rural Development and Growth Management in Colorado* (Denver: Industrial Economics Division — Denver Research Institute, University of Denver, 1973), pp. A–24. This document was prepared for the Colorado Rural Development Commission.

2. Estimates of the capitalization requirements of oil shale plants ranged from $500,000, as advanced by Floyd W. Parsons in "Oil from Shale: Everybody's Business," *Saturday Evening Post* (20 March 1920), p. 37, to $5,000,000, as stated in Paul L. Russell, *History of Western Oil Shale* (East Brunswick, N.J.: Center for Professional Advancement, 1980), p. 12. In contrast to those figures, few oil shale companies spent as much as $100,000 on their processing plants.

3. Russell, *History of Western Oil Shale*, p. 5.

4. William Edward Beilke, "Colorado's First Oil Shale Rush, 1910–1930" (Ph.D. diss., University of Colorado, 1984), p. 13. This is a very well researched and exhaustive economic history of the first oil shale boom, though it does not describe the boom's impact on local communities.

5. Ibid., p. 14.

6. E. G. Woodruff and David T. Day, *Oil Shale of Northwestern Colorado and Northeastern Utah*, U.S. Geological Survey Bulletin 581-A (Washington, D.C.: U.S. Government Printing Office, 1914) and Dean E. Winchester, *Oil Shale in Northwestern Colorado and Adjacent Areas*, U.S. Geological Survey Bulletin 641-F (Washington, D.C.: U.S. Government Printing Office, 1916). The tremendous impact of the Winchester bulletin on the first oil shale rush was confirmed by John W. Savage, Jr., grandson of one of the earliest surveyors of oil shale claims. Oral history interview by author with John W. Savage, Jr., 1122 293 Road, Rifle, Colorado, 6 January 1986.

7. Beilke, "Colorado's First Oil Shale Rush," p. 24, and Russell, *History of Western Oil Shale*, p. 5. Estimates on the number of barrels of oil contained in oil shale continue to rise and now stand at almost two trillion barrels, though less than half of that is potentially recoverable. For information on the oil shale acres placed in the Naval Oil Shale Reserve, see V. C. Anderson, *The Oil Shale Industry* (New York: F. A. Stokes, 1920), p. 5.

8. Walter Gallacher, "Shale's Beginnings: Doris Flynn Remembers," *Colorado River Journal* (Summer 1983), pp. 8–9. Among oil shale companies incorporated at this time were: American Shale Refining Company and its subsidiary Book Cliff Shale Company, Colorado Carbon Company, Colorado Shale Products Company, Columbia Oil Shale Company, Honolulu Consolidated Oil Company, Index Oil & Gas Company, Overland Mining & Refining Company, Monarch Oil Shale Company, Mount Logan Oil Shale & Refining Company, Mount Mamm Company, Prairie Oil & Gas Company, Shale Oil Company, Searchlight Oil Shale and Refining Company, Standard Shale Products Company, and the Ventura Oil Company.

9. Doris Stratton Flynn, New Castle Drugstore. Interviewed by the author on 22 July 1977. Text of this interview is in the Western History Department of the Denver Public Library. For a historical comparison to other mining promoters, see Lewis Atherton, "The Mining Promoter in the Trans-Mississippi West," *Western Historical Quarterly*, vol. 1, no. 1 (January 1970): 35–50.

10. Stock certificate #179, issued by the Oil Shale Mining Company on 18 August 1917 (800 shares at $1 per share), displays a dozen oil derrick frames with three

gushing wells — one at each side of the certificate and one in the middle. But heated oil shale drips; it never gushes and certainly not in a large, upward plume. Stock certificate facsimile in the Savage Family Oil Shale Collection, Rifle, Colorado.

11. Colorado Shale and Metals Company's precious metal dollar amounts are from Beilke, "Colorado's First Oil Shale Rush," p. 34, citing *Rocky Mountain News,* 15 October 1922. Russell gives different dollar amounts for the same company in *History of Western Oil Shale,* p. 23.

12. Colorado Oil, Shale and Refining Corporation incorporation papers facsimile in the Savage Family Oil Shale Collection, Rifle, Colorado.

13. Bureau of Mines, State of Colorado, *The Oil Shales of Northwestern Colorado,* Bulletin no. 8 (Denver: Eames Brothers, 1919), p. 1.

14. Guy Elliott Mitchell, "Billions of Barrels of Oil Locked Up in Rocks," *National Geographic,* vol. 33, no. 2 (February 1918: 195–196. Other contemporary articles on the petroleum shortage and oil shale include: Frank Crane, "When the Oil Gives Out," *Current Opinion,* 69 (August 1920); David T. Day, "Oil Famine and the Remedy," *Review of Reviews* 62 (September 1920); Arthur D. Little, "The Fuel Problem," *Atlantic Monthly,* 127 (February 1921); Frank Glenn, "Defeating the Oil Famine," *Century,* 101 (February 1921): 544; C. Lorimore Colburn, "Our Future Supply of Oil," *DuPont Magazine,* 20 (November 1926): 11, and "Oil Shale — Our Future Oil Supply," *Scientific American,* 136 (May 1927): 342.

15. Parsons, "Oil From Shale," p. 34.

16. Gallacher, "Shale's Beginnings," p. 9.

17. Beilke, "Colorado's First Oil Shale Rush," p. 33. He also states that one inspired promoter even attempted to produce oil shale perfume as a "seemingly lucrative product." Other by-products that were considered but never produced include electrical insulation, battery boxes, and automobile steering wheels.

18. The oil shale patent medicine business did not thrive for long. The Food and Drug Administration looked askance at such products and prohibited all distribution of them beginning with injunctions against the C. D. Smith Drug Company. Doris Flynn responded to the federal prohibition of Shalo Products by earning a pharmacist's degree in 1928, after which she continued to make patent medicines.

19. Beilke, "Colorado's First Oil Shale Rush," p. 31. For a brief overview of oil shale history with some references to by-products, see Steven F. Mehls, "Waiting for the Boom: Colorado Shale-Oil Development," *Journal of the West,* vol. 21, no. 4 (October 1982): 11–16.

20. Edwin E. Slossen, "Food from Shale," *Scientific Monthly,* 21 (July 1925): 106.

21. Record of Minutes of the Mt. Logan Oil Shale Mining & Refining Company, p. 3. Original in the Savage Family Oil Shale Collection, Rifle, Colorado. Additional Mt. Logan materials include a typescript by H. D. Locke, former secretary of the corporation, titled "History and Development of the Mt. Logan Oil Shale

Mining & Refining Company," 15 May 1964, and a circular issued by the company in 1920.

22. Mt. Logan Oil Shale Mining & Refining Company circular, p. 4. H. D. Locke, the corporate secretary, writes in his typescript, "The Mt. Logan oil shale activity was encouraged at an early date by St. Louis capital," however, when oil prices went from $3.50 a barrel to about $.40 a barrel in a few years, the Company was advised by its St. Louis prospects as follows:

> When we made you the offer to finance a commerical oil shale plant, there was a shortage of oil in this country, and the price of oil was high enough to justify shale oil production. Now we have an overproduction of oil in the country, and the present price of oil would not justify extracting it from oil shale. How long this condition will last, we do not know; but if there should be a change in the near future, more favorable to an oil shale plant operation, we will contact you.

23. John W. Savage, Jr., interview, 1986. The entire question of oil shale litigation deserves a separate volume. Court records and testimony have taken up dozens of square feet of courtroom space. Beilke devotes a chapter to "Claims and Patents." Also see Frederic J. Athearn, "The Parachute That Failed to Open: Colorado's First Oil Shale Mining District, 1890–1935," *Midwest Review*, 2nd Series, no. 6 (Spring 1984): 1–12, Harry K. Savage, *The Rock That Burns* (Boulder, Colo.: Pruett Press, 1967), pp. 1–39, and Chris Welles, *The Elusive Bonanza* (New York: E. P. Dutton, 1970), pp. 131–175.

24. Beilke, "Colorado's First Oil Shale Rush," pp. 53, 55.

25. Erlene Durrant Murray, *Lest We Forget: A Short History of Early Grand Valley Colorado, Originally Called Parachute, Colorado* (Grand Junction: Quahada, Corporation, 1973), pp. 134–136. She cites the coroner's jury report and claims seven men died. Beilke claims six men died and cites Thomas S. Chamblin, ed., *The Historical Encylopedia of Colorado*, 1 (Denver: Colorado Historical Association, 1960).

26. Oil shale output figures are from Russell, *History of Western Oil Shale*, pp. 21–25. Patent certificate numbers are from Beilke, "Colorado's First Oil Shale Rush," p. 87. One of the major problems with retorting oil shale is that heated shale expands and clogs retorts, thus, the term "popcorn effect." The industry hopes to mitigate that effect with new "fluidized beds."

27. Beilke, "Colorado's First Oil Shale Rush," p. 61. Information on the renowned D. D. Potter is from A. W. Quillian III, "Oil Shale Treasure Chest and/or Pandora's Box: (Manuscript from the collection of the author, 1981), p. 4. Quillian was a senior engineer with the Union Oil Company's oil shale project.

28. Beilke, "Colorado's First Oil Shale Rush," p. 63. The *Oil Shale Outlook,* 20 April 1921, was printed in Denver and baldly stated, "This Paper is Boosting What Will Be the Greatest Industry West of the Mississippi within Ten years." As for

oil shale land prices, "In this issue it [the *Oil Shale Outlook*] records a sale of a large tract of land near DeBeque at $45 an acre, the record high price. A large tract offered last fall at $2 per acre is now held at $20 per acre. Any good, well located oil shale land offered under $50 per acre is cheap."

29. John W. Savage interview, 1986. Though different companies had failed by 1924, the federal government remained interested in oil shale. That year, President Coolidge added 23,000 acres to the Colorado reserve and 4,880 acres to the Utah reserve. The boosters never gave up. The front page of the *Grand Valley News* of 3 July 1926 was headlined, "Senator Eaton Visits Grand Valley" and stated, "Senator Eaton is vitally interested in the oil shale product and is anxious for the time to arrive when the big hills of shale will flow rivers of oil."

30. Gallacher, "Shale's Beginnings," p. 9.

31. Doris Flynn interview, 1977.

32. Mabel Moore Harness, 0187 236 Road, Silt, Colorado. Interviewed by author on 26 June 1977. Text of this interview is in the Western History Department of the Denver Public Library.

33. John Issac Dwire, 1310 Charlin, Silt, Colorado. Interviewed by author on 28 July 1977. Text of this interview is in the Western History Department of the Denver Public Library.

34. This version of this Depression hunting tale was related by Donald Havens, Silt, Colorado, in fall 1980. Other local hunting stories include tales of the pioneer who killed three deer with one shot and hunters who claimed they could imitate a bull elk's mating call by blowing into empty beer bottles. Then, of course, there are the improbable stories of downing big bucks at 300 yards by shooting with a Winchester 30-30 from a moving horse.

35. James Frederick Wickens, *Colorado in the Great Depression* (New York: Garland Publishing, 1979), pp. 8, 30.

36. Frank Deyoe Green, 1110 Charlin, Silt, Colorado. Interviewed by author on 29 June 1977. Text of this interview is in the Western History Department of the Denver Public Library.

37. Richard Lowitt, *The New Deal and the West* (Bloomington: Indiana University Press, 1984), p. 219.

38. Ibid.

39. Frank Deyoe Green interview, 1977.

40. Representative Taylor quoted in Wallace Stegner, *Beyond the Hundredth Meridian* (Lincoln: University of Nebraska Press [1953], 1982), p. 355. For Taylor's numerous contributions to the Western Slope, see Steven F. Mehls, *The Valley of Opportunity: A History of West-Central Colorado,* Cultural Resources Series no. 12 (Denver: Bureau of Land Management, 1982).

41. Lowitt, *The New Deal and the West*, pp. 8–32.

42. Andrew Gulliford and Randall Teeuwen, *The Years Ahead: Life for the Aging in Northwest Colorado* (Glenwood Springs, Colo.: Colorado Mountain College, 1977), p. 10. The authors conducted multiple interviews with Esma Lewis in

1977 and 1978 that are in the Western History Department of the Denver Public Library.

43. Doris Flynn interview, 1977. Some of that personal loyalty remained despite the chaos of the oil shale boom. Claud M. Davidson, in "Retail Facilities in Colorado Boomtowns," *Social Science Journal,* vol. 24, no. 3 (1987): 247–259, explains that "residents of agricultural communities are supportive of local business firms, and represent the most stable and dependable market group for professionals and merchants within the area." In direct contrast to this were the "boomers" who shopped for goods and services miles away from the boom communities they were impacting.

44. Wickens, *Colorado in the Great Depression,* p. 103.

45. Gulliford and Teeuwen, *The Years Ahead,* p. 9. Text of the original oral history interview of Juanita Ulibarri by Randall Teeuwen is in the Western History Department of the Denver Public Library. For the role of herbal and folk medicine in Hispanic culture, see Joe Graham, "The Role of the *Curandero* in the Mexican American Folk Medicine System in West Texas," and Francisco Guerra, "Medical Folklore in Spanish America," both in Wayland D. Hand, ed., *American Folk Medicine* (Los Angeles: University of California Press, 1976) and Robert T. Trotter and Juan Antonio Chivera, *Curanderismo: Mexican-American Folk Healing* (Athens: University of Georgia Press, 1982).

46. Jim Farris, 231 North First, Silt, Colorado. Interviewed by Randall Teeuwen on 16 August 1977. Text of this interview is in the Western History Department of the Denver Public Library.

47. Other western pioneers also utilize the mailbox motif to make symbolic statements on the transmission of culture. See Austin and Alta Fife and Henry H. Glassie, eds., *Forms Upon the Frontier,* Monograph Series, vol. 16, no. 2 (Logan: Utah State University Press, 1969), p. 11.

48. Though no published folklore articles exist for the Colorado River Valley, parallels can be found in Ronald L. Ives, "Folklore of Eastern Middle Park, Colorado," *Journal of American Folklore,* vol. 54, no. 211–212 (January–June 1941): 24–43. Ives describes the Wampus Kitty, Jackalope, Augerino, Tripodero, and a Ratchet Owl with a unique head movement.

49. Gerald D. Nash, *The American West Transformed* (Bloomington: Indiana University Press, 1985), p. 10.

50. Tell Ertl, untitled speech before the Arkansas Valley District of the Colorado Watershed Conservation Association, 5 August 1957, pp. 5–8. Ertl speech titled "Oil Shale: The Prime Mineral Resource of the Colorado River Basin," presented before the Colorado River Water Users Association in Las Vegas, Nevada, 5 August 1957, p. 3. Ertl speech titled, "Where Does an American Oil Shale Industry Stand Today?" presented before the National Western Mining and Energy Conference, 21 April 1960, p. 8. Other general information is from Dr. Ertl's resume, the rough draft of a memorandum written in 1967, the text of a talk to School District 51 Social Studies In-Service Group, on 21 January 1965, his letters, and his obituary in the *Grand Junction Daily Sentinel* of 16 January 1975.

All documents are in the possession of Joseph Fox, co-trustee of the Ertl Family Estate, Lakewood, Colorado.

51. T. Michael Crowell, "Ertl Formula for Success: Buy 50 Acres, Then Wait for the Land Rush," in "The Boomtowns: A Special Report," *Grand Junction Daily Sentinel*, 10 September 1981, p. 30.

52. "Riches in Rock," *Newsweek*, 27 May 1957, p. 87 and Frank J. Taylor, "Colorado's Fabulous Mountains of Oil," *Reader's Digest*, June 1957, pp. 132–138. Despite the rosy predictions, Union's pilot plant was shut down within a year, and engineer Tell Ertl then went to South America in 1958 to become project manager for a surface mine and prototype oil shale plant constructed by Petrobras, S.A., in Parana, Brazil.

53. "Grand Valley, Colorado: A Plan for the Development of the Grand Valley of the Colorado River Prepared by the Graduate Students of City and Regional Planning" (Report by the students, Cornell University, 1958), p. 17. Copy in the Colorado Collection of the Garfield County Public Library, New Castle, Colorado.

54. Ibid., pp. iii–v.

55. Ibid., pp. 15, 17.

56. Ibid., p. v.

57. Ibid., p. 17.

58. Ibid., p. 25.

59. Atomic Energy Commission, *The Bronco Oil Shale Study*, PNE–1400 (Washington, D.C.: U.S. Government Printing Office, 1967). This study was prepared by the United States Atomic Energy Commission, the United States Department of the Interior, CER Geonuclear Corporation, and the Lawrence Radiation Laboratory.

Notes to Chapter 3

1. For a brief note on Rock Springs Sheriff Ed Cantrell, see Joel Garreau, *The Nine Nations of North America* (New York: Avon Books, 1981), p. 293. Rock Springs was the subject of the CBS "60 Minutes" documentary that resulted in the undercover operation and the fatal shooting. Information on Gillette's raging bulldozer is from the "Straight Shots" column in *Rocky Mountain Magazine,* vol. 3, no. 4 (July/August 1981): 15. Flip McConnaughey, the city administrator of Gillette, added a bumper sticker to his car that read, "When bulldozers are outlawed, only outlaws will have bulldozers."

2. For a quick overview of western booms, see William S. Ellis, "A West Wild with Riches: Boom Times Past and Present," in *The Majestic Rocky Mountains* (Washington, D.C.: National Geographic Society, 1976): 33–53. In the social science literature, a good beginning is Charles F. Cortese and Jane Archer

Cortese, *The Social Effects of Energy Boomtowns in the West: A Partially Annotated Bibliography,* Council of Planning Librarians, Exchange Bibliography 1557, June 1978. On negative impacts, see Charles F. Cortese and B. Jones, "The Sociological Analysis of Boomtowns," *Western Sociological Review,* 8 (1977); Garth Massey, "Critical Dimensions in Urban Life — Energy Extraction and Community Collapse in Wyoming," *Urban Life,* vol. 9, no. (July 1980); Kenneth P. Wilkinson, James G. Thompson, Robert R. Reynolds, Jr., and Lawrence M. Ostresh, "Local Social Disruption and Western Energy Development, *Pacific Sociological Review,* vol. 25, no. 3 (July 1982) and commentary in the same issue by William R. Freudenburg titled "Balance and Bias in Boomtown Research."

3. Terry Thoem data from the Grand Junction *Daily Sentinel,* 18 July 1980. Also see Douglas G. Fox, Dennis J. Murphy, and Dennis Haddow, technical coordinators, *Air Quality, Oil Shale, and Wilderness — A Workshop to Identify and Protect Air Quality Related Values of the Flat Tops,* January 13–15, 1981, Glenwood Springs, Colo. USDA Forest Service, General Technical Report RM–91, Rocky Mountain Forest and Range Experiment Station (Fort Collins: Colorado State University, 1982); and David C. Sheesley and Ellen M. Leonard, "An Air Quality Strategy for Oil Shale Development," in Kathy Kellogg Peterson, ed., *Oil Shale: The Environmental Challenges* (Golden, Colo.: Colorado School of Mines Press, 1981): 294–318. This is based on proceedings of an international symposium August 11–14, 1980, at Vail, Colorado, sponsored by the Oil Shale Task Force and U.S. Department of Energy.

4. Noel J. Brown, "Perspectives," in Terrell J. Minger and Sherry D. Oaks, eds., *Growth Alternatives for the Rocky Mountain West.* Papers from the Vail Symposium V (Boulder, Colo.: Westview Press, 1976), p. 248. On the recent energy crisis and the emerging energy paradigm, see the often cited Sam H. Schurr, *Energy in America's Future: The Choices Before Us* (Baltimore, Md.: Johns Hopkins University Press for Resources for the Future, 1979) and Robert Stobaugh and Daniel Yergin, eds., *Energy Future: The Harvard Business School Report* (New York: Random House, 1979). An illustrated reference is National Geographic Society, *Energy — A Special Report in the Public Interest: Facing Up to the Problem, Getting Down to Solutions,* February 1981.

5. Ford Foundation Energy Policy Project, *A Time To Choose: America's Energy Future — Final Report* (Cambridge, Mass.: Ballinger Publications, 1974).

6. Ralph W. Richardson, "Regional Environmental Management — A National Imperative," in *Growth Alternatives,* Terrell J. Minger and Sherry D. Oaks, eds., pp. 21–30. Wallace Johnson, "Resource and Energy Development and the Law," in *Growth Alternatives,* p. 35. Also see Malcolm Wallop, "Energy Development and Water: Dilemma for the Western United States," in *Journal of Energy and Development,* vol 8, no. 2 (Spring 1983) and John A. Folk-Williams and James S. Cannon, *Water for the Energy Market,* vol. 2 of *Water in the West* (Santa Fe, N. Mex.: Western Network, 1983).

7. Edward Abbey, *The Journey Home — Some Words in Defense of the American West* (New York: E. P. Dutton, 1977), p. 170.

8. Ibid., p. 163.

9: Ibid p. 163. For a timely account of pollution in the Southwest, see the film *The Four Corners Area: A National Sacrifice Area?* (1985) by Christopher McLeod, Randy Hayes, and Glenn Switkes.

10. William R. Freudenburg, "People in the Impact Zone: The Human and Social Consequences of Energy Boomtown Growth in Four Western Colorado Communities" (Ph.D. diss., Yale University, 1979) and "Women and Men in an Energy Boomtown: Adjustment, Alienation, and Adaptation," *Rural Sociology,* vol. 46, no. 2 (1981). For growth from the Craig city administrator's point of view, see Donald B. Cooper, "Coping with Boomtown Growth," *Colorado Municipalities* (August 1981), pp. 4–7.

11. Dede Feldman, "Boomtown," *Minetalk,* Southwest Research & Information Center (May–June 1981). Colstrip, Montana, is described in Michael Parfit, "Last Stand at Rosebud Creek," *Rocky Mountain Magazine* (May 1980), pp. 65–70. For boomtown pressures on Wyoming women, see Sandra Widener, "Boom Town Women," *Rocky Mountain Magazine* (January/February 1982), pp. 45–49 and 81–85. Also see Phil Primack, "West's Economic Upsurge is Rose With Sharp Thorns," *Rocky Mountain News,* 9 March 1980. National coverage of the energy boom included Wallace Stegner and Page Stegner, "Rocky Mountain Country" in *Atlantic Monthly,* vol. 241, no. 4 (April 1978): 44–64 and "Rocky Mountain High — Soaring Prospects for the '80s," a cover story in *Time* (15 December 1980).

12. Art Brannan and Pat Brannan, Hat Ranch, Box 102, Maybell, Colorado. Interviewed by author, 4 July 1977. Text of this interview is in the Western History Department of the Denver Public Library. For other ranchers' pessimistic views on energy development, see Edward Abbey, "The Second Rape of the West," in *The Journey Home,* pp. 158–188, and the interview with Ellen Cotton in Teresa Jordan, *Cowgirls: Women of the American West* (New York: Anchor Press, 1982): 94–102.

13. Brannan interview, 4 July 1977.

14. John S. Gilmore and Mary K. Duff, *Boom Town Growth Management: A Case Study of Rock Springs — Green River, Wyoming* (Boulder, Colo.: Westview Press, 1975). Also see Tom Clark, "Wyoming Boom," *Rocky Mountain Magazine* (June 1979), pp. 64–76.

15. John S. Gilmore, "Boom Towns May Hinder Energy Resource Development," *Science,* vol. 191, no. 561–2 (13 February 1976): 535–540. Also see John S. Gilmore interview with author at the University of Denver, Denver, Colorado, on 1 November 1985. A recent book that places boomtowns in a national and international context is Gary W. Malamud, *Boomtown Communities* (New York: Van Nostrand, 1984).

16. Governor's Office, State of Colorado, Oil Shale Planning and Coordination, *IMPACT: An Assessment of Oil Shale Development — Colorado Planning and Management Region 11,* vol. 1–5 (Denver: December 1974).

17. Jimmy Carter, "President's Proposed Energy Policy," in *Vital Speeches of the Day*, vol. 43, no. 14 (1 May 1977): 418–420.

18. Jimmy Carter, "The Moral Equivalent of War," in *Vital Speeches of the Day*, vol. 43, no. 14 (1 May 1977): 420–423.

19. Atomic Energy Commission, *The Bronco Oil Shale Study*, PNE-1400 (Washington, D.C.: U.S. Government Printing Office, 1967), pp. 49, 62, and 58. This study was prepared by the United States Atomic Energy Commission, the United States Department of the Interior, CER Geonuclear Corporation, and the Lawrence Radiation Laboratory.

20. Letter to the author and Piceance Basin Planning Area maps from Calvin W. Hickey, chief, Branch of Cartographic Services, Bureau of Land Management, Colorado State Office, 2020 Arapahoe Street, Denver, 23 December 1985. Also see John Singlaub, "Special Management Areas in Energy Regions, The Piceance Basin," in Lawrence G. Kolenbrander, ed., *Special Management Areas: Processes and Strategies*. Proceedings of the Special Management Areas Conference, April 24 and 25, 1984, Denver Botanic Gardens, Denver, Colorado. Sponsored by The Nature Conservancy, Denver Botanic Gardens, USDI Bureau of Land Management, Colorado, and USDA Forest Service Rocky Mountain Region (Denver, Colo., 1984).

21. Steve Campbell, "Energy Development Prompts Mule Deer Study," Grand Junction *Daily Sentinel*, 13 December 1981; Gary Gerhardt, "Energy Firms Facing Ecological Problems They Create," *Rocky Mountain News*, 13 December 1981; Lloyd Levy, "Wildlife Official Stresses Need for Habitat," *Grand Junction Daily Sentinel*, 3 February 1980; and Bill Haggerty, "Energy and Wildlife: Loss of Habitat Concerns Wildlife Officials As Energy Development Hits West Slope," *Grand Junction Daily Sentinel*, 8 March 1981.

22. Michael R. Grode, wildlife biologist, Colorado Division of Wildlife, "Management Considerations for Riparian Habitats in Garfield County, Colorado" (May 1982), pp. 1–6, and Lloyd Levy, "Bald Eagles Threaten Gravel Pit (and vice versa)," *Grand Junction Daily Sentinel*, 26 September 1980.

23. Richard D. Lamm and Michael McCarthy, *The Angry West: A Vulnerable Land and Its Future* (Boston: Houghton Mifflin, 1982), p. 48.

24. Ralph Franklin quoted by Gary Schmitz in the *Glenwood Post*, 11 April 1980.

25. William R. Freudenburg, "People in the Impact Zone," 1976, p. 11. For full-length treatments of social impacts in the West, though without reference to bust cycles, see Steve H. Murdock and F. Larry Leistriz, *Energy Development in the Western United States — Impact on Rural Areas* (New York: Praeger Publishers, 1979). For critiques of social impact assessments, see H. Paul Friesma and Paul J. Culhane, "Social Impacts, Politics, and the Environmental Impact Statement Process," *Natural Resources Journal*, 16 (April 1976): 339–354; William M. Rohe, "Social Impact Analysis and the Planning Process in the United States: A Review and Critique," *Town Planning Review*, vol. 53, no. 4 (October 1982): 367–382; and William R. Freudenburg and Kenneth M. Keating, "Increasing the

Impact of Sociology on Social Impact Assessment: Toward Ending the Inattention," *American Sociologist,* vol. 17, no. 2 (May 1982): 71–79.

26. Larry Kozisek testimony before the Subcommittee on Regional and Community Development of the Committee on the Environment and Public Works of the United States Senate, 2 August 1977.

27. Annette Brand, former Silt town administrator. Interviewed by author 11, March 1986 at Denver, Colorado.

28. Ibid.

29. Ibid.

30. Andrew Gulliford, "From Boom to Bust: Small Towns and Energy Development on Colorado's Western Slope," *Small Town,* vol. 13, no. 5 (March/April, 1983), p. 21. Interview with Floyd A. Thurston by author on 3 October 1977, Rifle, Colorado.

31. *Shale Country* (January 1981), p. 2. By 1981, concern mounted that the energy-rich western states would hold the frost belt states "hostage" with exorbitant fuel fees. See David F. Salisbury, "Energy: The War Between the States," *Christian Science Monitor,* 17 June 1981.

32. President Carter addressed the nation on inflation and energy on 14 March 1980. See Jimmy Carter, "The Nation's Economy," in *Vital Speeches of the Day,* vol. 46, no. 12, pp. 354–357.

33. *Rifle Tribune,* 30 April 1980.

34. Gulliford, "From Boom to Bust," p. 18. Interview with Esma Lewis by author on 15 June 1977 at 6926 233 Road, Silt, Colorado.

35. Bessie Lindauer, homemaker/rancher, 0929 215 Road, Parachute, Colorado. Interviewed by author 29 October 1985.

36. On rural Colorado "time affluence," see Risa Palm, "The Daily Activities of Women," in Elizabeth Moen, Elise Boulding, Jane Lillydahl, and Risa Palm, eds., *Women and the Social Costs of Economic Development: Two Colorado Case Studies* (Boulder, Colo.: Westview Press, 1981), pp. 99–118.

37. Pat O'Neill. Interviewed by author at Harvey Gap, north of Silt, Colorado, 18 October 1985.

38. Reverend Lynn Evans, United Methodist–Presbyterian Church, 200 E. 4th, Rifle, Colorado. Interviewed by author 25 October 1985.

39. Andrew Gulliford and Randall Teeuwen, *The Years Ahead: Life for the Aging in Northwest Colorado* (Glenwood Springs, Colo.: Colorado Mountain College, 1977), p. 19. Interview with Doris Flynn by author at the New Castle Drugstore, New Castle, Colorado, 22 July 1977.

40. J. P. Fox and T. E. Phillips, "Wastewater Treatment in the Oil Shale Industry," in Kathy Kellogg Peterson, ed., *Oil Shale: The Environmental Challenges,* pp. 253–293. The most comprehensive analysis of oil shale and the environment is Paul Ferraro and Paul Nazaryk, *Assessments of the Cumulative Environmental Impacts of Energy Development in Northwestern Colorado — Final Report* (Denver: Colorado Department of Health, 1983).

41. Grand Junction *Daily Sentinel*, 23 December 1981. Also see "Soil Conditions on Shale Lands Can Be Improved," *Rifle Tribune*, 29 September 1980, and Gary Schmitz, "Environmental Concern Rises As Oil Shale Seems Imminent," *Glenwood Post*, 3 December 1979.
42. John Colson, "C-b Companies Seek Less Strict Laws," *Rifle Telegram*, 17 September 1980. Also see David C. Sheesley and Ellen M. Leonard, "An Air Quality Strategy for Oil Shale Development," in Kathy Kellogg Peterson, ed., *Oil Shale: The Environmental Challenges*, pp. 294–318; Environmental Defense Fund, "'Acid Rain' in the Intermountain West," a report by the Environmental Defense Fund of a Survey of Acid Rain Research in the Rocky Mountain Region, n. d.
43. Geritol reference is from Donald I. McClung, Occidental Oil Corporation safety inspector. Interviewed by author at Silt, Colorado, 21 October 1985. For a scientific analysis of shale's carcinogenic qualities, see L. M. Holland, "Studies of the Biology and Toxicology of Oil Shale Materials," in Kathy Kellogg Peterson, ed., *Oil Shale: The Environmental Challenges*, pp. 87–104.
44. Pat O'Neill, former reporter/editor with the *Rifle Tribune*. Harvey Gap, Colorado. Interview with author 10, 11, and 18 October 1985.
45. Reverend Lynn Evans. Former minister of the United Methodist-Presbyterian Church, 200 E. 4th, Rifle, Colorado. Interview by author 25 October 1985.
46. Jim Sullivan. Interview by author at the *Grand Junction Daily Sentinel* building, Grand Junction, Colorado. 16 October 1985.
47. Ibid.
48. Ibid.

Notes to Chapter 4

1. Hart quote is from the *Rocky Mountain News*, 13 June 1980. Exxon refused to provide me with a copy of the "white paper." Its main office in New York referred me to the Houston office. Waldo Leggett from the synthetic fuels division returned my call but said the "white paper" was no longer available because of the criticism they had received from it. When I asked if he could send me a copy of it from his office, he declined to do so because it was "a matter of policy." I finally found a copy in the files of the *Rifle Tribune*. It was dated 28 August 1980 and had been received from Les Rogers of Exxon on 2 September 1980.
2. Elizabeth W. Moen, "Voodoo Forecasting: Technical, Political and Ethical Issues Regarding the Projection of Local Population Growth," *Population Research and Policy Review*, 3 (1984): 1–25.
3. Meyer's statement is from the *Rocky Mountain News*, 12 June 1980. Also see Jim Sullivan, "Experts Assess Exxon's Shale Scenario," *Rifle Tribune*, 3 September 1980.

4. Neal Pierce, "Exxon's Shale Scenario," *Grand Junction Daily Sentinel,* 26 September 1980.

5. Information on construction activity is from Frank P. Barrow, project director, Exxon Colony Project. Interviewed by author at 10 Huntwick Lane, Englewood, Colorado, on 12 March 1986.

6. W. T. Slick, Jr., testimony before the Senate Budget Committee in Denver, Colorado, on 17 July 1980, and in Rifle, Colorado, 29 August 1980. There are variations in text between the two testimonies. Citation is from Rifle testimony, pp. 1–2.

7. Roger Ludwig, interviewed by author on 18 October 1985.

8. Paul Ferraro and Paul Nazaryk, *Assessments of the Cumulative Environmental Impacts of Energy Development in Northwestern Colorado — Final Report* (Denver: Colorado Department of Health, 1983), p. 1.

9. Slick testimony given in Rifle, pp. 3, 5, 6.

10. On 1,000-megawatt power plants, see Mary Louise Giblin, "Shale Plans Inadequate, Officials Tell Hart," *Grand Junction Daily Sentinel,* 12 August 1980. On interbasin water transfers, see Dr. Peter House, director, Office of Environmental Assessments, Office of Environment, Department of Energy, testimony before the Senate Budget Committee in Rifle, Colorado, 29 August 1980, pp. 15–17; press release from Exxon Company, U.S.A., Public Affairs, 800 Bell Avenue, Houston, "Water Transfer Feasible, Exxon Official Explains." For release October 23, 1980, 3:30 P.M. CDT. Original in *Rifle Tribune* files; "Exxon Chief Restates Shale Development Plan," *Grand Junction Daily Sentinel,* 22 November 1980; and Michael Rounds, "Water Transfer to Develop West Oil Shale 'Feasible'" *Rocky Mountain News,* 6 December 1980. Recent pertinent studies on the Colorado River and water in the West include Gary D. Weatherford and F. Lee Brown, *New Courses for the Colorado River: Major Issues for the Next Century* (Albuquerque: University of New Mexico Press, 1986); Marc Reisner, *Cadillac Desert: The American West and Its Disappearing Water* (New York: Viking Penquin, 1986); and *High Country News,* ed., *Western Water Made Simple* (Washington, D.C.: Island Press, 1987).

11. Slick testimony given in Rifle, p. 4. Exxon's Public Affairs office, 800 Bell Avenue, Houston, had a prepared press release to accompany Slick's testimony. Dated 29 August 1980, it was titled "Synfuels Potential Can Be Achieved in Acceptable Manner, Says Exxon."

12. Hart quote, in Jim Sullivan, "Experts Assess Exxon's Shale Scenario," *Rifle Tribune,* 3 September 1980. Hart letter to Exxon Corporation Chairman Clifford C. Garvin (undated) from Friends of the Earth files.

13. Slick quote in Sullivan, "Experts Assess Exxon."

14. Slick testimony given in Rifle, p. 14.

15. Gary Schmitz, "Dirt in the Blood: Catskinner's Job is Pushing Out the Road," in "The Boomtowns: A Special Report," *Grand Junction Daily Sentinel,* 10 September 1981, p. 15. "The Boomtowns: A Special Report" is the best compilation of articles on the boom period in Garfield County. Also see Russell Martin, "The

Great Western Shale Game," *Rocky Mountain Magazine* 1981, pp. 32–39; Bob Anderson, "Oil Shale Future: Jewel or Synfuel?" 13–1 *High Country News* (April 1981): 1, 10–11; Donald P. Scrimgeour, "Coping with the Oil Shale Boom," *Planning* (August, 1980): pp. 19–21; and David R. Hill and Daniel J. Schler, "Early Boom Town Planning in Colorado's Oil Shale Country," in James L. Regens, Robert W. Rycroft, and Gregory A. Daneke, eds., *Energy and the Western United States* (New York: Praeger, 1982), pp. 49–67.

16. Alan Isbell, "Is There Life After Exxon," *Colorado River Journal* (July 1982): p. 11. For a good account of the impact of development on agriculture, see Catherine Kilker, "Ranching: Tough Times and Top Land Prices," *Shale Country* (April/May 1982): pp. 2–4.

17. Elise Boulding, "Women as Integrators and Stabilizers," in Elizabeth W. Moen, Elise Boulding, Jane Lillydahl, and Risa Palm, eds., *Women and the Social Costs of Economic Development, Two Colorado Case Studies* (Boulder, Colo.: Westview Press, 1981), pp. 119–150. This is one of the finest essays on boom-town change.

18. Ludwig interview, 18 October, 1985. Also see Patrick Noel, "The County Commissioners: A Changing Role," *Colorado River Journal* (January/February 1982), pp. 10–13, 27–39.

19. William Davis, Office of Technology Assessment, United States Congress, published comments made after the session "Oil Shale Development: The Need for and Problems of Socioeconomic Impact Management and Assessment," in Kathy Kellogg Peterson, ed., *Oil Shale: The Environmental Challenges* (Golden, Colo.: Colorado School of Mines Press, 1981), p. 350.

20. Ronald R. Johnson in a letter to Hon. Richard D. Lamm, 9 September 1981, now in the Garfield County Human Services housing file, Garfield County Courthouse in Glenwood Springs, Colorado. Also see Pat O'Neill, "Parachute Beginning to Resemble Boomtowns of Old," *Rifle Tribune*, 22 April 1981. Lloyd Levy, "Garfield County Feels Weight of Shale 'Squatters'" and Joe McGowan, Jr., "Growing Pains: Parachute, People, Petroleum,"*Grand Junction Daily Sentinel*, 13 May 1981. Pat O'Neill, "Teepee Dwellers Ordered by County to Break Camp," *Rifle Tribune*, 20 May 1981. Alan Isbell, "Along the River: Coping with Squatters," *Colorado River Journal,* vol. 3, no. 5 (March/April 1982): 36; and Vicki Felmlee and Alan Isbell, "The Housing Crisis," *Colorado River Journal,* vol 3, no. 5 (March/April 1982): 10–15.

21. Johnson letter to Governor Lamm.

22. Ludwig interview, 18 October 1985.

23. Union Oil Company of California, Parachute Creek Shale Oil Program, Community Impact Mitigation data from Christopher J. Treese, public affairs administrator, Union Energy Mining Division, 2717 County Road #215, Parachute, Colorado. Information sheet in possession of the author.

24. Charles Pence, former president of Battlement Mesa Incorporated, interviewed by author on 7 March 1986, at 1929 Allen Parkway, Houston, Texas. For information on Battlement Mesa, Inc., see "Battlement Mesa: A New Community,"

Mines Magazine, Colorado School of Mines, vol. 71, no. 2 (February 1981): 29. Also see John Colson, "Lamm Interview: Bracing for the Energy Boom," *Rifle Tribune,* 20 May 1981.

25. Pence interview, 7 March 1986.

26. Ibid.

27. Ibid.

28. Joyce Illian, social worker, interviewed by author 25 October 1985 at Valley View Hospital, 1806 Blake Avenue, Glenwood Springs, Colorado.

29. Constance Albrecht, interviewed by author at Palisade, Colorado, on 16 October, 1985.

30. Pat O'Neill, interviewed by author on 18 October 1985. Also "Parachute Bar Doubles as a Church," *Rifle Tribune,* 2 March 1982. The story also received national publicity when it ran on the Associated Press wire service.

31. O'Neill interview, 18 October 1985.

32. Ibid.

33. Ibid.

34. Ibid.

35. Ibid.

36. Richard D. Lamm and Michael McCarthy, *The Angry West: A Vulnerable Land and Its Future* (Boston: Houghton Mifflin, 1982), p. 40.

37. Jim Sullivan, former editor *Rifle Tribune* and writer for *Grand Junction Daily Sentinel,* interviewed by author 16 October 1985 in the offices of the *Grand Junction Daily Sentinel.*

38. Ibid.

39. Randall Meyer, "Western States Energy Resources Development," *Mines Magazine,* Colorado School of Mines, vol. 71, no. 6 (June 1981): 3–7.

40. Ibid.

41. Lloyd Levy, "Presiding, With Ulcers, Over the Urbanization of Ranch Country," *Grand Junction Daily Sentinel,* "The Boomtowns: A Special Report," 10 September 1981, p. 11, and "Hazards of Growth: The Brain Drain," *Colorado River Journal* (January/February 1982), p. 37.

42. Henry Lee, "Oil Shale Development: A Perspective on Certain Regional Economic Issues," Energy & Environmental Policy Center, Discussion Paper Series E–80–06, John F. Kennedy School of Government, Harvard University, October, 1980, pp. 24–25.

43. This chronology of oil shale's Black Sunday events is compiled from excellent reporting by Pete Chronis and Gail Pitts of the *Denver Post* in several stories that ran the week of Black Sunday. In particular, see Chronis and Pitts, "Colony Pullout Came as Shock to Thousands," *Denver Post,* 9 May 1982.

44. Frank P. Barrow, former project director, Colony Project, Exxon, U.S.A., interview by author 12 March 1986 at 10 Huntwick Lane, Englewood, Colorado.

Notes to Chapter 5

1. The $920 million figure comes from Eleanor Johnson Tracy, "Exxon's Abrupt Exit from Shale," *Fortune* (May 31, 1982), p. 106. The exact figure may be impossible to determine. In my interview with Colony Project Director Frank P. Barrow, he refused to answer my question about the total cost "for proprietary reasons." In Exxon's press release, a $700 million figure was used. For an excellent news story, in which the sense of the bust impact was heightened by the use of the word "overnight" as a sentence lead-in (a journalistic device that I have borrowed), see the entire issue of *The Free Weekly Newspaper,* vol. 6, no. 41 (May 1982). The two-inch headline states "BUST!" and the smaller headline reads "JOLT: Exxon's Overnight Shutdown Stuns County."
2. Tracy, "Exxon's Abrupt Exit from Shale," p. 105
3. Pat O'Neill, "The Week The 'Chute Didn't Open," *Colorado River Journal* (July/August 1982), p. 13. As reporter, writer, editor, and O'Leary's owner and bartender, he knew the Parachute boomtown story inside and out. Of all the newspaper and television reports, his accounts are consistently the best. In the same issue of the *Colorado River Journal,* also see Sherri Poe Bernard, "The Tiger Empties the Tank," Alan Isbell, "Is There Life After Exxon?" Donald G. Berger, "A View from the State House," and Andrew Gulliford, "Shale's Rocky Road."
4. Douglas Martin, "Exxon Abandons Shale Oil Project," *New York Times,* 3 May 1982: 1; William E. Schmidt, "Uncertainty in Shale Oil Town," *New York Times,* 3 May 1982; Business section, p. 1 and D21. Douglas Martin, "The Singular Power of a Giant Called Exxon," *New York Times,* 9 May 1982, Business Section, p. 1. Steve Frazier, "Union Oil Keeps Its Shale Project Despite Shakeout," *Wall Street Journal,* 4 May 1982; Dan Balz, "Parachute Fails to Open — Workers Stranded by Exxon's Pullout," *Washington Post,* 7 May 1982.

   Colorado bust headlines for the week after Black Sunday in 1982 included: May 3—Gail Pitts, "Exxon Will Close Shale Oil Project" and Pete Chronis, "Parachute May Become Town of Lost Dreams," *Denver Post;* Jerry Funk, "Exxon Closing Oil Shale Project — Reaction Cautious, Not Panic" and Michael Paludan, "Lamm Assessing Exxon Impact," *Glenwood Post;* Gary Schmitz, "Exxon Closing: 180-Degree Turn for Shale Leader" and "Garfield, Parachute Leaders Glad They Prepared for Worst," *Grand Junction Daily Sentinel;*

   May 4 — Cindy Parmenter, "4,100 Jobs May Be Lost in Oil Shale Shutdown" and Kit Miniclier and Pete Chronis, "Life Turns Upside Down for Shale Plant Workers" and Ray Flack, "Housing Hit Hard by Closure," *Denver Post;* Sandy Graham, "Shale Economy Limps on One Leg," *Rocky Mountain News;* Jerry Funk, "Exxon Workforce Halved Today — Workers Steaming," *Glenwood Post;* T. Michael Crowell, "1,000 at Colony Get Layoffs, Last Checks" and "Firms

Tied to Colony May Lose Millions in Shutdown," *Grand Junction Daily Sentinel*; Deborah Frazier, "Shale Dreams Shatter," *Rocky Mountain News*;

May 5 — Sandy Graham, "Pink Slips and Paychecks Prevail" and Deborah Frazier, "Parachute's 'Pioneers' Bailing Out," *Rocky Mountain News*; John Colson, "Shale Shock — Parachute Officials Re-evaluate Plans After Exxon Pullout," *Rifle Tribune*; Gary Schmitz, "Officials Rap Exxon's Method," *Grand Junction Daily Sentinel*; "Exxon's Shutdown Surprises County," *Rifle Telegram*;

May 6 — Jerry Funk, "Exxon Actions May Kill School Plans," *Glenwood Post;* "Exxon Pulls Plug; Officials Express Concern," *Meeker Herald*.

National news magazines published "Setback for Synfuels," *Time* (17 May 1982), pp. 58–59; "The Death of Synfuels," *Newsweek* (17 May 1982), pp. 75–76; and "Oil-Shale Fiasco: The Death Knell for Synfuels?" *U.S. News & World Report* (17 May 1982), p. 58.

5. On the 1983 Black Sunday anniversary, see: "1983 Showcase — Energy and the Environment," special editon of the *Grand Junction Daily Sentinel*, 13 March 1983; Robert Unger, "Shale's Empty Promises Bust Colorado Boom Town," *Kansas City Times*, 6 April 1983; "Town Sees a Bright Side After Boom Goes Bust," *Kansas City Star*, 1 May 1983; Gary Schmitz, "Oil Shale Prospects Continue to Worsen" and Steve McMillan, "Parachute Takes a Breather," and "Foreclosures Mount as Growth Recedes," *Grand Junction Daily Sentinel*, 1 May 1983; Jerry Funk, "Towns Survive 'Black Sunday'" and "Officials Review Colony Shale Project" and Alan Isbell, "Shale's Welcome is Cautious Since Bust," *Glenwood Post*, 2 May 1983; Peter G. Chronis, "Remembering Black Sunday — Boomtown Now Awaits Bust No. 2" and "Streets, but No Houses," *Denver Post*, 1 May 1983; Robert Cross, "Boom Busts; Hope Sustains Town" and "Oil Boomtown Counts its Blessings After the Crash," *Chicago Tribune*, 7 June 1983. The best reporting, of course, was in the "Ghost Town Tribune," a special edition of the *Rifle Tribune*, 4 May 1983.

By 1984, the bust was taking its toll. See "Oil Shale Comes on Hard Times," a special issue of *High Country News*, 2 April 1984; Julie Asher, "Life Is Damn Hard, but There Are Still Hopes and Dreams in Oil Shale Country," *Denver Catholic Register*, 25 April 1984; Jon Klusmire, "Exxon Forgotten," *Weekly Newspaper* (Glenwood Springs), 9 May 1984; "Parachute Remembers in a Pleasant Way," *Rifle Tribune*, 9 May 1984; and Joe Garner, "Grand Junction Less Grand after Oil 'Bust'," *Los Angeles Times*, 23 November 1984.

6. Elisabeth Kubler-Ross, *On Death and Dying* (New York: Macmillan, 1969). For a synopsis of Kubler-Ross's arguments, see Daniel Goldman, "We Are Breaking the Silence About Death," *Psychology Today* (September 1976.) Every person interviewed by the author after the bust vividly remembered what he or she was doing on Black Sunday or on the day after.

7. Robert Nuffer, associate director, Sopris Mental Health Center, Glenwood Springs, Colorado. Interviewed by author on 16 January 1986.

8. John S. Gilmore, "Boom Towns May Hinder Energy Resource Development," *Science*, vol. 191, no. 561–562 (13 February 1976): 535–540. Also see Ellen Hirschberg Geier, "Boomtown Shock: Looking Beyond the Illness." (Manuscript from the collection of the author, undated, but ca. 1983).

9. Very little has been published on the recent state of economic chaos in western energy boomtowns. Two contemporary articles, however, are Jane H. Lillydahl and Elizabeth W. Moen, "Planning, Managing, and Financing Growth and Decline in Energy Resource Communities: A Case Study of Western Colorado, " *Journal of Energy & Development*, vol. 8, no. 2 (Spring 1983): 211–229, and Elizabeth W. Moen, "Voodoo Forecasting: Technical, Political and Ethical Issues Regarding the Projection of Local Population Growth," *Population Research and Policy Review*, 3 (1984): 1–25.

10. Lynn Evans, minister, United Methodist-Presbyterian Church, 200 E. 4th Street, Rifle, Colorado. Interviewed by author on 25 October 1985.

11. Rhonda Atchetee, Exxon accountant. Interviewed by author at Exxon headquarters in Houston, Texas, on 7 March 1986.

12. Ibid.

13. Ibid.

14. Ibid.

15. Ibid.

16. O'Neill, "The Week the 'Chute Didn't Open," *Colorado River Journal* (July/August 1982), p. 14. O'Neill delighted his pub patrons by having a "rumor jar" set up at O'Leary's for a "rumor of the week contest." Winner of the best rumor for a given week received a pitcher of beer.

17. O'Neill, "The Week the 'Chute Didn't Open," p. 14

18. "Dreams Dashed for Shale Workers," *Denver Post*, 4 May 1982. Also see "Shale Workers Are Bitter," *Rocky Mountain News,* 4 May 1982.

19. Joyce Illian, social worker. Interviewed by author at Valley View Hospital, 1906 Blake Avenue, Glenwood Springs, Colorado, on 25 October 1985.

20. Charles Pence, former president of Battlement Mesa, Inc., interviewed by author at 1929 Allen Parkway, Houston, Texas, on 7 March 1986.

21. John Colson, "Sorrow and Rage With the Bust That Was Not Supposed to Happen," *Rifle Tribune*, 5 May 1982. In that same issue of the *Tribune*, see Jim Sullivan, "Panic Cautioned Against in Face of Certain Economic Downturn" and "Limited Vandalism, Fights in Parachute Area."

22. Pence interview.

23. O'Neill, "The Week the 'Chute Didn't Open," p. 14

24. Colson, "Sorrow and Rage," *Rifle Tribune*, 4 May 1982.

25. Kit Miniclier and Pete Chronis, "Life Turns Upside Down for Shale Plant Workers," *Denver Post*, 4 May 1982.

26. Ibid.

27. *Rocky Mountain News*, 4 May 1982.

28. "Exxon Cuts and Runs," *Grand Junction Daily Sentinel,* 4 May 1982. For additional editorials, see: "Exxon Pulls Out," *Grand Junction Daily Sentinel,* 3 May 1982; "Bust," *Rifle Telegram,* 5 May 1982; "We Will Survive," *Rifle Tribune,* 5 May 1982; "Boom and Bust . . . Live and Learn," *Meeker Herald,* 6 May 1982; "Slow on Shale," *Washington Post,* 6 May 1982.

29. Cindy Parmenter, "4,100 Jobs May Be Lost in Oil Shale Shutdown," *Denver Post,* 4 May 1982.

30. Ray Flack, "Housing Hit Hard by Closure," *Denver Post,* 4 May 1982.

31. O'Neill, "The Week the Chute Didn't Open," p. 29.

32. Charles Pence quoted in the *Grand Junction Daily Sentinel,* 5 May 1982.

33. Cumulative Impact Task Force cover letter, draft, 6 May 1982. Proposed revisions 18 August 1982. Paul Ferraro and Paul Nazaryk, *Assessment of Cumulative Environmental Impacts of Energy Development in Northwestern Colorado — Final Report* (Denver: Colorado Department of Health, 1983).

34. "Colony Shutdown Shocks Workers," *Denver Post,* 9 May 1982.

35. "World's Largest Oil Company Leaves a Streak of Rage and Fear," *Washington Post,* 7 May 1982.

36. All interview excerpts are from T. Michael Crowell, "Exxon Kicks Off Slope's Economic Dominoes," *Grand Junction Daily Sentinel,* 9 May 1982.

37. "Speaking the Public Mind" — Letters to the Editor, *Grand Junction Daily Sentinel,* 9 May 1982. Letter was signed "Charline (Benson) Jones, Parachute."

38. "Editor's Mailbox," *Rifle Telegram,* 12 May 1982. Letter was signed "Blane Colton." Also see "The Collapse of the Colony Project — Where Do We Go From Here?" a letter to the editor by Connie Albrecht, Colorado West representative, Friends of the Earth, that appeared in the *Meeker Herald,* 13 May 1982.

39. Jim Sullivan, former editor of the *Rifle Tribune* and writer for the *Grand Junction Daily Sentinel.* Interviewed by author at the offices of the *Grand Junction Daily Sentinel,* Grand Junction, Colorado, on 16 October 1985.

40. Ibid.

41. Andrew Alexander, "Following the Boom: A Story of Persistence, Determination," *Grand Junction Daily Sentinel,* 4 May 1986.

42. Alice Boulton, letter to author, received 17 June 1986. For information on contract stipulations imposed by boomtown developers see John A. Savage, interview with author at 1122 293 Road, Rifle, Colorado, on 16 January 1986.

43. Frank P. Barrow, former project director, Colony Project, Exxon, U.S.A. Interviewed by author at 10 Huntwick Lane, Englewood, Colorado, on 12 March 1986.

44. Ibid.

45. Ibid.

46. Pence interview.

47. Ibid.

48. Ibid.

49. Ibid.

50. Ibid.

51. Evans interview.

52. Andrew Gulliford, "Boomtown Blues: When Dreams Don't Pan Out," *Not Man Apart — the Newsmagazine of Friends of the Earth*, vol. 16, no. 2 (March-April 1986): 14–15.

53. Sullivan interview.

54. Sonja Fritzlan, homemaker. Interviewed by author at 0391 332 Road, Rifle, Colorado, on 24 October 1985.

55. Sullivan interview.

56. Ibid.

57. Nicholas Lemann, "Grand Junction Can't Win for Losing," *Atlantic Monthly*, vol. 255, no. 18 (April 1985): 22. For insight into the retail sector during a boom-and-bust, see Claud M. Davidson, "Retail Facilities in Colorado Boomtowns," *Social Science Journal*, vol. 24, no. 3 (June 1987): 247–259.

58. "The Mayor Steps Down, But Still Keeps Tabs on Energy," *Shale Country* (April 1981), p. 20.

59. James T. Bernath, "Survey Results: 10 Percent of Families Say They Intend to Pull Up Stakes, Move," *Grand Junction Daily Sentinel*, 17 September 1984. "Foreclosure Isn't Always Fatal," *Grand Junction Daily Sentinel*, 16 February 1986.

60. Charley Blaine, "Oil Glut Puts Boom Town on the Rocks," *USA Today*, 18 November 1985.

61. Nuffer interview.

62. On the "whole new tier beginning to fall," see the previously cited Andrew Alexander, "Following the Boom: A Story of Persistence, Determination" in the *Grand Junction Daily Sentinel*.

63. Ralph Freedman, Parachute Town Administrator, interviewed by author in the Town Hall, Parachute, Colorado, on 21 October 1985.

64. Ed Marston, "What Happened to the Oil Shale Towns," *Planning*, vol. 50, no. 5 (May 1984): 25–29. Gary Schmitz, "Local Officials Feel Pinch of Strained Finances," *Grand Junction Daily Sentinel*, 1 May 1983. "Oil Shale Gifts Expensive to Maintain," *Rifle Telegram*, 26 October 1983. Also see interview with Jerry Smith, local affairs director, Colorado State Impact Office, 1313 Sherman, Room 523, Denver, Colorado. Interviewed by author on 11 March 1986.

65. Frederick Rose, "Coming Up Dry: Unocal Struggles on with Attempt to Get Crude Oil from Shale," *Wall Street Journal*, 14 May 1986.

66. Craig Kacskos, "McInnis Says He'll Ax Shale Value Provision," *Glenwood Post*, 28 February 1985.

67. Gary Schmitz, *Denver Post* reporter. Interviewed by author in the Press Club Building, Washington, D.C. , on 28 April 1986.

68. Bernard DeVoto, "The Plundered Province," in *Forays and Rebuttals* (Boston: Little, Brown, 1936), pp. 52–53.

Notes to Chapter 6

1. See Elise Boulding, "Women as Integrators and Stabilizers" in Elizabeth Moen, Elise Boulding, Jane Lillydahl, and Risa Palm, *Women and the Social Costs of Energy Development: Two Colorado Case Studies* (Boulder, Colo.: Westview Press, 1981).
2. Patricia Nelson Limerick, *The Legacy of Conquest* (New York: W. W. Norton, 1987), p. 31.
3. W. F. Cottrell, "Death by Dieselization," *American Sociological Review,* vol. 16, no. 3 (June 1951): 360.
4. Garvin quote from John J. Petillo, "Social Responsibility: The Role of the University," *Christian Science Monitor,* 27 February 1986. For an expanded discussion of corporate obligations, see Douglas J. Den Uyl, *The New Crusaders: The Corporate Social Responsibility Debate* (Bowling Green, Ohio: Social Philosophy & Policy Center, 1984).
5. Recent assessments of EISs include William R. Freudenburg and Kenneth M. Keating, "Applying Sociology to Policy: Social Science and the Environmental Impact Statement," *Rural Sociology,* vol. 50, no. 4 (Winter 1985): 578–605; Freudenburg, "Social Impact Assessment," *Annual Review of Sociology,* vol. 12, 1986: 451–478; and James G. Thompson, Robert R. Reynolds, Jr., and Kenneth P. Wilkinson, "Contributions Toward a Conceptual Framework for Social Impact Assessment in Semi-Arid Lands of the Western United States," ERIC/CRESS microfiche RC 015643, March 1986. ERIC clearinghouse on Rural Education and Small Schools, Las Cruces, New Mexico. ERIC/CRESS is now located at Appalachia Educational Laboratory, Charleston, West Virginia.
6. Roger M. Olien and Diana Davids Olien, *Oil Booms: Social Change in Five Texas Towns* (Lincoln: University of Nebraska Press, 1982), p. 18. Reporting on the boom-and-bust in Grand Junction, Nicholas Lemann wrote, "But nearly every conversation one hears . . . turns to the possibility of a new boom." Nicholas Lemann, "Grand Junction, Can't Win for Losing," *Atlantic Monthly,* vol. 255, no. 18 (April 1985): 24.
7. Patrick O'Neill, former reporter/editor of the *Rifle Tribune* interviewed by author at Harvey Gap, Colorado, on 10, 11, and 18 October 1985.
8. Ibid.
9. Ibid.
10. John A. Savage, attorney, 1122 293 Road, Rifle, Colorado. Interviewed by author on 6 January 1986. Letter to author dated 2 June 1986. Material quoted from both sources.
11. Clifton Garvin speech cited in Garry B. Smith, Danny Arnold, and Bobby G. Bizzell, *Business Strategy and Policy*. Case 11 — The Exxon Colony Project. (Boston: Houghton, Mifflin, 1985), p. 376.
12. Douglas Martin, "The Singular Power of a Giant Called Exxon," *New York Times,* Business section 3, 9 May 1982, p. 1.

13. Exxon Company, U.S.A., "The Role of Synthetic Fuels in the United States Energy Future," [the "white paper"] presented at Club 20, Grand Junction, Colorado on 25 August 1980. Also see original press releases from Exxon Public Affairs, 800 Bell Avenue, Houston titled "Synfuels Potential Can Be Achieved In Acceptable Manner, Says Exxon," 29 August 1980, and "Water Transfer Feasible Exxon Official Explains." For release 23 October 1980, 3:30 P.M. CDT.

14. Allanna Sullivan, "Exxon Workers Offered Option To Retire Early," *Wall Street Journal*, 24 April 1986; "Colony Closing Cited: Exxon Profit Down by 51.5%," Associated Press story in the *Grand Junction Daily Sentinel*, 22 July 1982.

15. Bill Ekstrand statements quoted by Jim Sullivan of the *Grand Junction Daily Sentinel* on 14 May 1984. Eckstrand was speaking before the Garfield County commissioners. He knew he had a lot of explaining to do as the new Colony Oil Shale Project resident manager. See Joan Isenberg, "Colony Manager to County: 'We Are Here. We Are Real People'," *Rifle Tribune*, 16 May 1984.

16. Garry B. Smith, Danny Arnold, and Bobby G. Bizzell, *Business Strategy and Policy*, pp. 366–367.

17. Linda Wollen, letter to the editor, *Grand Junction Daily Sentinel*, 31 May 1984. Area bust-related suicides included the president of the First National Bank of Grand Junction in 1984 and the chief financial officer of a rehabilitation center in 1985. See Lemann, "Grand Junction Can't Win For Losing," *Atlantic Monthly*, April 1985: 23.

18. Information on the oil bust for 1985 includes Laurent Belsie, "Energy Boom Gone Bust Overshadows Efforts to Restart Denver Economy," *Christian Science Monitor*, 15 October 1985; "OPEC's Bold Attempt to Save Itself," *U S. News & World Report*, 23 December 1985; Douglas R. Bohi, "The World Oil Market — The Future Will Not Resemble the Past," *Resources*, 79 (Winter 1985): 10–12. For information on the bust in 1986, see "Shale Oil Companies Pull Up Stakes in Utah, Return Leases," *Glenwood Post*, 2 January 1986; Laurie P. Cohen, "Hard Times: Plunge in Oil Prices Brings Economic Woes to Energy-Belt States," *Wall Street Journal*, 4 February 1986; John Yemma, "Oil-price Drop Causing Profound Changes in World," *Christian Science Monitor*, 19 February 1986; Charles Richards, "West Texans Tighten Their Belts to Ride Out the Oil Slump," *Austin American-Statesman*, 10 March 1986; Roy J. Harris, Jr., "Occidental Cuts Its Work Force And '86 Outlays," *Wall Street Journal*, 18 March 1986; John Yemma, "Falling Oil Prices Squeeze the Profit From US Producing Wells," *Christian Science Monitor*, 21 March 1986; Barbara Bradley, "Texas Bankers Scurry to Limit Oil Losses," *Christian Science Monitor*, 21 April 1986; "Texas: Boom to Bust," *Newsweek*, 31 March 1986, pp. 16–19. William Serrin, "For Texas Oil Workers, Economy Has Gone Dry," *New York Times*, 7 May 1986: A 20.

19. Statement by Clifford C. Garvin, chairman and chief executive officer, Exxon Corporation, is taken from a purchase recommendation prospectus on Paraho Development from Morgan Stanley Investment Research, Anne S. McBride, broker, dated 8 May 1981. Original is in the Senator Gary Hart Oil Shale files.

20. Exxon and Tosco, *Colony — The Colony Shale Oil Project*, 1982, from the Senator Gary Hart Oil Shale files. Copy is in the possession of the author courtesy of Ronald D. Elving, professional staff member, United States Senate Committee on Environment and Public Works Minority Staff, Senator Gary Hart's Office.

21. Ralph Freedman, Parachute town administrator. Interviewed by author in the Parachute Town Hall on 21 October 1985.

22. John S. Gilmore, "Boom Towns May Hinder Energy Resource Development," *Science,* vol. 191, no. 561–562 (13 February 1976): 535–540, and John S. Gilmore and Mary K. Duff, *Boom Town Growth Management* (Boulder, Colo.: Westview Press, 1975). For his experiences in the uranium boom and the statements cited here, see John S. Gilmore, senior research fellow, Denver Research Institute, interview with author at the University of Denver, Denver, Colorado, on 1 November 1985.

23. Gary Schmitz, *Denver Post* reporter. Interviewed by author in the Press Club Building, Washington, D.C., on 28 April 1986.

24. Ibid.

25. On 5 September 1985, I wrote the research director of the Exxon Education Foundation about dissertation support and stated, "I am also interested in access to company records, memos, etc. which will shed light on Exxon's decision to begin involvement with oil shale and then to back out completely." I was told that the Exxon Foundation did not fund student research, but I received no answer to my question about information access. On 27 November 1985, I called Exxon's main office in New York City to try to receive a copy of the "white paper " and was told to call Houston. On 3 December 1985, I called Houston and was told my call would be returned. On 4 December, Waldo Leggett, with synthetic fuels, said that the "white paper" was no longer available, but "when you do find it, I want you to read it as an example of what could be done, not what can or will be done by Exxon." Subsequently, I wrote Exxon Chairman Clifton Garvin and again requested information. I received a letter back from J. B. Davis of the Public Affairs Office on 15 January 1986. He stated:

> The "white paper" on projected synthetic fuels development you referred to is out of date and unavailable. We cannot agree to your request to access Exxon files or provide you material which we consider proprietary.
> Nor can we make available for interviews employees who have been associated with Colony. As a part of our ongoing business, Colony is a proprietary subject from Exxon's point of view. We trust the materials concerning Colony which are already on the public record will be adequate for your needs in pursuing your dissertation.

26. Schmitz interview, 28 April 1986.

27. Ibid.

28. Ibid.

29. Ibid.
30. Charles Pence, former president of Battlement Mesa, Inc. Interviewed by author on 7 March 1986 at 1929 Allen Parkway, Houston, Texas.
31. The shutdown announcement came on May 2, 1982. The next official Exxon announcement was the press release, "Exxon Announces Continuation Of Battlement Mesa Development On Reduced Scale," of 26 May 1982, from Donald E. Smiley, vice-president, Washington Office, Exxon Company, U.S.A. Original is in the Senator Hart Oil Shale files. Colorado officials responded more quickly. Randy Russell, in the Division of Commerce and Development, addressed a 4 May 1982 memo to Steve Schmitz on "Implications of Colony Shutdown on Committed Mitigation Items." Memo in Friends of the Earth files. Also see "Freedman Calls Exxon Plans 'Realistic'; More Talks Planned," *Rifle Tribune*, 2 June 1982. According to Friends of the Earth files, no more talks occurred. See Jerry Funk, "Exxon Revises Final Colony Closing Plans," *Glenwood Post*, 21 September 1982.
32. Reverend Lynn Evans, United Methodist-Presbyterian Church, 200 E. 4th, Rifle, Colorado. Interviewed by author on 25 October 1985.
33. Michael Rounds, "Exxon Consults CU, Mines on Handling Synfuels Boom," *Rocky Mountain News*, 22 November 1980.
34. Rev. Lynn Evans interview, 25 October 1985.
35. O. James Taylor, ed., *Oil Shale, Water Resources and Valuable Minerals of the Piceance Basin, Colorado: The Challenge and Choices of Development*, U.S. Geological Survey Professional Paper 1310. (Washington, D.C. : U. S. Government Printing Office, 1987).
36. Recent historiography chronicling investments in the West include Rodman W. Paul and Michael P. Malone, "Tradition and Challenge in Western Historiography," *Western Historical Quarterly*, vol 16, no. 1, (January 1985): 27–53, and Gerald D. Nash, *The American West in the Twentieth Century: A Short History of an Urban Oasis* (Albuquerque: University of New Mexico Press, 1977).
37. Chuck Hook, "BMI Faces Animosity," *Free Weekly Newspaper* (Glenwood Springs) 3 August 1988. Exxon also has caused antagonism in Wyoming. See Steve Hinchman and Ed Marston, "Exxon Tangles with Wyoming Over Taxes," *High Country News*, 28 March 1988.
38. For the ups and downs of Union Oil's shale plant, see Bob Silbernagel, "Pioneer Problems: Hot Rocks Freeze Work at Union Oil," *Grand Junction Daily Sentinel*, 13 August 1985; Bill Conrad, "Union Oil Plans 'Major Fix' at Plant," *Rifle Telegram*, 14 August 1985; "Hope Hinges on Fluidized Fed," *The Free Weekly Newspaper*, 28 January 1987; Steve McMillan, "Shale Plant Scrutinized by Unocal," *Grand Junction Daily Sentinel*, 7 August 1988, and Jon Klusmire, "An Oil Shale Project Hangs on, but Barely," *High Country News*, 27 February 1989.
39. On Texas real estate, see Kerry Elizabeth Knobelsdorff, "Real Estate Keeps Texas Thrifts in the Hole," *Christian Science Monitor*, 12 September 1988. For an excellent series on the oil patch, see Howard LaFranchi, with photos by Patty Wood, "The 'New Poor' in the Oil Patch," *Christian Science Monitor*, 31 August

1987; "Public Aid in Stricken Oil Patch," *Christian Science Monitor*, 1 September 1987; and "'Diversification' is Oil-patch Rallying Cry," *Christian Science Monitor*, 2 September 1987.

40. "Two Cheers for $5 Oil," *New York Times*, 9 October 1988.

41. "Long Gasoline Lines Predicted Again in 2–5 Years," *Denver Post*, 12 February 1987; Earl W. Foell, "No World Oil Crisis Now, but Wait a Generation," *Christian Science Monitor*, 26 January 1988; John Yemma, "Plenty of Oil, but Much Is in the Wrong Places," *Christian Science Monitor*, 12 February 1988; and John Yemma, "The Oil Weapon: Could Shocks of the '70s Repeat Themselves?" *Christian Science Monitor*, 9 September 1988.

42. John Yemma, "The Oil Weapon."

43. Jon Klusmire, "An Oil Shale Project Hangs On, but Barely," *High Country News*, 27 February 1989.

44. Telephone interview with B. D. Wims, synthetic fuels coordinator, Exxon, U.S.A., Houston, Texas, on 1 March 1989.

45. Local folklore from Mark Clayton, "Wringing High-grade Oil From Rock," *Christian Science Monitor*, 12 October 1988.

46. Chuck Hook, "Drinkhouse Fined $4,110.00," *The Free Weekly Newspaper* (Glenwood Springs), 3 August 1988.

Primary Sources

Documents/Manuscripts

Antlers Orchard and Development Company papers. In the posssession of Lovena Michelsen, 4951 233 Road, Rifle, Colorado.

Barthell, Robert J. "Mobile Home Architecture in Wyoming: Its Implications." Paper presented at the Popular Culture Association Annual Meeting. 21 April 1978. Manuscript in the collection of the author.

Bean, Mark L., Garfield County planning director, Garfield County Planning Office, Garfield County Courthouse, Glenwood Springs, Colorado. Letters to author 9 May 1986 and 29 May 1986.

Beard, Daniel, deputy assistant secretary of land and water resources, United States Department of the Interior. Letter to Ted Nation, Two Rivers Citizen Association, Grand Junction, Colorado, 15 August 1980. In the Friends of the Earth files.

Berger, Lisa. Files, interviews, publications, notes, and nonfiction manuscript "Boomtown (1980–1982)." Publishing contract originally with Simon & Schuster. Manuscript in the possession of the author.

Boulton, Alice, 5440 331 Road, Silt, Colorado. Letter to author received 17 June 1986.

Boulton, Margaret Irene Trusty. "Dry Hollow Ranch Memories." 1965. Copy of manuscript in the possession of John and Alice Boulton, Silt, Colorado.

Boulton, Sarah Jane. "Sketch of Divide Creek and Dry Hollow from Early Days." 1954, rev. 1956. Manuscript in the collection of the author.

Cayton, Jim. "The Fred Light Test Case." No date. Manuscript in the possession of the White River National Forest, Rifle Office, Rifle, Colorado.

Colorado Oil, Shale and Refining Corporation papers. Copy in the Savage Family Oil Shale Collection. Rifle, Colorado.

Colorado West Area Council of Governments. "Testimony Submitted During the Senator Hart Oil Shale Impact Hearings in Rifle, Colorado on August 29, 1980." In the *Rifle Tribune* files.

Cornell University. "Grand Valley, Colorado: A Plan for the Development of the Grand Valley of the Colorado River Prepared by the Graduate Students of City and Regional Planning." Autumn 1958. In the Colorado Collection, Garfield County Public Library, New Castle, Colorado.

Davis, J. B., coordinator, Public Affairs Department, Communication Services, Exxon Company, U.S.A., P.O. Box 2180, Houston, Texas. Letter to author 15 January 1986.

Doak, Libby. "The New Castle Mine Disaster." No date. Manuscript in the Garfield County Public Library, New Castle, Colorado.

Environmental Defense Fund. "Acid Rain' in the Intermountain West." Report by the Environmental Defense Fund of a Survey of Acid Rain Research in the Rocky Mountain Region. No date. In the Friends of the Earth files.

Ertl, Tell. Untitled speech text before the Arkansas Valley District of the Colorado Watershed Conservation Association, 5 August 1957. Speech titled "Oil Shale: The Prime Mineral Resource of the Colorado River Basin," presented before the Colorado River Water Users Association in Las Vegas, Nevada, 5 December 1957. Speech titled "Where Does an American Oil Shale Industry Stand Today?" presented before the National Western Mining and Energy Conference, 21 April 1960. Text of a talk to School District 51 Social Studies In-Service Group, 21 January 1965. Also excerpts from letters, the rough draft of a 1967 memorandum, and his professional resume. All documents in the possession of Joseph Fox, co-trustee, Ertl Family Estate, Lakewood, Colorado.

Exxon Company, U.S.A. Southwestern/Rocky Mountain Area. Original press release. "Exxon to Acquire Arco Interest in Colorado Oil Shale Project." 13 May 1980. In the *Rifle Tribune* files.

——. "The Role of Synthetic Fuels in the United States Energy Future" [The "white paper"]. Presented to Club 20, Grand Junction, Colorado. 25 August 1980.

——. Original press release. Public Affairs, 800 Bell Avenue, Houston. "Synfuels Potential Can Be Achieved in Acceptable Manner, Says Exxon." 29 August 1980. In the *Rifle Tribune* files.

——. Original press release. Public Affairs, 800 Bell Avenue, Houston. "Water Transfer Feasible, Exxon Official Explains." For release October 23, 1980 3:30 P.M. CDT. In the *Rifle Tribune* files.

——. Original press release. Public Affairs, 800 Bell Avenue, Houston. "Exxon to Discontinue Funding of Present Colony Oil Shale Project." 2 May 1982. In the Senator Gary Hart Oil Shale files.

——. Original press release. Public Affairs, 800 Bell Avenue, Houston. "Exxon Announces Continuation of Battlement Mesa Development on Reduced Scale." 26 May 1982. From Donald E. Smiley, Vice-President, Washington Office, Exxon Company, U.S.A. In the Senator Hart Oil Shale files.

Fisher, Thelma. "Are You Going Out This Week?" February, 1982. Manuscript in the collection of the author.

Garfield County Citizens Association. Original press release. "Colony Project Position Statement," Glenwood Springs, Colorado, 10 May 1982. In possession of the author.

Geier, Ellen Hirschberg. "Boomtown Shock: Looking Beyond the Illness." No date, but ca. 1983. Manuscript copy in possession of the author.

George, Jasper. "Cowcamps on the Flat Tops." November 1981. Manuscript in the collection of the author.

Grigor, John. "Rounding Up the Strays." 17 January 1921. Poetry manuscript in the Western History Collections of the Rifle Public Library, Rifle, Colorado.

Grode, Michael R., Colorado Division of Wildlife. "Management Considerations for Riparian Habitats in Garfield County, Colorado." May 1982. Manuscript in the collection of the author.

Hadigan, Dorothy, project officer, Exxon Education Foundation, 111 West 49th Street, New York, New York. Letter to author 2 October 1985.

Haptonstall, Judy. "A History of New Castle." 1977. Manuscript in the Garfield Public Library, New Castle, Colorado.

Hart, Gary. Letter to Clifford C. Garvin, chairman, Exxon Corporation. No date. In the Friends of the Earth files.

——. "Colorado's Energy Challenge." Address given in Denver. 23 March 1981. In the Friends of the Earth files.

——. Oil Shale Files, partial listing by subject heading: Union Oil, Colony, Chevron, Synfuels Corporation, Oil Shale—The Environmental Effects, Oil Shale Reclamation Bill, Colorado Synfuels 98th Congress, Oil Shale—Financial Incentives, Oil Shale Leasing—Others Positions, Senator Warner's S.B. 1484 vs. Senator Hart's S.B. 1383. Original materials from Senator Gary Hart's Office, 237 Russell Building, Washington, D.C.

House, Peter, director, Office of Environmental Assessments, Office of Environment, Department of Energy. "Testimony before the Senate Budget Committee, August 29, 1980, Rifle, Colorado." In the *Rifle Tribune* files.

Johnson, Ronald R., to Hon. Richard D. Lamm, September 9, 1981. Garfield County Camp Survey [squatters] 8/27/81. In the Garfield County Human Services file, Garfield County Courthouse, Glenwood Springs, Colorado.

Kohrs, E. L. and Dean V. "Social Consequences of Boomtown Growth in Wyoming," Paper presented at the regional meeting of the American Association for the Advancement of Science at Laramie, Wyoming, 1974. Paper in possession of Dr. William R. Freudenburg, Department of Sociology, University of Wisconsin at Madison.

Kozisek, Larry, mayor of Grand Junction, Colorado. "Testimony before the Subcommittee on Regional and Community Development of the Committee on the Environment and Public Works of the United States Senate." 2 August 1977. In the Colorado West Area Council of Government files, Rifle, Colorado.

Locke, H. D. "History and Development of the Mt. Logan Oil Shale Mining & Refining Company." 15 May 1964. In the Savage Family Oil Shale Collection, Rifle, Colorado.

Markey, Kevin L. "Comments of Friends of the Earth and the Environmental Defense Fund on EPA's Proposed Conditional Approval of a PSD Permit for the Colony Development Operation." 21 May 1979. In the Friends of the Earth files.

——. "Costs of Oil Shale." August 1979. In the Friends of the Earth files.

——. "Testimony of Friends of the Earth Regarding Oil Shale, Air Quality and Public Policy before the Senate Budget Committee, Rifle, Colorado, August 29, 1980."

McDermott, William F., chairman of the Community Affairs Subcommittee of the Rocky Mountain Oil and Gas Association, Inc. "Testimony before the Senate

Budget Committee, Rifle, Colorado, August 29, 1980." In the *Rifle Tribune* files.

McNeel, John A., Jr., Garfield County sheriff. Letter to Ray Baldwin, Garfield County planner, 12 December 1980. In the Garfield County Planning Office files, Garfield County Courthouse, Glenwood Springs, Colorado.

Moran, Stephanie. "The New Kids in Town: Tips for Boomtown Teachers," July 1981. Manuscript in the collection of the author.

Morgan Stanley Investment Research. Purchase Recommendation [prospectus] on Paraho Development. Broker, Anne S. McBride. 8 May 1981. Original in the Senator Hart Oil Shale files.

Mt. Logan Oil Shale Mining & Refining Company. Record of minutes, and a company circular, 1920. In the Savage Family Oil Shale Collection, Rifle, Colorado.

Oil Shale Mining Company. Stock certificate #179, issued 18 August 1917. Stock certificate facsimile in the Savage Family Oil Shale Collection, Rifle, Colorado.

O'Neill, Patrick. Letter to author 16 August 1984.

Pascoe, Monte. "Statement to United States Budget Committee, Rifle, Colorado, August 29, 1980." In the *Rifle Tribune* files.

Pence, Charles L. 2000 Post Oak Boulevard, Suite 2180. Houston, Texas. Letter to author 23 April 1986.

Quillian, A. W., III. "Oil Shale Treasure Chest and/or Pandora's Box." 1981. Manuscript in the collection of the author.

Russell, Randy. Colorado Division of Commerce and Development. Memo to Steve Schmitz on "Implications of Colony Shutdown on Committed Mitigation Items." 4 May 1982. In the Friends of the Earth files.

Savage, John A. 1122 293 Road, Rifle, Colorado. Letters to author 29 April 1986, and 2 June 1986.

Slick, W. T., Jr., vice-president, Exxon, U.S.A. "Synthetic Fuels Testimony before the Senate Budget Committee." Denver, Colorado, 17 July 1980, and Rifle, Colorado, 29 August 1980. There is a difference in the texts. In the *Rifle Tribune* files.

Slover, Charlene, coordinator, Garfield County Legal Services, Garfield County Courthouse, Glenwood Springs, Colorado. Letters to author on 18 February 1986, and 21 April 1986.

Union Oil [Company] Special Use Permit—Conditions on Construction Camp, and Union Oil Special Use Permit Conditions. In the Garfield County Planning Office files, Garfield County Courthouse, Glenwood Springs, Colorado.

——. Community Impact Mitigation data from Public Affairs administrator, Union Energy Mining Division, 2717 County Road, #215, Parachute, Colorado.

Wade, Mary, and Prendergast, Gladys. "History of New Castle, Colorado." 1966. Manuscript in the Garfield County Public Library, New Castle, Colorado.

Oral History Interviews

[All interviews by author unless otherwise stated. Interviews conducted prior to 1983 are in the Western History Department of the Denver Public Library. Interviews conducted after 1983 are in the possession of the author.]

Albrecht, Constance, Friends of the Earth staff member. Palisade, Colorado. 16 October 1985.

Atchetee, Rhonda M., Exxon accountant. Houston, Texas. 7 March 1986.

Barrow, Frank P., former project director, Colony Project, Exxon, U.S.A. 10 Huntwick Lane, Englewood, Colorado. 12 March 1986.

Berger, Lisa, energy writer. 810 3rd Street, S.W., Washington, D.C. 16 May 1986.

Bird, John William, rancher. Yampa, Colorado. 2 July 1977. Interviewed by Randall Teeuwen.

Boulton, Owen, rancher. 435 Hutton Avenue, Rifle, Colorado. 23 October 1985.

Brand, Annette, former Silt Town adminstrator. 1926 Newton, Denver, Colorado. 11 March 1986.

Brannan, Art and Pat, ranchers. Hat Ranch, Maybell, Colorado. 4 July 1977.

Burrows, Elmer, laborer. Burns, Colorado. 23 August 1977. Interviewed by Randall Teeuwen.

Carpenter, Farrington, retired lawyer and rancher. 13250 U.S. 40, Hayden, Colorado. 29 June 1977. Interviewed by Randall Teeuwuen.

Carpenter, Julia, ranch wife/homesteader. Craig, Colorado. 14 June 1977. Interviewed by Randall Teeuwen.

Craig, Mills, rancher. Craig, Colorado. 28 June 1977. Interviewed by Randall Teeuwen.

Cramer, Ira William, retired geologist. Rangely, Colorado. 12 July 1977.

Dodo, Ralph, rancher. 7717 245 Road, New Castle, Colorado. 25 July 1977.

Dow, Jim, former reporter/editor with *Rifle Tribune*. Avon, Colorado. 14 October 1985.

Dwire, John Issac, retired farmer. 1310 Charlin Street, Silt, Colorado. 28 July 1977.

Duffy, Ruth Louise, homemaker. Silt, Colorado. 13 June 1977.

Ebler, Sharon, realtor. VIP Investments, 100 E. 11th, Rifle, Colorado. 23 October 1985.

Elving, Ronald, professional staff member, United States Senate Committee on Environment and Public Works Minority Staff. Senator Gary Hart's Office, 237 Russell Building, Washington, D.C. 8 May 1986.

Engleman, Lulu, homesteader. Craig, Colorado. 27 June 1977. Interviewed by Randall Teeuwen.

Estrada, Salomon, retired railroad section hand. 832 Home Avenue, Silt, Colorado. 12 July 1977.

Evans, Reverend Lynn, former minister of the United Methodist—Presbyterian Church. 200 E. 4th. Rifle, Colorado. 25 October 1985.

Farris, Jim, farmer with draft horses. 231 North First Street, Silt, Colorado. 16 August 1977. Interviewed by Randall Teeuwen.

Flynn, Doris Stratton, druggist. New Castle Drugstore, New Castle, Colorado. 22 July 1977.

Fox, Joseph, co-trustee, Tell Ertl Estate. 3000 Youngfield, Suite 326, Lakewood, Colorado. 10 March 1986.

Freedman, Ralph, Parachute town administrator. Town Hall, Parachute, Colorado. 21 October 1985.

Fritzlan, Sonja I., homemaker. 0391 332 Road, Rifle, Colorado. 24 October 1985.

Gilmore, John S., senior research fellow, Denver Research Institute, University of Denver, Denver, Colorado. 1 November 1985.

Green, Frank Deyoe, retired rancher. 1110 Charlin Street, Silt, Colorado. 29 June 1977.

Harness, Mabel Moore, rancher. 0187 236 Road, Silt, Colorado. 26 June 1977.

Johnson, Nellie, homesteader. Craig, Colorado. 27 June 1977. Interviewed by Randall Teeuwen.

Illian, Joyce, social worker. Valley View Hospital, 1906 Blake Avenue, Glenwood Springs, Colorado. 25 October 1985.

Lewis, Esma, retired teacher. 6926 233 Road, Silt, Colorado. 15 June 1977.

Lighthizer, Leonard, rancher. Grand Junction, Colorado. 22 June 1977. Interviewed by Randall Teeuwen.

Lindauer, Bessie, rancher. 0929 215 Road, Parachute, Colorado. 29 October 1985.

Ludwig, Roger, Garfield County administrator. Glenwood Springs, Colorado. 18 October 1985.

McClue, Larry, construction worker. Silt, Colorado. 22 October 1985.

McClung, Donald I., Occidental Oil Corporation safety inspector. 795 North 7th Street, Silt, Colorado. 21 October 1985.

Mello, Wendy, counselor. White River Counseling, Western Garfield County Offices, Rifle, Colorado. 21 October 1985.

Nuffer, Robert, associate director, Sopris Mental Health Center. Glenwood Springs, Colorado. 16 January 1986.

O'Neill, Patrick, Jr., former reporter/editor with *Rifle Tribune*. Harvey Gap, Colorado. 10, 11, and 18 October 1985.

Pence, Charles, former president, Battlement Mesa Incorporated. 1929 Allen Parkway, Houston, Texas. 7 March 1986.

Savage, John A., Jr., attorney and oil shale investor. 1122 293 Road, Rifle, Colorado. 6 January 1986.

Schmitz, Gary, *Denver Post* energy reporter. Press Club Building, Washington, D.C. 28 April 1986.

Schmitz, Steve, director, Colorado West Area Council of Governments. Rifle, Colorado. 4 September 1977. Interviewed by Randall Teeuwen.

Smith, Jerry, local affairs director, Colorado State Impact Office. 1313 Sherman, Room 523, Denver, Colorado. 11 March 1986.

Staton, Steve, boomtown bartender. Dillon, Colorado. 11 October 1985.

Sullivan, Jim, former editor *Rifle Tribune*, and writer *Grand Junction Daily Sentinel*. Grand Junction, Colorado. 16 October 1985.

Sundberg, Lucille Martha, ranch wife. Hayden, Colordo. 7 June 1977. Interviewed by Randall Teeuwen.

Thurston, Floyd Alvin, retired county employee. 337 West Avenue, Rifle, Colorado. 3 October 1977.

Treese, Christopher J., public affairs administrator, Union Oil Company. 2712 County Road, #215, Parachute, Colorado. 29 October 1985.

Wims, B. D., synthetic fuels coordinator, Exxon, U.S.A. Houston office. 1 March 1989, telephone interview.

Zato, John, rancher. Craig, Colorado. 23 June 1977. Interviewed by Randall Teeuwen.

Unpublished Theses and Dissertations

Beilke, William Edward. "Colorado's First Oil Shale Rush, 1910–1930." Ph.D. dissertation, University of Colorado at Boulder, 1984.

Chapman, Mary Margaret. "Boomtown in Transition: Changing Patterns of Local Decision Making." Ph.D. dissertation, University of Colorado at Denver, 1982.

Fahys-Smith, Virginia Ellen. "The Migration of Boomtown Construction Workers: Wanderlust or Adaptation." Ph.D. dissertation, University of Colorado at Boulder, 1982.

Freudenburg, William R. "People in the Impact Zone: The Human and Social Consequences of Energy Boomtown Growth in Four Western Colorado Communities." Ph.D. dissertation, Yale University, 1979.

Gulliford, Andrew. "Boomtown Blues: A Community History of Oil Shale Booms in the Colorado River Valley, 1885–1985." Ph.D. dissertation, Bowling Green State University, 1986.

Jurie, Jay Dorian. "Oil Shale in Western Colorado: Public Policy and Regional Development." Ph.D. dissertation, Arizona State University, 1985.

Kinney, Paul. "The Impact of Selected Policy Objectives on the Funding Process: The Local Government Mineral Impact Assistance Fund Program, Colorado Department of Local Affairs." Master's thesis, University of Colorado at Denver, 1978.

Rait, Mary. "Development of Grand Junction and the Colorado River Valley to Palisade from 1881 to 1931." Master's thesis, University of Colorado at Boulder, 1931.

Shaw, Luther Gardner. "The Impact of Energy Facility Development on Local Government Revenues." Ph.D. dissertation, University of West Virginia, 1982.

Conference Proceedings and Policy Papers

Alcohol and Drug Abuse Division, Colorado Department of Health. *The Impact of Energy Development on Alcohol and Drug Problems and Treatment, Prevention and Intervention Services in Two Specific Catchment Areas of Northwest Colorado 1980–1985*. 1 November 1981.

Brown, Noel J. "Perspectives." In *Growth Alternatives for the Rocky Mountain West: Papers from the Vail Symposium V*, edited by Terrell J. Minger and Sherry D. Oaks. Boulder, Colo.: Westview Press, 1976, pp. 247–257.

Colorado Division of Planning. "Human Settlement Policies." Planning Division, 1313 Sherman Street, Room 520, Denver. 17 January 1979.

Davenport, Judith A., and Davenport, Joseph, III. *Proceedings of the First International Symposium on the Human Side of Energy*. Laramie: University of Wyoming, Department of Social Work, 1981.

Davenport, Judith A.; Davenport, Joseph, III; and Wiebler, James R. *Social Work in Rural Areas: Issues and Opportunities*. Laramie: University of Wyoming, Office of Conferences and Institutes, 1980.

Davenport, Joseph, III, and Davenport, Judith A., eds. *The Boom Town: Problems and Promises in the Energy Vortex*. Laramie: University of Wyoming, Department of Social Work, Wyoming Human Services Project, 1980.

Environmental Defense Fund. "Acid Rain' in the Intermountain West, A Report by the Environmental Defense Fund of a Survey of Acid Rain in the Rocky Mountain Region." n.d.

Etulain, Richard W. "A New Historiographical Frontier: The Twentieth Century West." Paper presented at the Western Historical Association, Sacramento, California, October 1985.

Ford, Gerald R. "Remarks." In *Growth Alternatives for the Rocky Mountain West: Papers from the Vail Symposium V*, edited by Terrell J. Minger and Sherry D. Oaks. Boulder, Colo.: Westview Press, 1976, pp. 215–223.

Fox, Douglas G.; Murphy, Dennis J.; and Haddow, Dennis, technical coordinators. *Air Quality, Oil Shale, and Wilderness—A Workshop to Identify and Protect Air Quality Related Values of the Flat Tops*. 13–15 January 1981, Glenwood Springs, Colorado. USDA Forest Service, General Technical Report RM–91. Rocky Mountain Forest and Range Experiment Station. Fort Collins: Colorado State University, September 1982.

Fox, J. P., and Phillips, T. E. "Wastewater Treatment in the Oil Shale Industry." In *Oil Shale: The Environmental Challenges*. Proceedings of an international symposium, sponsored by the Oil Shale Task Force and U.S. Department of Energy, 11–14 August 1980 at Vail, Colorado, edited by Kathy Kellogg Peterson. Golden, Colo.: Colorado School of Mines, 1981, pp. 253–291.

Garfield County Economic Development Steering Committee, Nick Massaro, Chairman. *Garfield County Economic Development Report*. Glenwood Springs, Colo.: December 1985.

Gilmore, John S., and Duff, Mary K. *Policy Analysis for Rural Development and Growth Management in Colorado*. Prepared for Colorado Rural Development Commission. Denver: University of Denver, Denver Research Institute, March 1973.

Gilmore, John S. *Observation and Comments on the Roles of Federal, State, and Local Governments in Socioeconomic Impact Mitigation*. Paper presented at Alaska Symposium on Social, Economic and Cultural Impacts of Natural Resource Development, Alaska Pacific University, Anchorage, 27 August 1982.

Gilmore, John S.; Duff, Mary K.; and Stenehjem, Erik J. "Oil Shale Development: The Need for and Problems of Socioeconomic Impact Management and Assessment." In *Oil Shale: the Environmental Challenges*. Proceedings of an international symposium, sponsored by the Oil Shale Task Force and U.S.

Department of Energy, 11–14 August 1980 at Vail, Colorado, edited by Kathy Kellogg Peterson. Golden, Colo.: Colorado School of Mines, 1981, pp. 319-376.

Gilmore, John S. *Socioeconomic Impact Management: Are Impact Assessments Good Enough to Help?* Paper presented at Conference on Computer Models and Forecasting Impacts of Growth and Development, University of Alberta, Jasper Park Lodge, Alberta, Canada, 21 April 1980, rev. June 1980.

Grode, Michael R. wildlife biologist, Colorado Divison of Wildlife. *Management Considerations for Riparian Habitats in Garfield County, Colorado.* Prepared for Garfield County Planning Department, May 1982.

Growth Impact Group. *Quality of Life, Expectations of Change, and Planning for the Future in an Energy Production Community—A Report to the People of Meeker and Walden, Colorado.* Boulder, Colo.: University of Colorado, January 1982.

Gruen, Lori, ed. *The Quality of Life in Colorado: Proceedings of a Conference.* Center for the Study of Values and Social Policy, Department of Philosophy, University of Colorado, 1982.

Hill, A. David. *What People in Western Colorado Said Last Summer When the Boom Was On.* Studies in the Quality of Life vol. 1, no. 1. Center for the Study of Values and Social Policy, Department of Philosophy, University of Colorado, March 1983.

Hirschberg, Ellen. *The Socioeconomic Impacts of Oil Shale Development.* Paper presented at the "Island" Conservation Summit Meeting at Glade Park near Grand Junction, Colorado, 18 September 1981. Copy in Friends of the Earth files.

Holland, L. M. "Studies of the Biology and Toxicology of Oil Shale Materials." In *Oil Shale: The Environmental Challenges.* Proceedings of an international symposium, sponsored by the Oil Shale Task Force and U.S. Department of Energy, 11–14 August 1980 at Vail, Colorado, edited by Kathy Kellogg Peterson. Golden, Colo.: Colorado School of Mines, 1981, pp. 87–104.

Howell, Robert E., and Bentley, Marion T. *Assessing, Managing and Mitigating the Impacts of Economic Decline: A Community Perspective.* WREP 91. Western Rural Development Center, Corvallis: Oregon State University, June 1986.

Johnson, Wallace. "Resource and Energy Development and the Law." In *Growth Alternatives for the Rocky Mountain West: Papers from the Vail Symposium V,* edited by Terrell J. Minger and Sherry D. Oaks. Boulder, Colo.: Westview Press, 1976, pp. 31–40.

Jurie, Jay D. *Arizona Mining Towns: Public Policy During Boom and Bust.* Public Policy Papers Series, No. 1. Center for Public Affairs, College of Public Programs, Arizona State University, n.d.

Kassover, Jodi, and McKeown, Robert L. *Resource Development, Rural Communities and Rapid Growth: Managing Social Change in the Modern Boomtown.* Policy paper by Rocky Mountain Consulting Associates and the Colorado West Regional Mental Health Center, n.d.

Lee, Henry. *Oil Shale Development: A Perspective on Certain Regional Economic Issues.* Paper Series E–80–06. Energy & Environmental Policy Center, John F.
Kennedy School of Government, Harvard University, October 1980.

Leutwiler, Nels R. "The Mancamp Issue: Toward a Good Neighbor Policy for Major
Energy/Minerals Developments." Western Oil Shale/Synfuels Symposium at
Grand Junction, Colorado, 22-26 April 1985.

Loper, D. R., president, Chevron Shale Oil Company. *Cooperation Versus Crunch
for Energy Impacted Communities. Synthetic Fuels—Problems and Prospects.*
U.S. National Committee. The World Energy Conference. Washington, D.C.,
16 April 1981.

Martin, William E.; Deeds, Dana; Carpenter, Edwin; Ayer, Harry; Arthur, Louise;
and Gum, Russell. *Reduction in Labor Force in a Single Company Town:
Who is Selected and How Do They Adapt?* Discussion Paper #8. Western
Rural Development Center, Corvallis: Oregon State University, 1976.

Minger, Terrell J., ed. *The Vail Symposium/Six: The Future of Human Settlements in
the Rocky Mountain West.* Papers from the Vail Symposium VI. Vail, Colo.:
The Printery, 1978.

Richardson, Ralph W. "Regional Environmental Management—A National Impera-
tive." In *Growth Alternatives for the Rocky Mountain West: Papers from the
Vail Symposium V*, edited by Terrell J. Minger and Sherry D. Oaks. Boulder,
Colo.: Westview Press, 1976, pp. 21–30.

Sheesley, David C., and Leonard, Ellen M. "An Air Quality Strategy for Oil Shale
Development." In *Oil Shale: The Environmental Challenges.* Proceedings of
an international symposium, sponsored by the Oil Shale Task Force and U.S.
Department of Energy, 11–14 August 1980 at Vail, Colorado, edited by Kathy
Kellogg Peterson. Golden, Colo.: Colorado School of Mines, 1981, pp. 294–
317.

Siegel, Michael, Colorado West Area Council of Governments impact coordinator
and housing specialist. "Construction Worker Housing Issues Paper." Rifle,
Colorado, January 1981.

Singlaub, John. "Special Management Areas in Energy Regions, The Piceance
Basin." In *Special Management Areas Conference.* Proceedings of the Special
Management Areas Conference, sponsored by the Native Conservancy, Den-
ver Botanic Gardens, USDI Bureau of Land Management, Colorado, and
USDA Forest Service, Rocky Mountain Region, 24–25 April 1984 at Denver
Botanic Gardens, Denver, Colorado, edited by Lawrence G. Kolenbrander.

Thompson, James G.; Reynolds, Robert R., Jr.; and Wilkinson, Kenneth P. "Con-
tributions Toward A Conceptual Framework for Social Impact Assessment in
Semi-Arid Lands of the Western United States." Educational Resources Infor-
mation Center (ERIC), Clearinghouse for Rural Education and Small Schools
(CRESS). Document #RC 015643. Las Cruces: New Mexico State University,
March 1986.

Uhlmann, Julie M., and Olson, Judith K. *Human Services Handbook for Rural Rapid
Growth Communities.* Working Paper #1: Regional Profile Analysis.

Washington, D.C.: U.S. Department of Health and Human Services, Grant No. 90–PD–10002101, October 1981.

Uhlmann, Julie M.; Olson, Judith K.; and Turshak, Paulette. *Human Services Handbook for Rural Rapid Growth Communities*. Working Paper #2: Human Services Standards. Washington, D.C.: U.S. Department of Health and Human Services, Grant No. 90–PD–10002101, October 1981.

Uhlmann, Julie M.; Olson, Judith K.; Turshak, Paulette; Slaughter, Ellen L.; Taylor Kenneth C. *Human Services Handbook for Rural Rapid Growth Communities*. Working Paper #3: Social Indicators Analysis. Washington, D.C.: U.S. Department of Health and Human Services, Grant No. 90–PD–10002101, September 1981.

Williams, David C. *Boom, Then Bust: Managing Rapid Growth Cities*. Management Information Service Project. International City Management Association. vol. 9, no. 3 March 1977.

Socioeconomic Impact Statements

Ashland Oil, Inc. *Oil Shale Tract C-b Socio-Economic Assessment*, vol. 1 "Baseline Description," and vol. 2 "Impact Analysis." March 1976.

BMML, Inc. *Chevron Shale Oil Company Clear Creek Project—Socioeconomic Assessment Existing Conditions*. vol. 1 and 2. Boulder, Colorado, July 1982.

Colorado West Area Council of Governments. *Illustrative Information and Analysis Regarding Socioeconomics of Oil Shale Development*. Rifle, Colorado, September 1980.

Denver Research Institute and Browne, Bortz & Coddington. *Socioeconomic Impacts of Power Plants*. Prepared for the Electric Power Research Institute, Environmental Risk and Issues Analysis Program/Energy Analysis and Environment Division, February 1982.

Geoecology Associates, Marlatt and Associates, and Voorhees Associates. *Socio-Economic Studies*. Prepared for Colony Development Operation, Atlantic Richfield Company, operator, July 1974.

Governor's Office. Oil Shale Planning and Coordination. *Impact: An Assessment of the Impact of Oil Shale Development*—Colorado Planning and Management Region 11 vol. 1 "Executive Summary," vol. 2 "Human Services—Health," vol. 3 "Human Services—Other Than Health," vol. 5. "Population Analysis." Denver: December 1974.

Gulf Oil Corporation. *Rio Blanco Oil Shale Project: Social and Economic Impact Statement for Tract C-a*. March 1976. Addendum, May 1977.

Leistritz, F. Larry, and Maki, Karen C. *Socioeconomic Effects of Large-Scale Resource Development Projects in Rural Areas: The Case of McLean County, North Dakota*. Agricultural Economics Reports no. 151. Fargo: North Dakota State University, December 1981.

Monarchi, David, and Rahe, Charles. *A Study of the Social and Economic Needs Created by the Proposed Craig Power Installation*. Prepared for Yampa Project participants, n.d.

Mountain West Research, Inc. *A Guide to Methods for Impact Assessment of Western Coal/Energy Development*. Prepared for the Missouri River Basin Commission and Resource and Land Investigations Program, U.S. Geological Survey, January 1979.

———. *A Proposal to Conduct an Economic Base and Secondary Impact Analysis for Mesa County, Colorado*. 22 May 1981.

National Institute for Socioeconomic Research. *Colony/Battlement Mesa Socioeconomic Monitoring Report Second Quarter of 1982*. Boulder, Colorado, July 1982.

———. *Colony/Battlement Mesa Socioeconomic Monitoring Report Third Quarter of 1982*. Boulder, Colorado, October 1982.

Piatt, Susan P. *Regional Socio-Economic Impact Monitoring System—Region 11*. Prepared for the Colorado West Area Council of Governments, November 1981, rev. February 1982.

Quality Development Associates. *Cathedral Bluffs Shale Oil Project, Socioeconomic Monitoring Report Number 6*. Denver, 1979.

———. *Development Patterns and Social Impacts: A Focus on the Oil Shale Region*. Denver, July 1979.

Rahenkamp/Oldham, Inc. *Garfield County [Colorado] Comprehensive Plan*. May 1981.

Schmueser & Associates, Inc. *Union Oil Company Parachute Creek Shale Oil Program Third Quarter Report*. Glenwood Springs, Colorado, 1982.

———. *Colony/Battlement Mesa Socioeconomic Monitoring Report Fourth Quarter of 1982*. Glenwood Springs, Colorado, January 1983.

———. *Colony/Battlement Mesa Socioeconomic Monitoring Report First Quarter of 1983*. Glenwood Springs, Colorado, April 1983.

Stenehjem, Erik J. *Summary Description of SEAM: The Social and Economic Assessment Model*. Energy and Environmental System Division, Argonne National Library, Argonne, Illinois, April 1978.

THK Associates, Inc. *Impact Analysis and Development Patterns for the Oil Shale Region—Mesa, Garfield and Rio Blanco Counties, Colorado*. Prepared for the Colorado West Area Council of Governments and the Oil Shale Regional Planning Commission, February 1974.

VTN Colorado. *Socioeconomic and Environmental Land Use Survey: Moffat, Routt and Rio Blanco Counties, Colorado—Summary Report*. Prepared for W. R. Grace, April 1975.

Government Documents and Technical Reports

Abt/west. *Energy Activity in the West: Data Book*. Prepared for Western Governors Policy Office, 1980.

Ashland Oil, Inc. *Oil Shale Tract C-b, Detailed Development Plan and Related Materials*, Vol. 1 and 2. February 1976.

Athearn, Frederic J. *An Isolated Empire: A History of Northwest Colorado*. Denver: Bureau of Land Management, 1982.

Atomic Energy Commission. *The Bronco Oil Shale Study* PNE–1400. Prepared by the United States Atomic Energy Commission, the United States Department of the Interior, CER Geonuclear Corporation, and the Lawrence Radiation Laboratory. Washington, D.C.: U.S. Government Printing Office, 13 October 1967.

Bechtel Petroleum, Inc. *White River Shale Project. Detailed Development Plan, Oil Shale Tracts Ua and Ub,* Vol. 1 and 2. San Francisco, August 1981.

Bickert, Browne, Coddington & Associates, Inc. *Attitudes and Opinions Related to the Development of an Oil Shale Industry.* Prepared for The Oil Shale Regional Planning Commission and the Colorado West Area Council of Governments, July 1973.

——. *Boom Town Financing Study, Vol. 2 Estimates of Public Sector Financial Needs, Six Western Colorado Communities.* Denver: Colorado Department of Local Affairs, July 1976.

Bolt, Ross M.; Luna, Dan; and Watkins, Lynda A. *Boom Town Financing Study, Vol. 1 Analysis and Recommendations.* Denver: Colorado Department of Local Affairs, November 1976.

Bowers, James M. and Associates. *Housing Report.* Prepared for Colorado West Area Council of Governments, January 1974.

Bureau of Land Management, U.S. Department of the Interior. *Draft Environmental Impact Statement for the White River Resource Area. Wilderness Planning Amendment.* Denver: Bureau of Land Management, 1982.

——. *Draft Piceance Basin Resource Management Plan and Environmental Impact Statement,* vol. 1 and 2. April 1984, vol. 3. March 1985.

——. *Piceance Basin Planning Area Maps.* Branch of Cartographic Services, BLM Colorado State Office, 2020 Arapahoe Street, Denver, n.d.

Bureau of Mines, State of Colorado. *The Oil Shales of Northwestern Colorado,* Bulletin no. 8. Denver: Eames Brothers, 1 August 1919.

Business Research Division, Graduate School of Business Administration, University of Colorado. *The Plateau Region, Colorado Planning and Management Region No. 11, Colorado Regional Development Profile.* Prepared for Community Development Section, Division of Commerce and Development, Colorado Department of Local Affairs, December 1975.

Center for Community Development and Design. *Town Halls Workbook.* Prepared for Division of Energy Impact Assistance, Colorado Department of Local Affairs, Summer 1981.

Colorado Division of Planning. *From Bonanza to Last Chance: Changing Economic Expectations in Colorado,* vol. 1. (Statewide approach). October 1977.

Colorado Energy Research Institute, Colorado School of Mines. *Colorado Oil Shale Development Scenarios 1981–2000.* Prepared for Governor's Blue Ribbon Panel, March 1981.

Committee on Oil Shale. *Shale Oil Status Report.* Denver: Rocky Mountain Oil and Gas Association, January 1985.

Covey, Herb. *Colorado's Energy Boom: Impact on Crime and Criminal Justice .* Colorado Division of Criminal Justice, 9 February 1981.

Department of Local Affairs, Division of Impact Assistance. *Construction Workforce Housing—Assembled Materials.* State of Colorado, n.d.

Duncan, Donald C., and Swanson, Vernon E. *Organic Rich Shales of the U.S. and World Land Areas.* U.S. Geological Survey Circular 523. Washington, D.C.: U.S. Government Printing Office, 1966.

Energy Development Consultants, Inc., and Wright–Ingraham Institute. *Colorado Oil Shale: The Current Status.* U.S. Department of Energy Grant # DE–FG48–79R800212.001. Denver: Colorado Geological Survey, 1979.

Energy Security: A Report to the President of the United States. Washington, D.C.: United States Department of Energy, March 1987.

Environmental Research & Technology, Inc. *Phililips Petroleum Company Mahogany Oil Shale Project.* Exhibit to Lower Colorado River Basin Proceedings to Set Stream Classification and Establish Numeric Standards. October 1982.

Exxon Company, U.S.A., Public Affairs Department. *Energy Outlook 1980–2000.* Houston, December 1979.

—— and Tosco (The Oil Shale Company). *Colony—The Colony Shale Oil Project.* 1982.

Exxon Corporation. Annual Reports. 1251 Avenue of the Americas, New York, New York. 1979–1984.

Ferraro, Paul, and Nazaryk, Paul. *Assessments of the Cumulative Environmental Impacts of Energy Development in Northwestern Colorado —Final Report.* Denver: Colorado Department of Health, March 1983.

First Biennial Report of the Bureau of Labor Statistics of the State of Colorado, 1886–1888. Denver: Collier & Cleaveland Lithography Co., 1888.

Folk-Williams, John A., and Cannon, James S. *Water for the Energy Market—Vol. 2 of Water in the West.* 2 vols. Santa Fe, N.M.: Western Network, 1983.

Gallacher, Walter. *The White River National Forest 1891–1981.* Rev. ed. Glenwood Springs, Colo.: White River National Forest Regional Office, 1983.

Garfield County Commisioners. "Resolution Concerned With Amending The Garfield County Zoning Resolution of 1978 by the Inclusion of a New Section 5.08 Fiscal Impact Mitigation Program," Resolution No. 82–318. 20 December 1982.

Gilmore, John S., and Duff, Mary K. *The Oil Shale Regional Economic Base: Regional Development and Land Use Study.* Prepared for the Oil Shale Regional Planning Commission and Colorado West Area Council of Governments, January 1973.

Gilmore, John S.; Duff, Mary K; and Jaeckel, Eric F. *Estimate of Local Service Employment and Diversification Potential Related to Development of a Single Oil Shale Plant in Garfield County and an Eight Plant Regional Complex.* Prepared for Atlantic Richfield Company, Operator Colony Development Operation, September 1973.

Gilmore, John S., and Duff, Mary K. *Analysis of Financing Problems in Coal and Oil Shale Boom Towns.* Prepared for the Federal Energy Administration, Of-

fice of Energy Conservation and Environment, Office of Environmental
    Programs, Washington, D.C., July 1976.
Hayden, F. V. *Tenth Annual Report of the United States Geological and Geographi-
    cal Survey of the Territories Embracing Colorado and Parts of Adjacent Ter-
    ritories, Being a Report of Progress of the Exploration for the Year 1876*.
    Washington, D.C.: U.S. Government Printing Office, 1878.
Industrial Economics and Management Division and Denver Research Institute. *Sum-
    mary of Fiscal Impact Assessment for Phase II of Union Oil Company's
    Parachute Creek Shale Oil Program*. June 1984.
Ludwig, Roger. *Garfield County 1983 Human Service Plan*. Glenwood Springs,
    Colo.: Garfield County Human Service Planning Department, January 1983.
Mehls, Steven F. *The Valley of Opportunity: A History of West-Central Colorado*.
    Cultural Resources Series no. 12. Denver: Bureau of Land Management, 1982.
Mineral Resources Work Group of the Upper Colorado Region, State-Federal Inter-
    Agency Group. *Upper Colorado Region Comprehensive Framework Study*,
    Appendix 7, Mineral Resources. Prepared for the Pacific Southwest Inter-
    Agency Committee, Water Resources Council, June 1971.
Montana Energy Advisory Council. *Energy Information Booklet: Supplement*.
    Helena, Mont.: Office of the Lieutenant Governor, 1975.
Morris, Lynne Clemmons, and Morris, Judson Henry, Jr. *Meeting Educational Needs
    in Rural Communities Confronting Rapid Growth*. Educational Resources In-
    formation Center (ERIC), Clearinghouse on Rural Education and Small
    Schools (CRESS). Las Cruces: New Mexico State University, February 1981.
Morse, J. G., Colorado Energy Research Institute. *Colorado Energy Resources Hand-
    book. Vol. 2: Oil Shale*. Golden, Colo.: Colorado School of Mines, October
    1976.
National Park Service, U.S. Department of the Interior. *Energy Impacted Com-
    munities: Challenges in Recreation, Open Space and Historic Preservation*.
    No place of publication or date.
National Petroleum Council. *Factors Affecting U.S. Oil and Gas Outlook*.
    Washington, D.C.: National Petroleum Council, 1987.
Neal, Arthur G.; Groat, H. Theodore; and Wicks, Jerry W. *Social and Demographic
    Correlates of Household Energy Use and Conservation—Final Report*. Ohio
    Inter-University Energy Research Council, Ohio Board of Regents, Contract
    No. OBR–ER–4 July 1981.
Petrock, Edith M., and Bauman, Paul C. *Energy and Education: Planning for Higher
    Prices and Potential Shortages*. Report N. I82–2. Denver: Education Commis-
    sion of the States, July 1982.
Powell, John Wesley. *Report on the Lands of the Arid Region of the United States*.
    Washington, D.C.: U.S. Government Printing Office, 1878.
Prien, Charles H.; Schanz, John J., Jr.; and Doran, Richard K. *Profile Development
    of an Oil Shale Industry in Colorado*. Prepared for the Oil Shale Regional
    Planning Commission and the Colorado West Area Council of Governments,
    February 1973.

Russell, Kenneth R.; Williams, Gary L.; Hughes, Betty Ann; and Walsworth, Daniel S. *Wildmis—A Wildlife Mitigation and Management Planning System—Demonstrated on Oil Shale Development.* Final Administrative Report, Oil Shale Project, Fish and Wildlife Service, Contract #14-16-0008-2016. Performed for Western Energy and Land Use Team, Office of Biological Services, Fish and Wildlife Service, U.S. Department of the Interior, April 1980.

Rycroft, Robert W., and Monaghan, James E. *Cumulative Impacts of Energy and Defense Projects in the West: Synfuels and the MX.* Columbus, Ohio: Mershon Center and Program for Energy Research, Education, and Public Service, 1981.

Science and Public Policy Program, University of Oklahoma. *Energy from the West: Draft Policy Analysis Report.* Prepared for Office of Research and Development, U.S. Environmental Protection Agency, Washington, D.C., n.d.

Segall, Mary, project director, *Project Genesis—An Ethnography of Rifle and Parachute Colorado.* Denver: Community Health Nursing, University of Colorado Health Sciences Center, Spring 1982.

——. *An Ethnography of Rifle and Parachute, Colorado.* Denver: Community Health Nursing, University of Colorado Health Sciences Center, April 1983.

Sikorowski, Linda. *Assessment of Concerns and Informational Needs Involving Wildlife in Northwest Colorado.* Department of the Interior, U.S. Fish and Wildlife Service, Contract No. 14–16–0006–81–914, April 1982.

Taylor, O. James, ed. *Oil Shale, Water Resources and Valuable Minerals of the Piceance Basin, Colorado: The Challenge and Choices of Development.* U.S. Geological Survey, Professional Paper 1310. Washington, D.C.: U.S. Government Printing Office, 1987.

Trahan, Richard, and Dietz, John. *IDEAS: Impact of Developing Energy on Administration of Schools.* Greeley, Colo.: University of Northern Colorado, September 1983.

Uhlmann, Julie M., and Olson, Judith K. *Planning for Rural Human Services: The Western Energy-Impact Experience.* U.S. Department of Health and Human Services, 1983.

United States Department of the Interior. *Final Environmental Statement for the Prototype Oil-Shale Leasing Program. Regional Impacts of Oil Shale Development,* vol. 1–6. Prepared in compliance with Section 102 (2)(c) of the National Environmental Policy Act of 1969, Stock No. 2400–00785. Washington, D.C.: U.S. Government Printing Office, 1973.

——. *Proposed Development of Oil Shale Resources by the Colony Development Operation in Colorado—Final Environmental Statement,* vol. 1. N.d.

URS Engineers. *Meeker-Piceance Basin Rail Feasibility Study, Colorado State Rail Plan, Status Report.* 27 March 1981, and *Technical Memorandum on Evaluating the Alternatives.* 14 May 1981.

West, Stanley A. *Opportunities for Company-Community Cooperation in Mitigating Energy Facility Impacts.* Prepared for the United States Energy Research and Development Administration, August 1977.

Winchester, Dean E. *Oil Shale in Northwestern Colorado and Adjacent Areas.* U.S. Geological Survey Bulletin 641–F. Washington, D.C.: U.S. Government Printing Office, 1916.

Woodruff, E. G., and Day, David T. *Oil Shale of Northwestern Colorado and Northeastern Utah.* U.S. Geological Survey Bulletin 581–A. Washington, D.C.: U.S. Government Printing Office, 1914.

Secondary Sources

Multimedia Productions

Do We Really Need the Rockies? Videotape. NOVA for PBS/WGBH. 1980.

Oil Shale Now! Videotape in two parts. Oil Shale Association, 1676 Pleasant Plains Road, Annapolis, Md. October 1988.

Rifle, Colorado: Boomtown of the Seventies. Videotape. Produced by Candi Harper for Grassroots Television. Aspen, Colo. 1975.

The Four Corners Area: A National Sacrifice Area? Film. Produced by Christopher McLeod, Randy Hayes, and Glenn Switkes for Four Corners Films. 1985.

The Years Ahead: Life for the Aging in Northwest Colorado. Slide/tape. Produced by Andrew Gulliford and Randall Teewuen for the Colorado Endowment for the Humanities. 1978.

Journal and Magazine Articles

"All Washed Up." *The Economist*, 8 May 1982.

Armitage, Susan H. "Household Work and Childrearing on the Frontier: The Oral History Record." *Sociology & Social Research* 63 (April 1979): 467–74.

Athearn, Frederic, J. "The Parachute That Failed to Open: Colorado's First Oil Shale Mining District, 1890-1935." *The Midwest Review* 6 (Spring 1984): 1–13.

"Battlement Mesa: A New Community." *Mines Magazine* 71 (February 1981): 28.

Berger, Donald G. "A View from the State House." *Colorado River Journal* 4 (July/August 1982): 15, 16, 34.

Bernard, Sherri Poe. "The Tiger Empties the Tank." *Colorado River Journal* 4 (July/August 1982): 8–10.

Bohi, Douglas R. "The World Oil Market — The Future Will Not Resemble the Past." *Resources* 79 (Winter 1985): 10–12.

Brose, David. "Cowboy Poets Maintain Long Tradition." *Colorado Heritage News*, January 1986, p. 3.

"Brown and Root. ". . . and Crime to Boot." *Colorado Labor Advocate*, 24 July 1981, p. 6.

Carter, Jimmy. "President's Proposed Energy Policy." *Vital Speeches of the Day* 43 (1 May 1977): 418–420.

———. "The Moral Equivalent of War." *Vital Speeches of the Day* 43 (1 May 1977): 420–423.

———. "The Nation's Economy." *Vital Speeches of the Day* 46 (1 April 1977): 354–357.

Clark, Tom. "Wyoming Boom." *Rocky Mountain Magazine*, June 1979, pp. 46–74.

Colburn, C. Lorimore. "Our Future Supply of Oil." *DuPont Magazine* 20 (November 1926): 11.

Cooper, Donald B. "Coping With Boomtown Growth." *Colorado Municipalities* 54 (July/August 1981): 4–7.

Cortese, Charles F. and Jones, B. "The Sociological Analysis of Boomtowns." *Western Sociological Review* 8 (1977): 76–90.

Cottrell, W. F. "Death by Dieselization." *American Sociological Review* 16 (June 1951): 358–365.

Crane, Frank. "When the Oil Gives Out." *Current Opinion* 69 (August 1920): 173.

Davidson, Claud M. "Retail Facilities in Colorado Boomtowns." *Social Science Journal* 24 (June 1987): 247–259.

Day, David T. "Oil Famine and the Remedy." *Review of Reviews* 62 September 1920): 295.

DeVoto, Bernard. "The West: A Plundered Province." *Harper's Magazine* 169 (August 1934): 355–364.

Donley, Edward. "Synfuels, Security, and the National Will." *Vital Speeches of the Day* 46 (1 June 1980): 507–510.

Exxon Corporation. 1981 Annual Report.

Exxon Corporation. 1982 Annual Report.

Feldman, Dede. "Boomtown." *Minetalk*, May-June 1981.

Felmlee, Vicki, and Isbell, Alan. "The Housing Crisis." *Colorado River Journal* 3 (March/April 1982)): 10–15.

Flint, J. "What to Expect from Synfuels." *Forbes* 130 (6 December 1982): 43–44.

Frank, Glenn. "Defeating the Oil Famine." *Century* 101 (February 1921): 544.

Fraser, Mark, and Dykes, Jeffrey. "Booms in the Rural West: A Review." *Human Services in the Rural Environment* 9 (April 1986): 5–11.

Freudenburg, William R. "Women and Men in an Energy Boomtown: Adjustment, Alienation, and Adaptation." *Rural Sociology* 46 (Summer 1981: 220–244.

——. "Balance and Bias in Boomtown Research." *Pacific Sociological Review* 25 (July 1982): 323–338

——. "Boomtown's Youth: The Differential Impacts of Rapid Community Growth on Adolescents and Adults." *American Sociological Review* 49 (1984): 697–705.

——. "The Density of Acquaintanceship: An Overlooked Variable in Community Research?" *American Journal of Sociology* 92 (July 1986): 27–63.

——. "Social Impact Assessment." *Annual Review of Sociology* 12 (1986): 451–478.

——. Bacigalupi, Linda M.; and Landoll-Young, Cheryl. "Mental Health Consequences of Rapid Community Growth: A Report from the Longitudinal Study of Boomtown Mental Health Impacts." *Journal of Health and Human Resources Administration* 4 (Winter 1982): 334–352.

——. and Keating, Kenneth M. "Applying Sociology to Policy: Social Science and the Environmental Impact Statement." *Rural Sociology* 50 (Winter 1985): 578–605.

——. "Increasing the Impact of Sociology on Social Impact Assessment: Toward Ending the Inattention." *The American Sociologist* 17 (May 1982): 71–80.

Friesma, H. Paul, and Culhane, Paul J. "Social Impacts, Politics, and the Environmental Impact Statement Process." *Natural Resources Journal* 16 (April
1976): 339–354.

Gallacher, Walter. "Shale's Beginnings: Doris Flynn Remembers." *Colorado River
Journal* 5 (Summer 1983): 8–9.

Gilmore, John S. "Boom Towns May Hinder Energy Resource Development."
Science 191 (13 February 1976): 535–540.

Glenn, Frank. "Defeating the Oil Famine." *Century* 101 (February 1921): 544.

Golman, Daniel. "We Are Breaking the Silence About Death." *Psychology Today* 10
(September 1976): 44–47, 103.

Graber, Edith E. "Newcomers and Oldtimers: Growth and Change in a Mountain
Town." *Rural Sociology* 39 (Winter 1974): 504–513.

Gressley, Gene M. "The West: Past Present and Future." *Western Historical Quarterly* 17 (January 1986): 5–24.

Gulliford, Andrew. "Boomtown Blues: When Dreams Don't Pan Out." *Not Man
Apart—the Newsmagazine of Friends of the Earth* 16 (March/April 1986): 14–
15.

———. "Little Man Alone: F. V. Hayden." *Directions, the magazine for Western
Colorado*, May 1983, p. 27.

———. "From Boom to Bust: Small Towns and Energy Development on Colorado's
Western Slope." *Small Town* 13 (March/April 1983): 15–22.

———. "Shale's Rocky Road." *Colorado River Journal* 4 (July/August 1982): 14, 28.

———. "The Vantage Point: Colorado Elderly Steadfast." *Perspective on Aging* 9
(January/February 1980): 4–8.

———. "The Years Ahead: Growth and the Elderly on the Western Slope." *People &
Policy—a journal of humanistic perspectives on Colorado Issues* 1 (Summer
1979): 18–20, 40–41.

Halaas, David F. "Josephine Roche, 1886-1976: Social Reformer, Mine Operator."
Colorado Heritage News, March 1985, p. 4.

———. and Morton, Gerald C. "Boom and Bust." *Colorado Heritage News,* no. 1 and
2 (1983), pp. 9–24.

Hurlburt, David. "The Day the Company Said Goodbye." *Rocky Mountain
Magazine*, March 1981, pp. 35–39.

Isbell, Alan. "Along the River: Coping with Squatters." *Colorado River Journal* 3
(March/April 1982): 36.

———. "Is There Life After Exxon?" *Colorado River Journal* 4 (July/August 1982):
11–12.

Iverson, Martha J.; Bertsche, Jon W.; and Clark, Frank W. "Comprehensive Community Care: The Potential of Informal Helping for Boomtowns." *Journal of
Health and Human Resources Administration* 4 (Winter 1982): 353–362.

Ives, Ronald L. "Folklore of Eastern Middle Park, Colorado." *Journal of American
Folklore* 54 (January-June 1941): 24–43.

James, Mary. "Shale Oil? Here?" *Exxon, U.S.A* 20 (Third Quarter 1981): 2–7.

Kilker, Catherine. "Ranching: Tough Times and Top Land Prices." *Shale Country*,
April/May 1982, pp. 2–4.

Lemann, Nicholas. "Grand Junction: Can't Win for Losing." *Atlantic Monthly* 255 (April 1985): 18–28.

Levy, Lloyd. "Hazards of Growth: The Brain Drain." *Colorado River Journal* (January/February 1982): 37.

Lillydahl, Jane H., and Moen, Elizabeth W. "Planning, Managing, and Financing Growth and Decline in Energy Resource Communities: A Case Study of Western Colorado." *Journal of Energy & Development* 8 (Spring 1983): 211–229.

Little, Arthur D. "The Fuel Problem." *Atlantic Monthly* 127 (February 1921): 195.

Maddox, Sam. "Mr. Johnson Goes to Town, Gives Away Millions." *Rocky Mountain Magazine*, October 1979, pp. 29–31.

Marbach, W. D. "The Death of Synfuels." *Newsweek* 99 (17 May 1982): 75–76.

Margolis, Eric. "Colorado's Coal People: Images from Turn-of-the-Century Coal Communities." *Colorado Heritage News*, 1984, pp. 10–24.

———. "Western Coal Mining As a Way of Life: An Oral History of the Colorado Coal Miners to 1914." *Journal of the West* 24 (July 1985): 5–15.

Marston, Ed. "What Happened to the Oil Shale Towns." *Planning* 50 (May 1984): 25–29.

Martin, Russell. "Be It Ever So Mobile—There's No Place Like Home." *Rocky Mountain Magazine* 2 (December 1979): 55–60.

———. "The Great Western Shale Game." *Rocky Mountain Magazine* 3 (January/February 1981): 32–39.

Massey, Garth. "Critical Dimensions in Urban Life: Energy Extraction and Community Collapse in Wyoming." *Urban Life* 9 (July 1980): 187–199.

McCarthy, Michael. "He Fought for His West: Colorado Congressman Wayne Aspinall," *Colorado Heritage News*, no. 1 (1988), pp. 33–44.

McHugh, Heather H. ed. *Shale Country: Special Edition.* 5 (1983).

Mehls, Steven F. "Waiting for the Boom: Colorado Shale-Oil Development." *Journal of the West* 21 (October 1982): 11–16.

Meyer, Randall. "Western State Energy Resources Development." *Mines Magazine* 71 (June 1981): 3–7.

Mitchell, Guy Elliott. "Billions of Barrels of Oil Locked Up in Rocks." *National Geographic* 33 (February 1918): 195–205.

Moen, Elizabeth W. "Voodoo Forecasting: Technical, Political and Ethical Issues Regarding the Projection of Local Population Growth." *Population Research and Policy Review* 3 (January 1984): 1–25.

"More Synfuel Projects May Run Out of Gas." *Business Week*, 27 September 1982, pp. 27–28.

Morse, Edward L. "After the Fall: The Politics of Oil." *Foreign Affairs* 64 (Spring 1986): 792–811.

Noel, Patrick. "The County Commissioners: A Changing Role." *Colorado River Journal* 3 (January/February 1982): 10–13, 27–39.

"Oil Shale: A Huge Resource of Low-Grade Fuel." *Science* 184 (21 June 1974): 1271.

"Oil Shale—Our Future Oil Supply." *Scientific American* 136 (May 1927): 342.

O'Neill, Patrick. "The Week the 'Chute Didn't Open." *Colorado River Journal* 4 (July/August 1982): 13.

"OPEC's Bold Attempt to Save Itself." *U.S. News & World Report*, 23 December 1985, p. 30.

Parfit, Michael. "Last Stand at Rosebud Creek." *Rocky Mountain Magazine* 2 (May/June 1980): 65–70.

Parsons, Floyd W. "Oil from Shale: Everybody's Business." *Saturday Evening Post*, 20 March 1920, pp. 34, 37.

Paul, Rodman W., and Malone, Michael P. "Tradition and Change in Western Historiography." *Western Historical Quarterly* 16 (January 1958): 27–53.

Pelham, Ann. "Synthetic Fuels Bill Nearly Ready for Carter." *Congressional Quarterly* 36 (21 June 1980): 1691–1695.

———. "House Shelves Energy Mobilization Board." *Congressional Quarterly* 36 (28 June 1980): 1790.

"Riches in Rock." *Newsweek*, 27 May 1957, p. 87.

Robbins, William G. "The *Plundered Province* Thesis and the Recent Historiography of the American West." *Pacific Historical Review*, 60 (1986): 577–597.

"Rocky Mountain High—Soaring Prospects for the '80s." *Time*, 15 December 1980, pp. 28–41.

Rohe, William M. "Social Impact Analysis and the Planning Process in the United States: A Review and Critique." *Town Planning Review* 53 (October 1982): 367–382.

Scamehorn, H. Lee. "John C. Osgood and the Western Steel Industry." *Arizona and the West* 15 (Summer 1973): 133–148.

Scrimgeour, Donald P. "Coping with the Oil Shale Boom." *Planning* 46 (August 1980): 19–21.

"Setback for Synfuels." *Time*, 17 May 1982, pp. 58–59.

Sheets, K. R. "Oil Shale Fiasco: The Death Knell for Synfuels?" *U.S. News & World Report* 92 (17 May 1982): 58.

Singer, Mark. "Annals of Finance (Penn Square Bank—Part I, II, III)." *New Yorker*, 22 and 29 April, and 6 May 1985.

Slossen, Edwin E. "Food From Shale." *Scientific Monthly* 21 (July 1925): 106.

Stegner, Wallace, and Stegner, Page. "Rocky Mountain Country." *Atlantic Monthly* 241 (April 1978): 44–64.

"Straight Shots." *Rocky Mountain Magazine* 3 (July/August 1981): 15.

"Surprise Withdrawal Shuts Down Oil Shale Project." *Chemical Engineering* 89 (17 May 1982): 17.

Sweierenga, Robert P. "Land Speculation and Its Impact on American Economic Growth and Welfare: A Historiographical Review." *Western Historical Quarterly* 3 (July 1977): 283–302.

"Synfuels Get Pushed Further into the Future." *Business Week*, 17 May 1982, pp. 30–31.

"Synfuels in Jeopardy" *Newsweek*, 19 April 1982, p. 74.

Taylor, Frank J. "Colorado's Fabulous Mountains of Oil." *Reader's Digest*, June 1957, pp. 132–138.

"The Colony Oil Shale Project: Turning Technology into Reality." *Industrial Development* 5 (March/April 1982): 25–27.

"The Colony Project." *Profile (an Exxon, U.S.A Employee Magazine)* 21 (June 1982): 22–23.

"The Death of Mining." *Business Week*, 17 December 1984, pp. 64–70.

"The Fading Synfuel Dream." *Forbes* 129 (7 June 1982): 14.

"The Mayor Steps Down, but Still Keeps Tabs on Energy." *Shale Country* 3 (April 1981): 20.

"The State of Exxon." *Profile (an Exxon, U.S.A Employee Magazine)* 21 (6 June 1982): 28–29.

Tirman, J. "Investing in the Energy Transition: From Oil to What?" *Technological Review* 85 (April 1982): 72.

"Tosco's Tottering Synfuels Plans." *Business Week*, 19 April 1982, p. 64.

Tracy, Eleanor Johnson. "Exxon's Abrupt Exit from Shale." *Fortune*, 31 May 1982, pp. 105–107.

Wallop, Malcolm. "Energy Development and Water: Dilemma for the Western United States." *Journal of Energy and Development*. 8 (Spring 1983): 203–209.

Webb, Geoff. "At Last Synfuels Corporation Is Dead." *Not Man Apart, Newsmagazine of Friends of the Earth*, January/February 1986, p. 1.

"Why Things Aren't Going Right for Exxon." *Business Week*, 7 June 1982, pp. 88–91, 93.

Widener, Sandra. "Boom Town Women." *Rocky Mountain Magazine* 4 (January/February 1982): 45–49, 81–85.

Wilkinson, Kenneth P.; Thompson, James G.; Reynolds, Robert R., Jr.; and Ostresh, Lawrence M. "Local Social Disruption and Western Energy Development." *Pacific Sociological Review* 25 (July 1982): 275–296.

Newspapers

Austin American - Statesman
Richards, Charles. "West Texans Tighten Their Belts to Ride Out the Oil Slump." 10 March 1986.

Chicago Tribune
Cross, Robert. "Boom Busts; Hope Sustains Town." 7 June 1983.
———. "Oil Boomtown Counts Its Blessings After Crash." 7 June 1983.

Christian Science Monitor
Belsie, Laurent. "Energy Boom Gone Bust Overshadows Efforts to Restart Denver's Economy." 15 October 1985.
Bradley, Barbara. "Texas Bankers Scurry to Limit Oil Losses." 21 April 1986.
Clayton, Mark. "Wringing High-grade Oil From Rock." 12 October 1988.
Foell, Earl W. "No World Oil Crisis Now, but Wait a Generation." 26 February 1988.

Germani, Clara. "Planners Try to Snap Cycle of Boom and Bust [in Alaska]." 8 February 1985.

Knobelsdorff, Kerry Elizabeth. "Real Estate Keeps Texas Thrifts in the Hole." 12 September 1988.

LaFranchi, Howard. "The 'New Poor' in the Oil Patch," 31 August 1987.

———. "Public Aid in Stricken Oil Patch." 1 September 1987.

———. "'Diversification' Is Oil-patch Rallying Cry." 2 September 1987.

Petillo, John J. "Social Responsibility: The Role of the University." 27 February 1986.

Salisbury, David F. "Energy: The War Between the States." 17 June 1981.

———. "Report Alerts US West to Acid Rain Effects." 1 April 1985.

Yemma, John. "Oil-price Drop Causing Profound Changes in World." 19 February 1986.

———. "Falling Oil Prices Squeeze the Profit From U.S. Producing Wells." 21 March 1986.

———. "The Oil Weapon: Could Shocks of the '70s Repeat Themselves?" 9 September 1988.

———. "Plenty of Oil, but Much Is in the Wrong Places." 1 September 1988.

Grand Junction Daily Sentinel

Alexander, Andrew. "Following the Boom: A Story of Persistence, Determination." 4 May 1986.

"All Right Already, the Sky Is Not Falling." Editorial. 12 May 1982.

Bernath, James T. "Summer Exodus Anticipated in GJ." 27 May 1984.

———. "Survey Results: 10 Percent of Families Say They Intend to Pull Up Stakes, Move." 17 September 1984.

———. "Two Safeways to Close Dec. 29." 2 December 1984.

Campbell, Steve. "Energy Development Prompts Mule Deer Study." 13 December 1981.

"Colony Closing Cited: Exxon Profit Down By 51.5%." 22 July 1982.

Crowell, T. Michael. "Ertl Formula for Success: Buy 50 Acres, Then Wait for the Land Rush" in "The Boomtowns: A Special Report." 10 September 1981.

———. "1,000 at Colony Get Layoffs, Last Checks." 4 May 1982.

———. "Firms Tied to Colony May Lose Millions in Shutdown." 4 May 1982.

———. "Exxon Kicks Off Slope's Economic Dominoes." 9 May 1982.

———. "Exxon to Purchase Shale Workers' Homes." 9 May 1982.

———. "Truck Firm Closes; 26 Layoffs Locally." 26 May 1982.

"Exxon Chief Restates Shale Development Plan." 22 November 1980.

"Exxon Cuts and Runs." Editorial. 4 May 1982.

"Exxon Pulls Out." Editorial. 3 May 1982.

Fishell, Dave. "The Vulcan Mine Disasters: Tragedy at New Castle." 18 February 1879.

Foster, Christi. "Mile High Seed Victim of Energy Bust, Owners Say." 1 December 1983.

"Garfield County's Housing Problem Triggers Formation of a Task Force." 25 November 1979.

Giblin, Mary Louise. "Shale Plans Inadequate, Officials Tell Hart." 12 August 1980.

———. "Gary Inc. [refinery] Files for Chapter 11 Reorganization." 4 March 1985.

———. "County's Valuation Takes Historic Drop." 18 July 1985.

———. "County to Look for More Budget Cuts." 18 October 1985.

Haggarty, Bill. "Energy and Wildlife: Loss of Habitat Concerns Wildlife Officials As Energy Development Hits West Slope." 8 March 1981.

Jones, Charline Benson. Letter to the editor. 9 May 1982.

Levy, Lloyd. "Wildlife Official Stresses Need for Habitat." 3 Feb 1980.

———. "Bald Eagles Threaten Gravel Pit (and Vice Versa)." 26 September 1980.

———. "Garfield County Feels Weight of Shale 'Squatters'." 13 May 1981.

———. "New in These Parts? Busybody Welcomes Strangers to Boomtown" in "The Boomtowns: A Special Report." 10 September 1981.

———. "Presiding, with Ulcers, over the Urbanization of Ranch Country." 10 September 1981.

Link, Tony. "Mammoth Machines Molder." 27 June 1985.

———. "Survey Shows Population Drop." 8 July 1985.

———. "Vacancy Rate Above 14%, Survey Says." 5 February 1986.

———. "Foreclosure Isn't Always Fatal." 16 February 1986.

McGowan, Joe, Jr. "Growing Pains: Parachute, People, Petroleum." 13 May 1981.

McMillan, Steve. "Parachute Takes a Breather." 1 May 1983.

———. "Foreclosures Mount as Growth Recedes." 1 May 1983.

———. "Howard Johnson's Shutters Restaurant; Motel Still Open." 12 June 1985.

———. "Shale Plant Scrutinized by Unocal." 7 August 1988.

"Oil Shale—View from the Editors" in a special edition. January 1979.

Peirce, Neal. "Exxon's Shale Scenario." 26 September 1980.

Rice, Ginger. "Safeway Closings No Surprise." 5 December 1984.

———. "Independent Grocer to Close Doors on 22-year-old Market." 30 January 1985.

———. "Chamber Asks for $200,000 Credit to Stay Afloat." 6 February 1985.

———. "Mall Medical Closes its Doors." 7 March 1985.

———. "Restaurant Closes Doors until August." 8 March 1985.

———. "Two 7-Elevens Shutting Down." 14 March 1985.

———. "Delta Products Inc. Closing Due to Steadily Falling Sales." 24 March 1985.

Schmitz, Gary. "Dirt in the Blood: Catskinner's Job is Pushing Out the Road" in "The Boomtowns: A Special Report." 10 September 1981.

———. "Colony's Job Office Attracts 'Shale Rush'." 21 April 1981.

———. "Work Force Estimate For Colony Project Revised up to 7,000." 29 January 1982.

———. "Exxon Closing: 180-degree Turn for Shale Leader." 3 May 1982.

———. "Garfield, Parachute Leaders Glad They Prepared for Worst." 3 May 1982.

———. "Officials Rap Exxon's Method." 5 May 1982.

———. "Oil Shale Prospects Continue to Worsen." 1 May 1983.

———. "Local Officials Feel Pinch of Strained Finances." 1 May 1983.

"Showcase—Energy and the Environment" in a special edition. 13 March 1983.

Silbernagel, Bob. "Pioneer Problems: Hot Rocks Freeze Work at Union Oil. " 13
	August 1985.
"Two Developers Lose Suit against Exxon." 1 May 1983.
Wollen, Linda. Letter to the editor. 31 May 1984.
Wright, Alice. "Room for All of Us" in "Westworld: The Sunday Magazine." 14
	August 1977.

Denver Catholic Register
Asher, Julie. "Life Is Damn Hard, but There Are Still Hopes and Dreams in Oil
	Shale Country." 25 April 1984.

Denver Post
Chronis, Peter. "Parachute May Become Town of Lost Dreams." 3 May 1982.
———. "Streets, but No Houses." 1 May 1983.
———. "Remembering Black Sunday—Boomtown Now Awaits Bust No. 2." 1 May
	1983.
Chronis, Peter, and Pitts, Gail. "Colony Pullout Came as Shock to Thousands." 9
	May 1982.
"Colony Shutdown Shocks Workers." 9 May 1982.
"Dreams Dashed for Shale Workers." 4 May 1982.
Flack, Ray. "Housing Hit Hard by Closure." 4 May 1982.
"Long Gasoline Lines Predicted Again in 2-5 Years." 12 February 1987.
Miniclier, Kit, and Chronis, Pete. "Life Turns Upside Down for Shale Plant
	Workers." 4 May 1982.
Parmenter, Cindy. "4,100 Jobs May Be Lost in Oil Shale Shutdown." 4 May 1982.
Pitts, Gail. "Exxon Will Close Shale Oil Project." 3 May 1982.
"Shale: We Still Need It." Editorial. 5 May 1982.

Garfield County Democrat
"Vulcan Mine Explosion." 19 December 1913.

Glenwood Post
"Developers Claim Exxon Lied about Shale Project." 21 April 1983.
Funk, Jerry. "Exxon Closing Oil Shale Project—Reaction Cautious, Not Panic." 3
	May 1982.
———. "Exxon Workforce Halved Today—Workers Steaming." 4 May 1982.
———. "Exxon Actions May Kill School Plans." 6 May 1982.
———. "Exxon Figures Colony Recovery Costs Will Run near $30 Million." 27
	August 1982.
———. "Exxon Revises Final Colony Closing Plans." 21 September 1982.
———. "Towns Survive 'Black Sunday'." 2 May 1983.
———. "Officials Review Colony Shale Project." 2 May 1983.
Hrivnak, Barbara. "Families Are Being Priced out of Housing." 11 October 1979.
———. "Silt's Budget to Rely Heavily on Grants." 18 October 1979.
———. "Duncan Tours Oil Shale Sites." 23 October 1979.

Isbell, Alan. "Shale's Welcome Is Cautious Since Bust." 2 May 1983.
Kacskos, Craig. "McInnis Says He'll Ax Shale Value Provision." 28 February 1985.
Paludan, Michael. "Lamm Assessing Exxon Impact." 3 May 1982.
Schmitz, Gary. "Environmental Concern Rises As Oil Shale Seems Imminent." 3 December 1979.
———. "Garfield County: A Developer's Dream?" in "Update '79."
———. "Oil from Shale: Time Is on Its Side" in "Update '79."
———. "Exxon Plan Would Invest $500 Billion." 11 June 1980.
"Shale Oil Companies Pull Up Stakes in Utah." 2 January 1986.

High Country News (Paonia, Colorado)
"$34/Barrel Shale Oil Subsidy." February 16, 1987.
Anderson, Bob. "Oil Shale Future: Jewel or Synfuel?" 3 April 1981.
———. "Oil Shale Risks Shared by Nation's Water Users, Taxpayers." 17 April 1981.
———. "Tar Sands: Utah's Rocks Ooze with Oil." 14 November 1980.
"Backing Out of Shale." 16 July 1976.
"Confidential Oil Shale Study Reveals Independence Spells Push for Shale." 2 August 1974.
"Congress Squeezes Oil Shale Rules." 26 June 1981.
Dow, Jim. "Grand Junction Ran a High Gold Fever." 15 April 1985.
Edmonds, Carol. "Colorado Can Orchestrate State's Oil Shale Growth; Interview with Gov. Dick Lamm." 18 July 1975.
"Exxon Leaves Colorado Shale Behind." 14 May 1982.
"Exxon Plans Temporary Reclamation." 28 May 1982.
Gorham, Dan. "Oil Prices Have Synfuels Struggling." 29 April 1983.
———. "Synthetic Fuels: Less from More." 10 June 1983.
———. "Synthetic Fuels: Money in Search of an Idea." 10 June 1983.
Hamilton, Bruce. "Beginning of the End? Colony Pulls Out of the Oil Shale Race." 11 October 1974.
———. "Oil Shale Fever Rises in West." 18 January 1974.
Harvey, Dorothy, and Hamilton, Bruce. "Utah Oil Shale Boom: Not If, but When Leases Suspended, What Next?" 3 December 1976.
Hinchman, Steve. "Congress to Look Again at Oil-Shale Lands." 2 March 1987.
Hinchman, Steve, and Marston, Ed. "Exxon Tangles with Wyoming over Taxes." 28 March 1988.
"Industry Rejected Watt's Oil Shale Giveaway Program." 31 October 1983.
"Interior Halts Colorado Oil Shale Leasing Program for One Year." 27 August 1976.
"Judge Nods to Piceance Basin Shale Development. Says One Environmental Statement Is Enough." 8 September 1978.
Jones, Carol. "Colorado Shale Gets SFC Cash." 5 August 1983.
Klusmire, Jon. "An Oil Shale Project Hangs On, but Barely." 27 February 1989.
Marston, Ed. "A Great Deal Rides on Unocal's Oil Shale Project." 15 April 1985.
———. "Industry and Government Charge Environmentalists with Bad Faith Negotiating." 2 April 1984.
———. "Kevin Markey Argues: Now Is the Time to Make a Deal." 2 April 1984.

——. "Life After Oil Shale." 15 April 1984.
——. "Oil Shale Foes End a Decade-long War." 20 December 1983.
——. "Shale Plant Given Last Chance." 15 August 1988.
——. "Synfuel Corp.'s Act Is Challenged." 23 June 1986.
——. "Synfuels Aid Is Moribund." 14 October 1985.
——. "The Clock Is Ticking on Union's Shale Project." 2 April 1984.
——. "The Oil Shale Boom Weakened Agriculture in the Fruita Area." 15 April 1985.
——. "Union Cited for Federal Violations." 2 April 1984.
——. "Union Oil's Fred Hartley Fights Wall Street Vultures and Conservationists." 2 April 1984.
——. "Yet Another Domino Falls in Colorado's Oil Shale Country." 1 September 1986.
Moffatt, Judy, "Oil Shale County Takes a Hit." 14 September 1987.
"Oil Shale Comes on Hard Times" in a special edition. 2 April 1984.
"Oil Shale Dropouts." 2 January 1976.
"Oil Shale Negotiations Are Alive, but Barely." 14 May 1984.
"Oil Shale v. Environment: The Great Balancing Act." 5 July 1974.
"Post Questions Shale Deal." 4 January 1974.
Robinson, Michael J. "Critic Says 'Reform' Bill is a Giveaway." 23 May 1988.
Rowenwald, Lonnie. "R & D Cuts Would Push Synfuel Firms West." 6 March 1981.
——, and Edmunds, Lavinia. "Noble Synfuels' Bermuda Triangle." 15 May 1981.
Schmitz, Gary. "An Oil Shale Land Settlement is Attacked." 1 September 1986.
——. "Denver Talks Positively Synfuel." 8 January 1982.
——. "SFC Will Act on Oil Shale Grants. . .Maybe." 28 November 1983.
"To Aid or Not to Aid Synfuels." 19 February 1982.
"Who Gave Away What at Oil Shale Talks?" 2 April 1984.
"Zero Interest." 21 January 1983.

Houston Chronicle
"Exxon Sells $3.2 Million Worth of Items from Shale Oil Project." 19 October 1982.

Houston Post
"Colorado Boom Towns Say They'll Pull Out of 'Bust.'" 3 October 1982.
"Exxon Expects to Resume Shale Project." 14 May 1982.
"Exxon Plans to Shut Down Oil Shale Project." 3 May 1982.
"Exxon Pullout 'Grave Setback.'" 4 May 1982.
"Hundreds Jobless as Project Ends." 5 May 1982.
"Oil Shale Pipeline Project Dropped." 7 May 1982.
"Oil Shale Project in Colorado Could be Restarted, Exxon says." 18 July 1982.

Kansas City Star
"Town Sees a Bright Side after Boom Goes Bust." 1 May 1983.
Unger, Robert. "Shale's Empty Promises Busts Colorado Boom Town." 6 April 1983.

Los Angeles Times
Garner, Joe. "Grand Junction Less Grand after Oil Bust." 23 November 1984.

Meeker Herald (Meeker, Colorado)
Albrecht, Connie. "The Collapse of the Colony Project—Where Do We Go from Here?" Opinion/editorial. 13 May 1982.
"Boom and Bust . . . Live and Learn." Editorial. 6 May 1982.
"Exxon Pulls Plug; Officials Express Concern." 6 May 1982.

New Castle News
"37 Lives Lost in Vulcan Disaster." 18 December 1913.
"Death Came without Warning." 22 February 1896, 7 March 1896, 14 March 1896, 21 March 1896.
"Statistics on Employed Coal Miners." 11 January 1896.

New York Times
Martin, Douglas. "Exxon Abandons Shale Oil Project." 3 May 1982.
——. "The Singular Power of a Giant Called Exxon." 9 May 1982: Business section 3, p. 1.
Schmidt, William E. "Uncertainty in Shale Oil Town." 3 May 1982: Business section, p. 1 and D21.
Serrin, William. "For Texas Oil Workers, Economy Has Gone Dry." 7 May 1986: A20.
"Tosco Forced to Review Total Strategy." 3 May 1982: Section IV, p. 4.
"Two Cheers for $5 Oil." 9 October 1988: 5.
"U.S. Aid Halt on Shale Oil." 15 June 1982: Section IV, p. 18.

Oil Shale Outlook (Denver, Colorado)
No author, no article title. 20 April 1921.

Rifle Telegram (Rifle, Colorado)
Brimhall, Mrs. Thomas J. Letter to the editor. 26 February 1986.
"Bust." Editorial. 5 May 1982.
Colton, Blane. Letter to the editor. 12 May 1982.
Conrad, Bill. "Union Oil Plans 'Major Fix' at Plant." 14 August 1985.
"Exxon's Shutdown Surprises County." 5 May 1982.
Frick, Jody. "Silt Citizens Favor Sales Tax Increase." 14 November 1979.

Rifle Tribune (Rifle, Colorado)
"Adios Amigos": Final Issue Ceasing Publication after Chronicling Boom and Bust." 9 January 1985.
"Colony Three-year Plan Delayed; Reclamation Estimate $30 Million." 1 September 1982.
Colson, John. "C-b Companies Seek Less Strict Laws." 17 September 1980.
——. "Parachute to Eliminate Marshall Law System." 20 May 1981.

——. "Lamm Interview: Bracing for the Energy Boom." 20 May 1981.

——. "Morrow Plans Determined Fight for Job." 24 July 1981.

——. "Shale Shock—Parachute Officials Re-evaluate Plans after Exxon Pullout." 5 May 1982.

——. "Sorrow and Rage with the Bust That Was Not Supposed to Happen." 5 May 1982.

——. "Exxon to Buy Back 105 Houses Belonging to Colony Workers." 12 May 1982.

——. "'Bust Fund' Called for to Offset Impacts of Project Pullouts." 12 May 1982.

——. "Out of Shale and into Jellybeans, Exxon Bounces Back." 19 May 1982.

"Developer Sues Exxon and Tosco." 11 August 1982.

Dow, Jim. "The Bottom: Indicators Show Economic Anemia, but Problems Might Be Leveling Off." 9 May 1984.

"Exxon Closer to Ruedi Rights." 27 May 1981.

"Exxon's Parking Lot Approved By County Commissioners." 20 May 1980.

"Freedman Calls Exxon Plans 'Realistic'; More Talks Planned." 2 June 1982.

"Ghost Town Tribune." Special edition. 4 May 1983.

Gulliford, Andrew. "Promises of Rainbows Cheap When Foreign Oil is Cheaper." 4 May 1983.

Isenberg, Joan. "Colony Manager to County: 'We Are Here. We Are Real People'." 16 May 1984.

"Oil Shale Gifts Expensive to Maintain." 26 October 1983.

O'Neill, Patrick. "Controversial Lawman Answers Detractors." 11 June 1980.

——. "Grand Valley Split over Support for Marshall." 11 June 1980.

——. "Parachute's Displaced People Feel Effects of Boom." 25 March 1981.

——. "Parachute Beginning to Resemble Boomtowns of Old." 22 April 1981.

——. "Exxon Called 'Inconsiderate'." 29 April 1981.

——. "Teepee Dwellers Ordered by County to Break Camp." 20 May 1981.

"Parachute Bar Doubles As a Church." 2 March 1982.

"Parachute Remembers in a Pleasant Way." 9 May 1984.

Quillian, A.W. III. "Oil Shale Treasure Chest and/or Pandora's Box?" 17 March 1982 and 24 March 1982.

"Silt Administrator Answers Allegations." 28 February 1979.

Sullivan, Jim. "Experts Assess Exxon's Shale Scenario." 3 September 1980.

——. "Limited Vandalism, Fights in Parachute Area." 5 May 1982.

——. "Panic Cautioned Against in Face of Certain Economic Downturn." 5 May 1982.

"We Will Survive." Editorial. 5 May 1982.

Rocky Mountain News (Denver, Colorado)

Baron, John. "Energy Boom Will Repaint Town Picture." 23 November 1980.

——. "Man's Mission: Create Western Slope Oil City." 23 November 1980.

——. "Old-timers Don't Mind Change on Their Mesa." 25 November 1980.

——. "Junction Mayor Articulates Energy Concerns." 26 November 1980.

Eizenstadt, Stuart E. "Our Energy Is Imperiled: Exxon's Termination of Oil-shale Plant Is An Act in a National Tragedy." Opinion/editorial. 2 June 1982.

Frazier, Deborah. "Shale Dreams Shatter." 4 May 1982.

——. "Parachute's 'Pioneers' Bailing Out." 5 May 1982.

Gerhardt, Gary. "Energy Firms Facing Ecological Problems They Create." 13 December 1981.

Gulliford, Andrew. "Colorado Future Shock." Opinion/editorial. 2 September 1979.

Graham, Sandy. "Shale Economy Limps on One Leg." 4 May 1982.

——. "Pink slips and Paychecks Prevail." 5 May 1982.

Primack, Phil. "West's Economic Upsurge Is Rose with Sharp Thorns." Opinion/editorial. 9 March 1980.

Rounds, Michael. "Water Transfer to Develop West Oil Shale 'Feasible.'" 6 December 1980.

——. "Oil Shale Boom has Come to Colorado." 23 November 1980.

——. "Exxon Consults CU, Mines on Handling Synfuels Boom." 22 November 1980.

"Shale Workers Are Bitter." 4 May 1982.

San Francisco Chronicle

Chamberlin, David. "A Boomtown Waits for the Boom" in "This World" Supplement. 25 October 1981.

The Free Weekly Newspaper (Glenwood Springs, Colorado)

"BUST! JOLT! Exxon's Overnight Shutdown Stuns County." 5 May 1982.

Hook, Charles. "BMI Faces Animosity." 3 August 1988.

——. "Drinkhouse Fined $4,110.00." 3 August 1988.

"Hope Hinges on Fluidized Bed." 28 January 1987.

Klusmire, Jon. "Rulison Nuke Blast Effect Questioned." 16 October 1985.

——. "Exxon Forgotten." 9 May 1984.

"Needed: Plans for Failure." Editorial. 12 May 1982

USA Today

Blaine, Charley. "Oil Glut Puts Boom Town on the Rocks." 18 November 1985.

Wall Street Journal

Cohen, Laurie P. "Hard Times: Plunge in Oil Prices Brings Economic Woes to Energy-Belt States." 4 February 1986.

Frazier, Steven. "Union Oil Keeps Its Shale Project Despite Shakeout." 4 May 1982.

Harris, Roy J. "Occidental Cuts Its Work Force And '86 Outlays." 18 March 1986.

"Metal Fatigue: Exxon Mining Unit Hits Tough Going." 31 August 1982.

Rose, Frederick. "Coming Up Dry: Unocal Struggles on with Attempt to Get Crude Oil from Shale." 14 May 1986.

Sullivan, Allanna. "Exxon Workers Offered Option to Retire Early." 24 April 1986.

Washington Post

Balz, Don. "Parachute Fails to Open—Workers Stranded by Exxon's Pullout." 7 May 1982.

"Exxon Pulls Out of $5 Billion Oil Shale Project." 3 May 1982.

"Exxon Pullout a Blow to Synfuels Industry." 4 May 1982.

"Exxon Says Shale Project in Mothballs." 14 May 1982.

"Letters to the Editor: On the Energy Front." 17 May 1982.

"Parachute, Abandoned by Exxon, Isn't Folding Up After All." 25 July 1982.

"Slow on Shale." Editorial. 6 May 1982.

"World's Largest Oil Company Leaves a Streak of Rage and Fear." 7 May 1982.

Books

Abbey, Edward. *The Journey Home: Some Words in Defense of the American West.* New York: E. P. Dutton, 1977.

Allen, James B. *The Company Town in the American West.* Norman: University of Oklahoma Press, 1966.

——. "The Company-Owned Mining Town in the West: Exploitation or Benevolent Paternalism?" In *Reflections of Western Historians.* John A. Carroll, ed. Tucson: University of Arizona Press, 1969.

Anderson, V. C. *The Oil Shale Industry.* New York: F. A. Stokes, 1920.

Barton, Allen H. *Communities in Disaster.* New York:Doubleday, 1970.

Bender, Thomas. *Community and Social Change in America.* Baltimore: Johns Hopkins University Press, 1986.

Bluestone, Barry, and Harrison, Bennett. *The Deindustrialization of America: Plant Closings, Community Abandonment, and the Dismantling of Basic Industry.* New York: Basic Books, 1982.

Blumenthal, Albert. *Small Town Stuff.* Chicago: University of Chicago Press, 1932.

Boulding, Elise. "Women as Integrators and Stabilizers." In *Women and the Social Costs of Energy Development: Two Colorado Case Studies.* Elizabeth Moen, Elise Boulding, Jane Lillydahl, and Risa Palm. Boulder, Colo.: Westview Press, 1981.

Bowles, Roy T., ed. *Social Impact Assessment in Small Communities.* Vancouver, British Columbia, 1984.

Burroughs, John Rolfe. *Where The Old West Stayed Young.* New York: Bonanza, 1962.

Buss, Terry F., and Redburn, F. Stevens. *Shutdown at Youngstown.* Albany: State University of New York Press, 1983.

Carlson, Richard C.; Hartman, Willis W.; and Schwartz, Peter. *Energy Futures, Human Values and Lifestyles.* Boulder, Colo.: Westview Press, 1982.

Cerquone, Joseph. *In Behalf of the Light: The Dominguez and Escalante Expedition of 1776.* Denver: Paragon Press, 1976.

Chamblin, Thomas S., ed. *Historical Encyclopedia of Colorado.* Denver: Colorado Historical Association, 1960.

Chavez, Angelico, trans. and Warner, Ted J., ed. *The Dominguez Escalante Journal: Their Expedition Through Colorado, Utah, Arizona, and New Mexico in 1776*. Provo: Brigham Young University Press, 1976.

Clark, John G. *Energy and the Federal Government: Fossil Fuel Policies, 1900–1946*. Urbana: University of Illinois Press, 1987.

Clark, Wilson, and Page, Jake. *Energy, Vulnerability and War*. New York: W. W. Norton, 1981.

Cortese, Charles F., and Cortese, Jane Archer. *The Social Effects of Energy Boomtowns in the West: A Partially Annotated Bibliography*. Council of Planning Librarians, Exchange Bibliography 1557. June 1978.

Coward, Raymond T., and Smith, William M., Jr. *The Family in Rural Society*. Boulder, Colo.: Westview Press, 1981.

Craycroft, Robert, and Fazio, Michael, eds. *Change and Tradition in the American Small Town*. Jackson: University of Mississippi Press, 1983.

Den Uyl, Douglas J. *The New Crusaders: The Corporate Social Responsibility Debate*. Bowling Green, Ohio: Social Philosophy and Policy Center, 1984.

Devine, Michael O. *Energy from the West: A Technology Assessment of Western Energy Resource Development*. Norman, Okla.: University of Oklahoma Press, 1981.

DeVoto, Bernard. *Forays and Rebuttals*. Boston: Little, Brown, 1936.

Edison, Carol A., ed. *Cowboy Poetry from Utah: An Anthology*. Salt Lake City: Utah Folklife Center, 1985.

Ellis, William S. *The Majestic Rocky Mountains*. Washington, D.C.: National Geographic Society, 1976.

Erikson, Kai T. *Everything in its Path: Destruction of Community in the Buffalo Creek Flood*. New York: Simon and Schuster, 1976.

Fife, Austin; Fife, Alta; and Glassie, Henry H., eds. *Forms Upon the Frontier*, Monograph series, vol. 16, no. 2. Logan: Utah State University Press, 1969.

Finsterbusch, Kurt, and Wolf, C. P. *Methodology of Social Impact Assessment*. Stroudsburg, Pa.: Dowden, Hutchinson & Ross, 1977.

Finsterbusch, Kurt, ed. *Social Impact Assessment Methods*. Beverly Hills: Sage, 1983.

Ford Foundation, energy policy project. *A Time to Choose: America's Energy Future—Final Report*. Cambridge, Mass.: Ballinger Publications, 1974.

Fradkin, Philip L. *The Colorado: A River No More*. Tucson: University of Arizona Press, 1984.

Freeman, S. David. *Energy: The New Era*. New York: Vintage Books, 1974.

Garreau, Joel. *The Nine Nations of North America*. New York: Avon Books, 1981.

Gates, Charles M. "Boom Stages in American Expansion." In *The West of the American People*. 3rd printing. Allan G. Bogue, ed. et al. Itasca: Peacock, 1973. 306–311.

Gilmore, John S., and Duff, Mary K.. *Boom Town Growth Management: A Case Study of Rock Springs–Green River, Wyoming*. Boulder, Colo.: Westview Press, 1975.

Goetzmann, William H. *Exploration and Empire: The Explorer and the Scientist in the Winning of the American West.* New York: Random House, 1966.

Goff, Richard; McCaffree, Robert H.; and Sterbenz, Doris. *Centennial Brand Book of the Colorado Cattlemen's Association.* Boulder, Colo.: Johnson Publishing, 1967.

——. *Century in the Saddle.* Boulder, Colo.: Johnson Publishing, 1967.

Gulliford, Andrew. *America's Country Schools.* Washington, D.C.: Preservation Press, 1984.

——. *Garfield County, Colorado: The First Hundred Years 1883–1983.* Glenwood Springs, Colo.: Grand River Museum Alliance, 1983.

——, and Teeuwen, Randall. *The Years Ahead: Life for the Aging in Northwest Colorado.* Glenwood Springs, Colo.: Colorado Mountain College, 1977.

Hand, Wayland D., ed. *American Folk Medicine.* Los Angeles: University of California Press, 1976.

Hawdon, David, ed. *The Energy Crisis—Ten Years After.* New York: St. Martin's Press, 1984.

Hayes, Lynton R. *Energy, Economic Growth, and Regionalism in the West.* Albuquerque: University of New Mexico Press, 1980.

High Country News, eds. *Western Water Made Simple.* Washington, D.C.: Island Press, 1987.

Hill, David R., and Schler, Daniel J.. "Early Boom Town Planning in Colorado's Oil Shale Country." In *Energy and the Western United States.* James L. Regens, Robert W. Rycroft, and Gregory A. Daneke, eds. New York: Praeger, 1982: 49–67.

Iskandar, Marwan. *The Arab Oil Question.* 2d edition. Privately printed, January 1974.

Johnson, Anna, and Yajko, Kathleen. *The Elusive Dream: A Relentless Quest for Coal in Western Colorado.* Glenwood Springs, Colo.: Gran Farnum Printing, 1983.

Jordan, Teresa. *Cowgirls—Women of the American West.* Garden City, N.J.: Anchor Press, Doubleday & Company, Inc., 1982.

King, Joseph E. *A Mine to Make a Mine: Financing the Colorado Mining Industry, 1859-1902.* College Station: Texas A&M University Press, 1977.

Kohl, Wilfrid L. *After the Second Oil Crisis.* Lexington, Mass.: Lexington Books, 1982.

Kubler-Ross, Elisabeth. *On Death and Dying.* New York: MacMillan, 1969.

Lamm, Richard D., and McCarthy, Michael. *The Angry West: A Vulnerable Land and Its Future.* Boston: Houghton Mifflin, 1982.

Lash, Jonathan, and King, Laura, eds. *The Synfuels Manual.* New York: Natural Resources Defense Counsel, 1983.

Leistritz, F. Larry, and Murdock, Steven H.. *The Socioeconomic Impact of Resource Development: Methods for Assessment.* Boulder, Colo.: Westview Press, 1981.

Limerick, Patricia Nelson. *The Legacy of Conquest.* New York: W. W. Norton, 1987.

Lingeman, Richard. *Small Town America.* Boston: Houghton Mifflin, 1980.

Lowitt, Richard. *The New Deal and the West*. Bloomington: Indiana University Press, 1984.

Lynd, Staughton. *The Fight Against Shutdowns*. San Pedro, Calif.: Singlejack Books, 1983.

MaKillop, Andrew. *The Oil Crisis and Economic Adjustments*. New York: St Martin's Press, 1983.

Malamud, Gary W. *Boomtown Communities*. New York: Van Nostrand, 1984.

Martindale, Hanson. *Small Towns and Nation: The Conflict of Local and Translocal Forces*. Westport, Conn.: Greenwood Press, 1969.

McCarthy, Michael. *Hour of Trial, The Conservation Movement in Colorado and the West, 1891-1917*. Norman: University of Oklahoma Press, 1977.

McCreanor, Emma, ed. *Mesa County, Colorado: A 100 Year History*. Grand Junction, Colo.: Museum of Western Colorado, 1983.

McGovern, George S. and Guttridge, Leonard F. *The Great Coalfield War*. Boston: Houghton Mifflin, 1972.

McKell, Cyrus M., et al. *Paradoxes of Western Energy Development*. Boulder, Colo.: Westview Press, 1984.

Mead, Walter; McKie, James; Quirin, David; Watkins, Campbell; and Walkers, Michael, eds. *Oil in the Seventies: Essay on Energy Policy*. Vancouver, B. C.: Fraser Institute, 1977.

Murdock, Steve H., and Leistriz, F. Larry. *Energy Development in the Western United States—Impact on Rural Areas*. New York: Praeger Publishers, 1979.

Murray, Erlene Durrant. *Lest We Forget: A Short History of Early Grand Valley, Colorado, Originally Called Parachute, Colorado*. 3d printing. Grand Junction, Colo.: Quahada Corporation, [1973] 1981.

Nash, Gerald D. *The American West in the Twentieth Century: A Short History of an Urban Oasis*. 3d printing. Albuquerque: University of New Mexico Press, 1977.

———. *The American West Transformed*. Bloomington: Indiana University Press, 1985.

National Geographic Society. *Energy—A Special Report: Facing Up to the Problem, Getting Down to Solutions*. Washington, D.C.: National Geographic Society, February 1981.

Odell, Peter R. *Oil and World Power*. Middlesex, England: Penguin Books, 1979.

Oilen, Roger M., and Oilen, Diana Davids. *Oil Booms: Social Change in Five Texas Towns*. Lincoln: University of Nebraska Press, 1982.

Ott, Richard, ed. *When The River Was Grand: Historical Views of Colorado's Grand Valley*. Palisade, Colo.: Gazette Press, 1976.

Palm, Risa. "The Daily Activities of Women." In *Women and the Social Costs of Economic Development: Two Colorado Case Studies*. Elizabeth Moen, Elise Boulding, Jane Lillydahl and Risa Palm. Boulder, Colo.: Westview Press, 1981.

Powell, John Wesley. *The Exploration of the Colorado River and Its Canyons 1895*. New York: Dover, [1895] 1961.

Progressive Men of Western Colorado. Chicago: A & W Bowen Co., 1905.

Reading Club of Rifle, Colorado, compiler. *Rifle Shots —The Story of Rifle, Colorado*. Rifle, Colo.: Reading Club of Rifle, Colorado, 1973.

Regens, James L.; Rycroft, Robert W.; and Daneke, Gregory A. *Energy and the Western United States: Politics and Development*. New York: Praeger Publishers, 1982.

Reisner, Marc. *Cadillac Desert: The American West and Its Disappearing Water*. New York: Viking Penguin, 1986.

Richardson, Elmo R. *The Politics of Conservation: Crusades and Controversies 1897-1913*. Berkeley: University of California Press, 1962.

Righter, Rober W. *Wright, Wyoming: The Birth of a Town*. Boulder, Colo.: Roberts Rinehart, 1985.

Roosevelt, Theodore. "A Colorado Bear Hunt." In *Chronicles of Colorado*, Frederick R. Rinehart, ed. Boulder, Colo.: Roberts Rinehart, 1984.

Ruland, Sylvia. *The Lion of Redstone*. Boulder, Colo.: Johnson Books, 1981.

Russell, Paul L. *History of Western Oil Shale*. East Brunswick, N.J.: Center for Professional Advancement, 1980.

Savage, Harry K. *The Rock That Burns*. Boulder, Colo. : Pruett Press, 1967.

Schamehorn, Lee. *Pioneer Steelmaker in the West: The Colorado Fuel & Iron Company 1892-1903*. Boulder, Colo.: Pruett Press, 1976.

Schurr, Sam H. *Energy in America's Future: The Choices Before Us*. Baltimore, Md.: Johns Hopkins University Press for Resources for the Future, 1979.

Smiley, Jerome, C., ed. *Semi-Centennial History of the State of Colorado*. Vol. 1 and 2. Chicago: Lewis Publishing Co., 1913.

Smith, Duane A. *Rocky Mountain Mining Camps: The Urban Frontier*. 1967. Lincoln: University of Nebraska Press, 1974.

——. ed. *Natural Resources in Colorado and Wyoming*. Manhattan,Ks.: Sunflower University Press, 1982.

Smith, Garry B.; Arnold, Danny; and Bizzell, Bobby G. *Business Strategy and Policy*. Boston: Houghton Mifflin, 1985.

Sprague, Marshall. *Massacre: The Tragedy at White River*. Boston: Little, Brown, 1957.

Stegner, Wallace. *The Big Rock Candy Mountain*. Lincoln: University of Nebraska Press [1938], 1983.

——. *Beyond the Hundredth Meridian*. Lincoln: University of Nebraska Press [1953], 1982.

——. *The Sound of Mountain Water*. New York: E. P. Dutton, 1980.

——. ed. *Report on the Lands of the Arid Region of the United States with a More Detailed Account of the Lands of Utah by John Wesley Powell*. Cambridge: The Belknap Press of Harvard University Press, 1962.

Shoemaker, Len. *Roaring Fork Chronicle*. 3d ed. Silverton, Colo.: Sundance Publications [1958], 1979.

Stobaugh, Robert, and Yergin, Daniel. *Energy Future: The Harvard Business School Report*. New York: Random House, 1979.

Toffler, Alvin. *Future Shock*. New York: Random House, 1970.

Trotter, Robert T., and Chivera, Juan Antonio. *Curanderismo: Mexican-American Folk Healing*. Athens: University of Georgia Press, 1982.

Twain, Mark. *Roughing It*. New York: New American Library [1871], 1962.

Udall, Stewart L. *The Quiet Crisis*. New York: Avon Books, 1963.

Underwood, Kathleen. *Town Building on the Colorado Frontier*. Albuquerque: University of New Mexico Press, 1987.

Urquhart, Lena M. *Cold Snows of Carbonate*. Denver: Golden Bell Press, 1967.

Vandenbusche, Duane, and Smith, Duane A. *A Land Alone: Colorado's Western Slope*. Boulder, Colo.: Pruett Press, 1981.

Vidich, Arthur J., and Bensman, Joseph. *Small Town in Mass Society: Class, Power and Religion in a Rural Community*. Princeton: Princeton University Press, 1968.

Warren, Roland L. *New Perspectives on the American Community*. Chicago: Rand McNally, 1977.

Waters, Frank. *The Colorado*. Athens: Ohio University Press [1946], 1984.

Weatherford, Gary D., and Brown, F. Lee. *New Courses for the Colorado River: Major Issues for the Next Century*. Albuquerque: University of New Mexico Press, 1986.

Weber, Bruce A., and Howell, Robert E., eds. *Coping With Rapid Growth in Rural Communities*. Boulder, Colo.: Westview Press, 1982.

Welles, Chris. *The Elusive Bonanza*. New York: E. P. Dutton, 1970.

Western Colorado Congress and Windstar Foundation. *Oil Shale: A Citizen's Perspective*. Montrose, Colo.: Western Colorado Congress, 1981.

Wickens, James Frederick. *Colorado in the Great Depression*. New York: Garland Publishing, 1979.

Wiley, Peter, and Gottlieb, Robert. *Empires in the Sun*. Tucson: University of Arizona Press, 1985.

Young, Helen Hawxhurst. *The Skin and Bones of Plateau Valley History*. Grand Junction, Colo.: Wilson & Young Printers, 1976.